You can return this item to any library but please
note that not all libraries are open every day.
Items must be returned on or before the due date.
Failure to do so will result in overdue charges.
Items may be renewed unless requested by
another customer, in person or by telephone, on
two occasions only. Your membership card number
will be required.
Please look after this item – you may be charged
for any damage.

Headquarters:
Information, Culture & Community Learning,
Town Hall, Bournemouth BH2 6DY

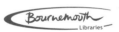

D1337891

BOURNEMOUTH LIBRARIES

300007721

© John Wickersham, 2008

First published February 2008

Every effort has been made to ensure the accuracy of the
information given but the author and the publisher accept no
responsibility for any injury, loss or inconvenience sustained by
anyone using this guide. If you have any comments, information or
photographs which would be useful to include in future editions of
The Motorcaravan Handbook, please send them to Books Division,
Haynes Publishing, Sparkford, Yeovil, Somerset BA22 7JJ.

ISBN 978 1 84425 428 6

British Library Cataloguing in Publication Data
A catalogue record for this book is available from the British Library

Printed by J. H. Haynes & Co. Ltd, Sparkford, Yeovil, Somerset BA22 7JJ, UK

Haynes Publishing
Sparkford, Yeovil, Somerset BA22 7JJ
Telephone: **01963 442030**
Fax: **01963 440001**
E-mail: **sales@haynes.co.uk**
Web site: **www.haynes.co.uk**

the
MOTORCARAVANNING
handbook
BUYING • OWNING • ENJOYING

JOHN WICKERSHAM

CONTENTS

CHAPTER ONE

FREEDOM
TO ROAM

Fresh milk is all that's needed before my motorcaravan is ready for action. The parked vehicle is always equipped with clothes, a basic supply of food, clean bedding, outdoor chairs and wellies. To escape for a break it's merely a matter of climbing aboard, starting the engine and turning right when leaving the drive. That's one of the benefits of owning a motorcaravan. Holidays can be taken with minimum fuss.

An increasing number of motorcaravans is purchased every year.

Launched in the 1950s, VW 'camper vans' have gained iconic status.

The increasing number of motorcaravans

The Society of Motor Manufacturers and Traders (SMMT) has announced that the total sales of new motorcaravans in 2006 reached a new high of 11,069. This amounted to a two per cent rise on the figures achieved in 2005. In addition, the National Caravan Council (NCC) had pointed out previously that the number of new motorcaravans registered at the DVLA in 2005 was over four per cent greater than the figure for 2004 – which in itself had been a record year.

So how many people actually own a motorcaravan in the UK? In a Press Release circulated in 2006, the NCC put the figure at 120,000 vehicles. In reality, it's probably more than that because a significant number of motorcaravans miss the data count for one simple reason. A surprising number of owners purchase a van and convert it themselves as a personal project!

More and more people have realised that ownership of a motorcaravan provides the freedom to roam. In fact, the growing popularity of this activity is easy to prove.

The sales of motorcaravans, for example, are consistently rising, as the figures alongside reveal. Whether this trend reflects people's discontent with airport delays, or disappointments when hotels don't attain the standards expected, is anyone's guess. But the facts reveal a clear picture: more and more people are buying motorcaravans.

Of course, the interest in motorcaravans isn't new. In the 1950s, many people were intrigued when Volkswagen introduced rear-engined light vans that turned out to be ideal for converting into camping vehicles. Over the years the 'V-Dub' became an icon, and people of all ages still display a fond affection for these basic but rather cute 'campers'.

This observation raises another issue. Is this book about 'campers', 'Dormobiles', 'caravanettes', 'coachbuilts', 'van conversions', 'motorcaravans', 'motorhomes' or 'RVs'? And what do these terms actually mean? It all sounds rather confusing. Furthermore, if you chuck an old mattress in the back of a van together with a camp table and a couple of folding chairs, could this be regarded as a motorcaravan?

The accompanying explanation helps to clarify the position as far as 'officialdom' is concerned. Chapter Two, which compares different types of leisure vehicle, also defines some of the classifications. Van conversions, coachbuilts, A-Class models, dismountables, American 'Recreational Vehicles' (RVs) are described in more detail and their respective merits are discussed.

But let's keep things simple, because the whole point of this book is to help readers to find out more about this leisure pursuit. As regards the vehicles, these will be referred to as motorcaravans and motorhomes, since both terms are commonly used in this country. In addition the term 'camper' is often

used to describe small van conversions, so this will also appear in the pages which follow. However, I won't refer to 'campers' or 'camper vans' as 'Dormobiles' – Dormobile was one of the early van converters whose trade name slipped into popular usage some 50 years ago. Even today a few people still describe van conversions as Dormobiles, just as many of us describe vacuum cleaners as Hoovers.

Now let's consider some of the reasons why this book has been written. No doubt you'll have already detected the author's enthusiasm for motorcaravanning. Having tested dozens for magazine articles, and having built two motorcaravans from scratch, I know the pleasures on offer to owners.

On the other hand, it's not easy for intending motorcaravanners to make an informed purchase. In fact the point is often made that a worrying number of owners concede they purchased the wrong model, and change if for another within a couple of years. That can be an expensive mistake.

With this in mind, there are many questions to ask. For instance, what kind of vehicle would best

Choosing the right model isn't as easy as you might imagine.

What is a motorcaravan?

In law-related publications, the term used for this kind of leisure vehicle is 'motor caravan' rather than 'motorhome'. If you check European Type Approval documents you'll also find that a 'motor caravan' is ' ... a special purpose M1 category vehicle constructed to include living accommodation which contains at least the following equipment: seats and table, sleeping accommodation (which may be converted from the seats), cooking facilities, storage facilities.' The statement also adds: 'This equipment shall be rigidly fixed to the living compartment; however, the table may be designed to be easily removable.'

Later in this book, the more complex issues about 'M1 vehicles' and elements like Vehicle Excise Duty will be discussed. But for the moment, it's clear that a panel van with a mattress in the back is not deemed to be a motor caravan. And whilst the term 'motorhome' is often used in this book and specialist magazines, you won't see the term in legal-type publications.

MAX HEIGHT 2.0m

LONG STAY CAR PARK

Sometimes parking places prohibit tall vehicles.

suit your particular needs? Where would you buy it? Where could you keep it? Are there any licensing issues to consider? Are you aware of height issues when searching for somewhere to park? And so on.

Then, having made a purchase, there's a lot to learn. For instance, an appliance like a leisure refrigerator is surprisingly different from the fridges we use in our homes. In addition, some items in the living area need checking and servicing on a regular basis.

One might presume that matters like this would be covered in the owners' manuals supplied by manufacturers, but be warned – some such 'manuals' comprise no more than a folder filled with leaflets supplied by appliance manufacturers. Even if there *is* a model-specific publication, purchasers of pre-owned models often discover that the original owner's manual has been lost.

Even the best handbooks supplied with new models aren't always easy to understand, and getting things to work can be as frustrating as coping with a new digital camera, a desktop computer or a multi-function washing machine. Mindful of this, some manufacturers of electronic goods supply 'quick-start guides' to supplement their instruction manuals. Indeed, the author has recently been commissioned

Some people use a motorcaravan as a base to support their active leisure interests.

by manufacturers of touring caravans to write similar guides for new owners. Curiously, however, quick-start guides have yet to be introduced for motorcaravanners.

Providing helpful guidance thus becomes another function of this book, and later chapters provide hints and tips relating to gas, water and electrical supply systems. Then, on a different note, advice is given about sites and some issues to consider when touring abroad.

Of course, this book isn't the only source of help. To keep abreast of changes in models, legal matters, new campsites, ferry operations and so on, readers are strongly recommended to look at magazines that specialise in motorcaravanning. These ensure you're up-to-date regarding legal issues, product developments and places deserving a visit.

Finally, motorcaravan users are like members of the population as a whole. We're all very different, and whereas some motorcaravanners are young, others are elderly. Some users buy a motorcaravan to pursue active leisure pursuits: others prefer more passive pleasures. Many motorhome owners have children or grandchildren; a number have dogs that get taken on holiday too. Also be aware that several manufacturers offer a service to adapt vehicles to render them suitable for users with physical disabilities.

Bearing all these points in mind, manufacturers produce a huge number of different types of motorcaravan. In fact the buyers' guide in a recent magazine listed 260 British-built models, around 400 European imports and 85 American products. Add to these all the second-hand models on sale and there's plenty of choice. But make sure you buy one that's just right for *you*. The pages that follow will prove a great help in achieving this.

Many owners enjoy outdoor activities and whilst some enjoy passive leisure pursuits, others want a motorcaravan that's able to tow a trailer . . .

Some motorcaravanners have young children or take grandchildren on holiday in their 'van . . .

. . . and some are dog owners. Several sites also provide special dog walks.

CHAPTER TWO

DIFFERENT TYPES OF MOTORCARAVAN

When planning to buy a motorcaravan there are many different types to choose from. You also need to decide on the tasks it will have to perform. Most people want a motorhome for touring in Europe, but some will be looking for expedition vehicles in which to traverse deserts and rocky terrain. Since different models are built to satisfy different needs, you'll have to check the options with care. Here's a way to narrow your choice.

13

With so many products on sale, it's hard to decide on a model you like.

One category of motorcaravans starts life as a panel van, a window van or a multi-purpose car.

Motorcaravans usually fall into one of two broad groups according to the way that they're built. Admittedly there are a few products that defy classification, but the majority fall into the following categories:

1. Van conversions. This type of motorcaravan starts life as a panel van, a multi-purpose vehicle or a van equipped with factory-fitted side windows. When fitted-out with domestic appliances, furniture and comfort items, the resulting motorcaravan is prosaically referred to as a 'van conversion'. Others call it a 'camper van'.

2. Coachbuilt models. These use base vehicles that comprise an engine and chassis; Chapter Three provides further description. All that need be said here is that some base vehicles start life with a cab; others have no cab at all. In automotive language the former is referred to as 'a chassis cab'; the latter is simply a 'chassis cowl'. Both form the base on which a 'coachbuilt' enclosure is mounted.

Coachbuilt motorcaravans are constructed either on a 'chassis cab' or a 'chassis cowl'.

Given that there are two different starting points, it's important to be mindful of their respective merits and weaknesses.

Van conversions

Plus points – If you want a vehicle that drives like a conventional car and is easy to park, a van conversion's the answer. In most cases they're not as large as coachbuilt models and are easier to drive through towns. Manoeuvrability is also important when parking a vehicle at home; some will even fit an ordinary garage, though height is often a problem.

Minus points – A panel van or a van fitted with side windows doesn't lend itself to high output production-line construction. For example, the restricted space inside limits the number of people who can work simultaneously during the fitting-out operation. Moreover, the intricate shape inside a steel shell means that furniture takes a considerable time to install. These factors contribute to the surprisingly high prices of most brand new models.

Coachbuilt motorcaravans

Plus points – By using prefabricated insulated panels for the floor, roof and flat sides, production-line assembly can be utilised. In fact several caravan

Above left: Van conversions are easy to drive, easy to park, and a large sliding door offers generous side access too.

Above: Converting a van is hindered by lack of space, so not many people can work inside at the same time.

To achieve working space, coachbuilt caravans and motorhomes are often assembled on a floor panel – walls are added much later.

Coachbuilt motorcaravans like this Auto-Trail can be spacious inside and a variety of different layouts are offered.

and motorhome manufacturers install furniture and appliances on an unenclosed floor panel, preserving the fitters' freedom of movement by not adding the wall panels until later. This facilitates speedy construction, which in turn is reflected in the vehicle's price. If you compare similarly priced van conversion and coachbuilt models, the latter usually offer a lot more space for your money. Coachbuilt models built with flat sides also provide greater scope for layout variations in the living area.

Minus points – Since the body is constructed using several separate panels, joints can't be avoided. In time these often become weak spots and water ingress then poses a threat.

The situation is made worse when dissimilar materials are used. For example, during extreme temperatures, steel panels forming the cab, aluminium-skinned plywood panels used for the walls and contoured plastic mouldings installed elsewhere all have different rates of expansion/ contraction. The inevitable thermal movements then challenge the flexibility of the joint sealant. In time it becomes brittle, and when it fails the body's weather-resistance is compromised. Examples of coachbuilt models afflicted by damp are often reported in magazine articles.

Bearing in mind that there are two distinct types of motorcaravan, a purchaser needs to consider their

Constructional differences

This chapter only looks at structural elements briefly; Chapter Four pursues the subject in greater depth. As regards base vehicles, these are also described more thoroughly in Chapter Three.

differences very carefully to avoid disappointment later. For example, coachbuilt models may offer spacious and opulent interiors, but, on the other hand, van conversions are better for driving on narrow lanes or exploring remote highland terrain. These comparisons are discussed in more detail in Chapter Five.

Some micro caravans like this Romahome Duo Hylo are sufficiently small to be parked in a typical domestic garage.

VAN CONVERSION MODELS

Micro conversions

At present, not many Micro motorcaravans are being manufactured, although well-maintained, pre-owned vehicles are sometimes offered for sale. Most Micro conversions include the installation of an elevating roof to increase internal headroom, but in road-ready state they can often be accommodated in a domestic garage. For some owners that's very important.

Recent examples

A well-respected designer, Barry Stimson of Design Developments, created models like the Provence. Based on the Citroën Berlingo, a similar conversion is now being sold by Lifestyle Vehicle Developments as La Parisienne.

Another Micro specialist is JC Leisure, whose recent models include the Porterhome, based on the Piaggio Porter, and the Rio, based on the Renault Kangoo.

When exhibited in 2000, the Romahome Duo Hylo also attracted attention. In addition to its garaging potential, the Hylo achieves an internal height of 1.83m when its roof is raised.

Plus points
- Usually the least expensive of all new models
- Easy to drive, park and store
- Good fuel economy
- Suitable as a daily commuting to work vehicle

Minus points
- Little space for storing your gear
- Tidy, organised living is imperative
- Beds formed using cab seats aren't noted for comfort
- On-board toilet provision is usually very basic
- Lounging comforts are lacking

Early VW vans were often used as low-roof 'camper vehicles' and occupants spent all their time in a seated position.

Low fixed-roof conversions

Most motorcaravanners would expect to be able to stand up in the living space, but that's out of the question in some fixed-roof conversions. The idea of cooking and generally living in a seated position was often adopted in converted Volkswagen T2 vans in the1950s. Today, a few van conversions are still built on short wheelbase vans with low rooflines.

Similarly, some manufacturers convert Multi Purpose Vehicles (MPVs) – especially to act as mobile offices for executives who work on the move, convene occasional meetings, and seldom expect the vehicle to provide overnight accommodation.

Recent examples

A well-constructed model, the Murvi Meteor, has been built using Fiat and Peugeot short wheelbase vans. However, versions bearing the Meteor name have also been built with elevating roofs. Fixed roof T4 Volkswagen vans have also been manufactured by Bilbo's Design and Young Conversions. Wheelhome, a company particularly noted for MPV conversions, has also fitted-out vehicles like the fixed-roof Suzuki Wagon R.

Plus points
- Easy to drive and park
- Good fuel economy
- Suitable for daily commuting to work
- Business versions built for mobile executives
- Some models can pass under car park height barriers

Minus points
- Intolerable if you want to stand up to stretch your legs
- Not particularly pleasant for long holidays
- Storage space is minimal
- Heat is lost if single-glazed windows are fitted throughout
- If used, an MPV is a far more expensive base than a light van

High fixed-roof conversions

Some light commercial panel vans have a longer wheelbase and a high roof. For example, the Fiat Ducato long wheelbase (lwb) Maxi van achieves an internal height around 1.88m (74in). That's slightly reduced when insulation material and plywood is added to the floor and ceiling, but high-roof vans on the Fiat Ducato/Peugeot Boxer and Mercedes Sprinter have often been converted into motorcaravans. For example, the Fiat-based Murvi Morello has won awards for its noteworthy design and pleasing comforts.

Overall this type of motorcaravan meets the needs of many people, though it may not be the best answer for really tall owners.

Recent examples

The Murvi Morello is particularly well-known and its converter in Devon has won numerous trophies in 'design and drive' competitions. Although the price is high compared with many van conversions, this model includes a long list of ancillary items. Bilbo's Design, a company well-known for VW conversions, has also developed the Fiat-based Cyclone in recent years.

As regards imported vehicles, the la strada Regent from Germany and the Adria Twin from Slovenia have been well-received in Britain. So has the Tribute from Trigano, which, though well-equipped, is noted for its competitive price. Since Trigano is the parent company behind Auto-Trail, the Tribute is often displayed on Auto-Trail's stand at exhibitions.

Some panel vans like this Renault Master are used for high fixed roof conversions such as the Oregon, built by IH Motor Campers.

Plus points
- Easy to drive
- Reasonable fuel economy
- No need for roof alterations during manufacture
- Good weather integrity
- Small enough to fit most servicing centres with ease
- A large sliding side door offers a wide point of entry

Minus points
- Not suitable for tall owners
- Costly when compared with large coachbuilts of similar price
- A sliding side door limits the number of layouts

Middlesex Motorcaravans offers elevating roof conversions that are individually built to suit clients' requirements.

Elevating (rising) roof conversions

Fitting elevating roofs on vans became a popular practice among converters of Volkswagen (VW) 'camper vans' in the 1950s. As the years passed different elevating systems were developed, and some models have been fitted with hinged wooden panels that fold upwards to form the sides of a box. The VW-based Trooper made by Auto-Sleepers is a well-known example; the Holdsworth Villa 3 was another example from the 1980s.

However, most elevating structures have canvas sides and a specially-built roof panel of glass-reinforced plastic (GRP). Some hinge along the side; others hinge from the front or rear. This is a clever way to create generous headroom, and once a vehicle is parked the elevated structure is sometimes equipped to support a high-level bed. Often it's a 'stretcher-bed' for young children but some manufacturers manage to fit a sturdy double bed for adults.

Today's elevating roof mechanisms are cleverly engineered but you can't overlook the fact that even a well-designed canvas-sided enclosure is not good at retaining heat in the winter.

Recent examples

Auto-Sleepers builds the Trooper with fold-up panel sides. Bilbo's Design offers fabric-sided models like the VW-based Celex, Komba and Nexa. Danbury Motorcaravans has been converting replica Type 3 VWs made under licence in Brazil, and these have been fitted with elevating roofs. However, the project is unlikely to run for much longer – reports suggest that Volkswagen is planning to relaunch these iconic models, albeit with modern engines.

Unusually, VW is one of the only vehicle manufacturers directly involved with motorcaravan conversions as well. The California Comfortline, SE, and Trendline are being built at the Hanover Plant in Germany. Each model features an elevating roof constructed on a VW T5 window van.

Plus points
- Easy to drive and park
- Good fuel economy
- Suitable for daily commuting to work
- More comfortable indoors than a low fixed-roof van
- Good access via the wide sliding side door

Minus points
- The interior can get cold in winter and hot in summer
- Packing away a damp roof leads to damage
- Useful high-level storage is seldom available
- Some lifting mechanisms are fine – but check this yourself

High-tops

Arguably, the high fixed-roof conversions described earlier could be classified in the 'high-top' category. However, in the motorcaravan industry the term is more often used for vans that have been retrospectively fitted with a GRP moulding in place of their original metal panel roof.

In high quality conversions, a GRP ('glass fibre') moulding will perfectly match the colour of the parent van. Its surfaces will also be free of undulations and the moulding will look as if it has always been part of the original vehicle. High-top vans built by Auto-Sleepers are a case in point. Using roof mouldings manufactured by Cheltenham Laminations, Auto-Sleepers is well-known for good body construction.

Of course, GRP roof mouldings can sometimes be added retrospectively and a number of manufacturers will cut away a steel roof panel for a client and install a high-top moulding in its place. Specialists like Middlesex Motorcaravans and Young Conversions are two of several small-scale converters who can offer this service.

Inside a GRP moulded roof shell, it's important that bare surfaces are insulated and this is usually done as part of a conversion package. Some owners also want cubbyholes fitted so that small items can be stored in the enclosure.

Recent examples

Many manufacturers include high-top van conversions in their product line-ups. Auto-Sleepers builds them using several base vehicles, eg the Duetto (Ford Transit panel van), Symbol (Peugeot panel van) and both the Topaz and Trident (VW T5 window van).

Models from Bilbo's Design are also well-known. Torbay Camper Conversions include the Nimbus and Sirius on VW T5 vehicles.

Numerous other converters manufacturing high-top models are listed in the buyers' guides published in motorcaravan magazines.

Small vans are often fitted with a GRP roof moulding to provide headroom – as with this high-top model.

Over-cab coachbuilts provide good space inside, but a large roof pod can lead to surprisingly high fuel consumption.

Above: Even with safety netting, not everyone likes sleeping in the confined space offered by a high-level bed over a cab.

Below: In some cases an over-cab space is used for storage as shown in this Auto-Trail Dakota.

COACHBUILT MODELS

Over-cab coachbuilts

Starting with a chassis cab, many manufacturers construct coachbuilt models that feature a large compartment built directly over the cab. Sometimes referred to as a 'Luton', this compartment is often used to house a fixed double bed.

An over-cab facility offers useful space in the living area, but externally it can detract from a vehicle's appearance. Moreover, some users dislike a high-level enclosed bed and opt to have cupboards fitted instead. Large 'pods' certainly don't help a vehicle's aerodynamic properties and fuel economy can be badly affected.

Underneath, a sturdy chassis supports the floor of the living space. This is either the original chassis supplied by the vehicle manufacturer or a lighter structure designed by AL-KO for motorcaravans. Further information about these chassis is given in Chapter Three.

As regards the living enclosure, this is usually built using prefabricated, bonded and insulated panels, and purpose-made plastic mouldings. Alternatively, a few manufacturers use monocoque construction in which a one-piece shell of GRP is mounted on the chassis.

Monocoque GRP body shells are usually rather heavy but the benefits of a seam-free, one-piece shell are indisputable. The lack of joints means that the weatherproofing qualities are as good as those of a GRP boat. The material also enables a builder to create an attractive, curvaceous shell without the prosaic flat sides found on most coachbuilt models.

Recent examples

Many manufacturers specialise in the construction of coachbuilt motorcaravans. In Britain, manufacturers like Autocruise, Auto-Sleepers, Auto-Trail, the Explorer Group and the Swift Group have dozens of models on offer. In fact the Swift Group presents models under the different badge names of Ace, Bessacarr and Swift.

Huge numbers of over-cab coachbuilts are also produced by manufacturers in mainland Europe, and several British dealers specialise in selling models imported from abroad.

As regards monocoque examples, Auto-Sleepers commissioned a celebrated car designer, the late William Towns, to create a GRP monocoque living compartment. His creations were built by Cheltenham Laminations and in 1980 Auto-Sleepers launched its first distinctive monocoque. Since then the product has been updated to reflect changes in vehicle design, and recent Auto-Sleepers monocoque coachbuilts include the Peugeot Boxer-based Executive, Mezan and Talisman, and the Ford-based Amethyst.

Monocoque models from manufacturers in mainland Europe include the Mobilvetta Kimu and la strada Nova.

One of the first GRP seam-free monocoque body shell designs was introduced in the 1980s and used on Auto-Sleepers' coachbuilts.

23

Plus points
- Coachbuilt motorcaravans offer spacious accommodation
- An over-cab bed involves little preparation at bedtime
- Considering size and price, coachbuilt models are particularly good value

Minus points
- Though easy to drive, a coachbuilt doesn't perform like a car
- Road-handling can be ponderous and punctuated by body roll
- Negotiating narrow lanes can be challenging
- Parking is sometimes difficult
- A typical coachbuilt isn't good for daily commuting

After a slow start, low-profile coachbuilt models such as this 2007 Knaus Sport Ti have become increasingly popular in the UK.

Low-profile coachbuilts

Most points relating to over-cab coachbuilts are applicable to low-profile models as well. The key difference is the omission of an over-cab 'Luton'.

Some owners find an over-cab bed too restrictive and it can easily become a 'dumping area' for sun-loungers, camp tables and other possessions. The issue of aerodynamics and fuel economy also renders 'Luton' designs questionable. In recognition of these points, low-profile models have been developed which offer a reduced height and a cleaner roofline. This style of motorcaravan was quickly accepted in mainland Europe, and UK manufacturers now produce examples as well.

Recent examples

Autocruise, together with its Pioneer range, includes more low-profile models than anything else. Other major manufacturers like Auto-Sleepers, Auto-Trail, the Explorer Group, Lunar and the Swift Group have been more cautious, but all now include examples of low-profile models in their ranges.

Imported low-profile models from Continental manufacturers include examples from Adria, Benimar, Burstner, Eura Mobil, Frankia, Hymer, Knaus, Laika, Maess, TEC and many more. The Hobby range in particular is noted for its high proportion of low-profile models, all of which bear the company's distinctive design cues.

Plus points
- Low-profiles share most of the points applicable to over-cab coachbuilts
- The reduced height is helpful when driving near trees
- They are likely to achieve better fuel economy figures

Minus points
- Most of the disadvantages of over-cab models also apply to low-profile models
- They offer reduced storage space
- Headroom may not be sufficient for tall users

A-class

Many discerning enthusiasts aspire to own an A-Class motorcaravan. There are undoubtedly smart examples but some features aren't to everyone's liking.

Using terms introduced earlier, an A-Class model is normally built using a 'chassis cowl' as opposed to a 'chassis cab'. In consequence, the manufacturer has to construct a body that's all-embracing. Since a chassis cowl doesn't have a cab and is open to the elements, the body design integrates the driving zone with the living accommodation.

Building an A-Class body is a major undertaking and it needs to include a windscreen, cab windows and a means of access for the driver. In the event, many manufacturers avoid the exacting task of building the kind of doors fitted to a normal cab. This means that the only way to reach the driving controls is by using the same door that provides entry to the living quarters. No other door is provided.

For many people, this is a poor arrangement, so Auto-Trail boldly fabricated hinged cab-like doors in the Grande Frontier A-Class. These are made using GRP and whilst they lack the rigidity of standard steel doors, the result's far better than having to rely on a single 'caravan' door to gain entry.

Replicating steel automotive doors complete with electric windows isn't easy, so Belgian manufacturer Maess used another strategy. Recognising that a standard cab has all the attributes needed apart from being too narrow, the company found ways to widen its steel shell. By skilfully adding small panels and subsequently installing a wider, commercial, stock-sized windscreen, they produced a masterpiece of modification.

Of course, one of the many opportunities presented by a wider cab in A-Class

This Pilote A-Class motorcaravan is built using a chassis cowl that supports a body embracing both the driving and living areas.

Right: By skilfully widening a standard chassis cab, Maess offers A-Class models with sturdy doors and wind-down windows.

Opposite: American RV models with their slide-out sides can be purchased in the UK from several import specialists.

Plus points
- The body design lends itself to clean, attractive lines
- An elevating bed in the cab can be left with its bedding in place
- Most models have well-appointed interiors
- Storage capacity is notably good

Minus points
- A cab bereft of doors is not to everyone's liking
- Replacement windscreens can be very expensive
- Large models are not suitable for use on narrow lanes
- Parking is often a problem
- Fuel economy on large models is usually disappointing
- If a large side panel gets damaged, repairs are often costly
- Some campsites are unable to accept large vehicles

motorcaravans is the chance to install a drop-down bed. Even though seats in the living area can normally be converted into beds, the one above the cab seats can be folded away with its bedding still in place. Clever geometry and gas spring assistance means that an elevating mechanism requires little operator-effort.

Apart from this feature, A-Class interiors aren't a great deal different from chassis cab coachbuilts – unless you include those grandiose monsters built on truck chassis that command six-figure prices.

Recent examples

Few British manufacturers have built A-Class models. The compact Autoking produced by Elddis in the 1980s achieved disappointing sales. The 1998 Bel-Air manufactured by Swift wasn't a big seller either and was withdrawn after just four years. Auto-Sleepers introduced the Luxor in 2002 but this was essentially a reworked version of the Italian-built Mirage. Finally, Auto-Trail introduced the Grande Frontier in 2005; this British-built model received much praise but production ended in 2007.

Far more A-Class models are available from manufacturers in mainland Europe. Maess products are imported from Belgium, the Pilote range from France, Laika from Italy, and many examples come from German manufacturers, including the ubiquitous Hymer models.

Among the largest vehicles are marques like Carthago and ClouLINER, which are undoubtedly impressive. So are models built in North Wales by MCL. Fitted-out to customer specifications, MCL's beautiful creations cost around £250,000.

American RVs

A significant number of big American recreational vehicles or RVs are purchased in this country. However, whether driving an inter-state leviathan on European roads is appropriate is a matter often debated. Furthermore, some campsite owners can't accommodate vehicles of this size and weight.

Surprisingly, American RVs are not as expensive to purchase as many people imagine. New models are hardly cheap, but if you calculate floor area and take account of all the standard equipment, you get an awful lot for your money. However, the purchase price is only one issue: servicing this type of vehicle and filling its fuel tanks is an aspect you mustn't ignore.

Another point to note relates to the build quality inside. The design of American furniture won't meet everyone's taste and buyers should look at it closely. Sometimes you'll find cabinets that were assembled in haste and the standard of craftsmanship is disappointing.

Recent examples

Motorcaravan magazines list several UK importers who specialise in the sale and servicing of RVs. It's probably best to purchase through a specialist dealer because electrical items and water components can be totally different from equivalent European products. Importers include Cheshire American Motorhomes, Dudleys American Motorhomes, Freedom Motorhomes, Gold RVs, Midland International Motorhomes, Oakwell Motorhomes, Travelworld, and Westcroft Motorhome Centre.

There are also active clubs whose members are usually eager to offer advice.

Plus points
- Storage space aplenty
- A veritable home on wheels
- Models offer items like hip baths, huge TVs, settees and so on

Minus points
- Some campsites can't accommodate large vehicles
- Fuel and maintenance costs are high
- Size limits touring possibilities; storage might also be difficult
- Few specialists have space for repairs, servicing and MOT tests
- Non-standard parts may be fitted; spares might be hard to obtain
- Build quality inside is sometimes disappointing

Anyone who owns a pickup truck like this powerful Nissan has an opportunity to use it for holidays too.

Plus points
- If you own a pickup truck, a pod is an inexpensive extra
- Detaching the pod releases the base vehicle for use

Minus points
- Cab space doesn't contribute to the living area
- With a top-heavy rig, dismountables can roll badly on twisting roads

OTHER MODELS

I conceded earlier that a few products defy classification. That's not to say that they aren't important options, although neither of the types described here are as popular in Europe as they are in North America. However, if pickup trucks become more common in Europe then both products listed below are likely to become popular here.

Dismountables

The amount of internal space in a dismountable 'pod' is surprisingly good, and once it's detached the base vehicle is ready for driving off-site.

Recent examples

Apollo, based in Lancashire, has manufactured dismountable units for more than a decade, with versions for both single and crew-cab pickup trucks. Ranger Motorhomes from the same county also manufactures dismountables. American products, including folding-roof versions, are imported by Niche Marketing. Easy Campers from Sweden are imported by Teknosys.

This dismountable unit manufactured by Ranger in Lancashire offers a surprising amount of living space.

Fifth wheelers

These articulated products require a pickup truck for towing. Not that it's like towing a caravan. Forget a poorly matched caravan's problem of snaking, and the difficulties of reversing an outfit. Fifth wheelers are far easier to control and deserve more acclaim in this country.

Of course, some of the American juggernauts are very large for Britain's small roads but they offer an excellent way to travel.

Recent examples

Products made by the Fifth Wheel Co in North Wales are built to extremely high standards. Arguably their original Celtic Rambler GRP monocoque is large for many of Britain's roads but now there's a smaller version too, albeit with slide-out sides. They're sold with or without a Nissan pickup and customer requirements can be built-in to order.

American products are imported by Nene Overland and Niche Marketing.

So is a fifth wheeler a caravan or a motorhome? Classification uncertainty is not the fault of the products, which have many points in their favour. But so do other models – as this chapter has already shown.

These high quality products made in North Wales by The Fifth Wheel Company are specially built to meet European standards.

Plus points
- Surprisingly easy to tow, reverse and manoeuvre on site
- Prices are not as high as many presume
- An ideal addition for owners of suitable pickup trucks
- A permanent bed fits into the half-height front
- Usually spacious inside

Minus points
- There's a need for even smaller models – one-off micro models have been built in the past
- Fifth wheelers might be hard to sell-on later

CHAPTER THREE

BASE VEHICLES

Though it's tempting to choose a motorcaravan solely on the basis of its living accommodation that would be a mistake. From an early stage in your decision-making process you need to consider its road-going characteristics and to check that it's pleasant to drive. This means you'll need to compare different types of base vehicle and decide which ones meet your particular needs. Products that look good in a showroom are sometimes quite dull on the road.

31

Motorcaravan driving courses are run by The Camping and Caravanning Club.

Courses to improve your driving skills are run by both The Camping and Caravanning Club and The Caravan Club.

Today's car drivers are pretty versatile people. The range of vehicles currently on sale means that one moment you might be driving a small town car, and the next an off-road vehicle, perched on a seat that's high above the ground.

Anyone who's had a range of experiences like these would find that driving most types of motorcaravan is relatively easy. If not, both The Camping and Caravanning Club and The Caravan Club run short training courses for prospective motorhome drivers.

Also bear in mind that the majority of motorcaravans are constructed using light commercial vehicles (LCVs), and modern examples are surprisingly car-like to drive. That's why many owners feel confident to take the wheel of a small or medium-sized motorhome. On the other hand, if your licence permits and you're eager to purchase an American RV or one of Europe's larger conversions, heavy goods vehicles (HGVs) are *not* like a car, and appropriate training is recommended.

Converted MPVs

In recent years the distinctions between cars, multi-purpose vehicle (MPVs) and vans have become increasingly blurred. In fact a few companies have specialised in the conversion of MPVs, into campervans, and Wheelhome is especially prominent in this field. Of course, these are fitted with a lining and finished inside like a car at the point of sale. In consequence converted MPVs are considerably more expensive than campervans based on light commercial vans.

 Technical Tip

Terminology

Throughout this book, the term 'base vehicle' is used to describe the automotive product on which a motorcaravan is built. Just to clear up potential confusion, note that when some people comment that they'd have liked their motorcaravan to have been built 'on a different chassis', what they actually mean is 'on a different base vehicle'.

When the word 'chassis' is used in this book it refers specifically to the structure that supports a coachbuilt motorcaravan body. To be pedantic, a panel van or side-window van doesn't have a traditional chassis; in fact it's like a modern car, which is built with a floorpan. Strengthened brackets that form part of this steel base accept items of running gear such as axles and suspension components.

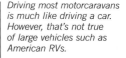

In the previous chapter, the point was also made that most motorhomes are either 'fitted-out' vans or coachbuilt constructions on top of a commercial chassis. This distinction also influences what they're like when you sit at the wheel.

Driving most motorcaravans is much like driving a car. However, that's not true of large vehicles such as American RVs.

To some people a 'chassis' refers to the base vehicle; in this book the term refers specifically to the support structure.

Van conversions, like cars, are built on a reinforced 'floor pan' as opposed to a traditional chassis.

Tall drivers often find that seats heightened by retrofitted swivels cause their eye-line to meet the top of the screen.

GENERAL MATTERS

Since a large number of potential owners haven't had experience driving a range of light commercial vehicles, they won't be aware of individual quirks. For example, taller drivers often find that in some LCVs the screen is too low for comfort. This arises if seats in the cab are retrofitted with 360° swivel systems, since these often add height to the seat squab and tall people then find their line of vision is too close to the top of the screen.

Shorter people might decide that high seats won't present a problem for them. That's certainly true where the screen is concerned, but they may have issue with the floor height instead. This may sound silly, but letters published in motorcaravan magazines reveal that many people sitting in the passenger seat find their feet barely touch the floor. The replies often report how owners solve this by using things like typists' foot-support platforms, hassocks from churches, and home-made plinths.

Details such as this can prove irritating and might come as a surprise to new motorcaravanners. This is why potential owners are advised to hire a motorcaravan for a short period to gain first-hand experience of its driving and habitation characteristics. Admittedly hiring can be costly during high season, but it's less costly outside peak periods.

Some dealers also run 'hire before you buy' schemes. Having hired one of their vehicles, clients often have the fee reimbursed if they subsequently buy a model from the dealer within a certain time frame.

All our comments so far have been concerned with matters of detail. Now let's look at the larger picture.

Useful Tip

Arrange a test drive

- There are far too many cases of new owners changing their motorcaravan a very short time after purchasing it. One reason for dissatisfaction concerns the driving experience and the base vehicle's features.
- It appears that many people don't insist on a test drive before making a purchase. That's certainly an oversight.
- If a dealer isn't prepared to arrange a test drive, it would be better to go elsewhere.

Seat height

Recognising that retrofitted seat swivel mechanisms often render the height of cab seats unsuitable, when Fiat launched its revised Ducato in 2006 one of its improvements involved a redesigned seating arrangement that addressed this.

Owners of earlier models can sometimes remedy the problem by fitting lower profile plinths sold by independent specialists such as TEK Seating. These fit in place of the original items and bring the seat squabs closer to the floor.

POINTS TO CONSIDER

From their 2006 models on, Fiat fitted lower bases and swivelling turntables so that the final seat heights are more acceptable.

In addition to idiosyncrasies like seat heights, potential owners obviously need to give due consideration to matters such as:

- Right- or left-hand drive?
- Engine capacity
- Choice of fuel – diesel or petrol?
- Economy
- Transmission – front-, rear- or four-wheel drive?
- Gears – manual gearbox, automatic or 'sprint shift'?
- Suspension – leaf spring, coil spring, torsion bars or air bellows?
- Chassis – vehicle manufacturer's or AL-KO Kober's products?
- Potential for towing
- Option lists – ABS, airbags, stability controls, GPS systems, upgraded stereos, central locking, electric windows, high output alternator, upgraded payload capacity and so on.

Many motorcaravans can't be fitted with a towing bracket – check this detail if you intend to tow a trailer like this EZrise air lifting model.

Many coachbuilt models have been paired with Fiat's 2.8 turbo diesel engine, which is pleasingly powerful.

Right- or left-hand drive?

Some imported motorcaravans are only available in left-hand-drive form. These can be difficult to sell at a later date and typically command a lower price during a trade-in transaction. This usually deters potential owners from being tempted into buying what's affectionately known as a 'left-hooker'.

On the other hand, some retired owners spend a considerable amount of time in the warmer parts of mainland Europe, especially during the winter months. If such trips are going to constitute a significant proportion of your own motorcaravanning activities, the purchase of a left-hand-drive model might make good sense.

Engine capacity

There are considerable differences between the performance characteristics of base vehicles' engines. Drivers' expectations differ as well. Some of us drive cautiously and are happy to potter along country lanes; others prefer a brisker pace and wish to proceed along motorways with purposeful zest.

Once again, first-hand experience is the best way to compare the performance of vehicles, as the author found for himself. A campervan he owned for ten years was notable for its lively driving. Then the editor of a motorcaravan magazine commissioned a report on a coachbuilt model and this produced some surprises. The vehicle was a 1995 Swift Royale over-cab model based on a Fiat Ducato with a 1.9 non-turbo diesel engine. Driving across France on motorways was one of the dullest drives imaginable. Even with the pedal pressed to the floor, speeds exceeding 60mph were only achieved with a struggle.

A similar test was requested several years later using a Fiat Ducato coachbuilt fitted with a 2.8 turbo diesel engine. The difference was hard to believe. Acceleration, general pulling power, top speeds and economy delivered the additional

performance that many of us expect. More recently motorcaravans built on a Renault Master base vehicle with a 3.0-litre turbo diesel engine have also made their mark. Having the extra power in reserve is appealing, especially when you recognise that from an aerodynamic viewpoint the body shape of coachbuilt motorcaravans is little more streamlined than a house brick.

Many readers won't share the author's preferences regarding acceleration, speed, emissions and fuel economy. But please recognise that engine performances vary a lot and that's why test drives are important.

Choice of fuel

The majority of today's motorcaravans are driven by turbo diesel engines, and the pedestrian performance of *non*-turbo diesels has already been described. It's also worth noting that non-turbo models are unlikely to offer improved fuel economy.

In recent years there have been significant improvements in diesel engine design, and compared with petrol-driven units they've achieved remarkable levels of efficiency. It's a shame, therefore, that fuel forecourt prices in the UK have been unfavourable to owners of diesel vehicles, whereas in much of mainland Europe the cost of diesel fuel is much lower.

Petrol-driven motorcaravans are far less common but they still have some points in their favour. The initial purchase price of a petrol-engined vehicle is often lower, the performance is good, and the power unit is usually less noisy.

Most commercial vehicles traditionally have diesel engines because they're more robustly built and typically achieve a longer working life than petrol units; and since motorcaravans are normally built on LCVs, this helps account for the preponderance of turbo diesel models. However, they're certainly good to drive and are a giant's leap away from the smelly, smoky and plodding power units that once gave diesel engines a bad name.

The Fiat 2.3 litre 120 Multijet engine in this 2007 Adria Twin is both lively and economical.

Some engines are more fuel-efficient than others, but large over-cab constructions also affect fuel economy.

Economy

In addition to fuel economy based on the type of base vehicle, don't forget issues related to conversion elements. Both the weight and shape of motorcaravans are key contributors to fuel economy. There's little doubt that a modern van conversion is going to stand a better chance of achieving good fuel economy than a coachbuilt model with an identical engine. Large over-cab lumps certainly don't enhance aerodynamic performance, though the disadvantages might not become significant until you attain higher speeds.

Work on alternative fuels is also being carried out with increasing vigour. It *is* possible to convert engines to run on LPG, though this is catching on in Britain only slowly. Biologically-produced versions of diesel fuel are also gaining a foothold, and are worth keeping an eye on.

Transmission

Like so many modern cars, LCVs have become predominantly front-wheel driven. However, Ford has only recently followed this trend on some Transit models, while the Mercedes Sprinter has remained wedded to its rear-wheel-drive configuration. As regards four-wheel drive, only a few models have offered this, including some VW Transporters and vans from Mazda and Toyota.

Whatever the benefits of rear-wheel drive, the long propshaft fitted to vehicles with a front-mounted engine and driven back axle can make it harder for a motorcaravan manufacturer to install components below floor level. It also precludes replacing a short chassis on a pre-converted chassis cab with a longer chassis made by AL-KO Kober. This is one reason why the Mercedes Sprinter hasn't been used more often by motorcaravan manufacturers.

Rear-wheel-drive vehicles have a prop shaft under the floor and this can present problems when fitting underfloor tanks.

The fifth gear ratio on some Fiats is too high for heavy vehicles but it's not expensive to alter the gearing.

Gears

LCVs have been fitted with manual gearboxes for many years. Models offering five gears gained ground in the 1990s, but many of these have now been superseded by six-gear versions.

Fiat won much acclaim when the Ducato was launched in 1993 with its cable-operated, fascia-mounted gear lever. Improved access to the living area was noted at once, and a decade later this had become the norm in all but a few base vehicles. However, in some post-2000 Ducatos the fifth gear proved too high when the vehicle was heavily laden, and a number of owners had a surprisingly inexpensive conversion carried out to achieve a lower ratio.

For many years automatic transmissions were seldom available in LCVs, although some firms installed retrospective electronic systems. The Sprintshift (Mercedes) and the Durashift (Ford) were among the first to appear, and now other manufacturers also offer several types of automatic systems, including Volkswagen on the new T5. There's clearly a need for such options, especially for elderly and partly disabled drivers.

Automatic gearboxes have been unusual on vans but the latest Volkswagen T5 includes this option.

Rear leaf springs are quite common on light commercial vehicles, but ride comfort isn't always pleasing.

Above: Motorhomes built on the distinctive lightweight chassis from AL-KO Kober benefit from torsion bar rear suspension.

Below: To enjoy first class comfort and an automatic self-levelling system, some vehicles have full 'air suspension'.

Right: Adding 'air assisters' can boost tired springs but don't confuse this with air suspension, which replaces steel springs.

Suspension

Although Volkswagen has been noted for its use of rear coil springs, this is an unusual feature. Most commercial vehicles use leaf springs at the rear, which are fine when carrying industrial loads but aren't the most comfortable suspension for 'people-carrying' vehicles. However, on base vehicles fitted with an AL-KO Kober motorhome chassis, the rear axle offers the benefits of torsion bar suspension.

A few motorcaravans also have the original leaf spring system removed and replaced by TVAC's computer-controlled, load-levelling 'air suspension' system. AL-KO has developed air suspension too.

This mustn't be confused with systems in which leaf springs are augmented by inflatable bellows. This retrofit strategy is correctly known as 'air assistance', in which the installation of air inflatable units helps compensate for tired springs. However, these products do *not* help to raise the permitted loading limits of a vehicle. It's also apparent that some suppliers are quite wrongly describing as 'air suspension', modified arrangements in which inflatable units are added to help weak steel springs. Retrofit 'air assistance' conversions do *not* offer the same benefits as a full 'air suspension' installation.

The chassis supplied with a base vehicle is a robust structure and many builders use this for their motorcaravans.

Chassis

Some coachbuilt motorcaravans are constructed on the vehicle manufacturer's original chassis and suspension. These structures are sound, but until Fiat introduced its 2006 chassis-cab range, original chassis have not been designed specifically for motorcaravans. This is why some motorcaravan manufacturers have preferred to use AL-KO Kober's purpose-made, lightweight motorcaravan chassis instead. These also have torsion bar suspension for improved comfort.

The AL-KO product offers several additional benefits including an opportunity to create a lower floor height in the living quarters. Alternatively, some motorcaravans are produced with a double floor so

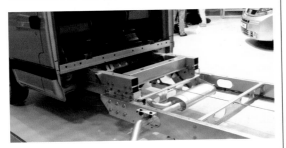

Lightweight AL-KO chassis are sometimes fitted as a replacement. This example offers a lower floor height.

This AL-KO chassis is specified by motorhome builders that want a double floor. Tanks and services use the lower section.

On some models, such as this 2004 model Bessacarr, the body extends too far rearwards of chassis members to safely fit an AL-KO towbar.

that water tanks, services and storage lockers can be placed in a dry area, which may even receive ducted heat from the living space.

The AL-KO chassis is also made to receive easy-fit add-on items such as a scooter rack or a towbar. However, these products can't be fitted where a coachbuilt manufacturer extends the rear part of the body enclosure beyond the last cross member on the chassis. For instance, several older models from the Swift Group – including some in the Bessacarr range – can't accept these accessories because the body extends beyond the AL-KO chassis more than the requisite distance. That's changed in 2008 models.

More information on chassis alternatives is provided in Chapter Four of *The Motorcaravan Manual* (2nd edition), also published by Haynes.

Potential for towing

Whether you plan to purchase a van conversion or any form of coachbuilt, if it's your intention to tow a trailer you need to check very carefully that it's possible to fit a tow bracket. Many vans appear in catalogues listing model-specific tow brackets, but on closer inspection you'll find these can't be installed once the vehicle has been converted into a motorcaravan. Items such as underfloor water tanks often obscure fixing points for brackets.

Independent specialist PWS designs and installs tailor-made towbars – but not all vehicles can be thus equipped.

Option lists

Consistent with the growing sophistication of commercial vehicles, the latest motorcaravans are often supplied with ABS braking, airbags, central locking, electric windows, high-quality sound systems, satellite navigation and computerised stability control devices, just like many cars. Decide what features you consider important, and check specification details with care.

Less well known is that you have the chance to specify a high output alternator, which clearly copes better with the task of running 12V components both on the base vehicle *and* inside the living area.

EXAMPLES OF BASE VEHICLES

This is a recent cab, although Fiat's convenient fascia-mounted, cable-operating gear lever first appeared on 1993 models.

Daihatsu

For a while the tiny Hijet van was converted by Devon and JC Leisure to create micro campervans. However, poor roadholding, susceptibility to crosswinds and minimal protection from front impact didn't help the number of sales. The Piaggio Porter, based on the Daihatsu, has also been made under licence.

Fiat Ducato

The first model was introduced in 1981 and over 900,000 were built. In 1991 it was subjected to a restyle but this revamped model was short-lived. The Mark 2 Ducato was launched in 1993 and its fascia-mounted, cable-driven gear selector was seen as a ground-breaking feature. Without the intrusion of a floor-mounted gear stick it became easy to move into the living area from the cab.

A facelift model appeared in 2002 with cab improvements and changes to the engine, but no automatic transmission versions for right-hand-drive vehicles. Similarly, four-wheel-drive versions were not available in the United Kingdom.

In recent years the Fiat Ducato has been the base vehicle for over half of all UK-built motorcaravans, and in order to retain this dominance a completely new model was introduced in 2006. Until then, most vehicle manufacturers regarded motorcaravan applications as a relatively insignificant segment of the market. The majority went to commercial users and few design/specification features were available for motorcaravan converters.

But Fiat changed its stance in 2006 by introducing vehicles specifically designed for conversion into motorhomes. These included anti-roll bars and a wider rear axle to create a track of 1.98m as opposed to the standard 1.79m. The top of the chassis members is also 145mm lower (around 5¾in).

When Fiat launched a new Ducato in 2006, the company introduced motorhome-specific chassis for the first time.

The ratings for spring and shock absorbers have also been amended to suit passengers, and there's a 3.8m long chassis version. Moreover, running the brake cables to one side of the chassis instead of adopting a central route has facilitated the installation of such items as underfloor tanks.

Cab changes include structural reinforcements and roofs that are pre-cut in the factory, improved B pillars for integration with a coachbuilt body, and swivelling cab seats attaining the appropriate height.

A range of Multijet engines has also been heralded as further improvements, both in terms of power and pulling performance ('torque'). Matched with this are significant reductions in exhaust emissions and improvements in fuel efficiency. Meanwhile, a new six-speed gearbox provides ratios especially suitable for motorhome driving.

Comparisons are certainly not easy to make with earlier models but general opinion has revealed that the Multijet engine is a vast improvement. For instance, the motorhome-only 2.3-litre 130 Multijet has greater power than the 2.8JTD engine used in previous generation vehicles (130 over 127bhp), greater torque (320Nm against 300) and a predicted 23 per cent improvement in fuel economy. Then

Below: The Fiat Multi-jet range of engines introduced in 2006 offers good economy, reduced emissions and improved performance.

Below right: The radically different bulbous-nosed front on Fiat models launched in 2006 didn't meet with universal approval.

Many models from the Fiat Ducato range are also available bearing Citroën Relay and Peugeot Boxer badges.

there's the 3.0-litre 160 Multijet, which is more powerful still.

Time will reveal how things turn out in practice, and the revised bulbous front on the latest Fiat Ducatos has certainly not appealed to everyone.

Ford Transit

The Ford Transit has been in production in various 'generations' for over 40 years. It is also worthy of note that it's been by far the best-selling light commercial vehicle in Britain. Enthusiasts point out there have been three 'generations' but five 'series' of Transits since it was launched in 1965. Originally, all but one model in the 1965 range had petrol engines; today that situation has been totally reversed and diesel is almost universal.

But the Transit hasn't been popular in a motorcaravan context, one reason being the fact that most versions have been rear-wheel-drive. As we've already seen, the existence of a prop-shaft running down the centre of a vehicle to drive the back axle can pose problems when installing underfloor items such as water tanks. A further disincentive has been the long-standing use of floor-mounted gear sticks. However, in September 2000 the Transit range broke with tradition when some models became available in front-wheel drive form.

In the general absence of automatic gear change systems in LCVs, it should be added that some Transits have been fitted with what Ford calls the 'Durashift' automatic gearbox.

In 2007 further revisions were made to Transits, including cosmetic features such as headlamp and grill alterations. In the cab, a dash-mounted gear stick and car-type instrumentation were noteworthy. Under the bonnet a range of new TDCi common-rail diesel engines was introduced, and it appears that a revised

The rear-wheel-drive Mercedes Sprinter has been a popular base vehicle with A-Class motorcaravan manufacturers.

electronic automatic transmission is likely to replace the Durashift system. These changes immediately prompted the manufacturer of Orian motorcaravans to use the Transit as the base for its Dorado and Gemini models, which were previously built on Peugeot vehicles.

Iveco

The large Daily van has been popular with a number of Italian converters and includes models with prodigious payloads. However, Iveco vehicles are more 'van-like' to drive than many models and some owners haven't found this to their liking.

Mercedes Vito and Sprinter

Though used by some converters, the Vito van hasn't been as popular in the motorcaravan industry as the Fiat Ducato and VW Transporter, and has been described in some reports as having heavier controls and less pleasurable drive characteristics.

The Sprinter has been more popular and is a commonly chosen base vehicle for A-Class motorcaravans. However, rear-wheel-drive vans have been used in conversions too. Depending on the model, the Sprinter can also be supplied with an automatic gearbox using the Mercedes 'Sprintshift' system. This is a hybrid model in the form of a clutchless manual/automatic.

Further changes occurred in 2007 following collaboration with Volkswagen. The Sprinter was launched with a number of wheelbase options and a Gross Vehicle Weight limit of between 3,000kg and 5,000kg depending on model. New engine options also appeared and diesel versions have a six-speed gearbox as standard. The not always popular Sprintshift system was replaced by a hybrid torque-converter/automated manual transmission that has proved popular in some Mercedes cars.

In spite of the Peugeot badge, the engine and major features of this vehicle will have been assembled in Fiat's factory.

Peugeot

These are 'badge-engineered' products. For instance, the Partner is virtually a Fiat Berlingo, the Expert is a Fiat Scudo/Citroën Dispatch and the Boxer is a Fiat Ducato/Citroën Relay.

Renault

In spite of their capable features, Renaults haven't very often been used as base vehicles in the past, but that started to change around 2005. However, some small campervans have been built using the Kangoo, which has been available with petrol and diesel engines, automatic transmission options and four-wheel drive.

Recent versions of the Trafic (shared with Vauxhall as the Vivaro) have been used by a number of converters. The latest Master is certainly becoming extremely popular and is likely to gain increasing prominence.

Recent Renault Masters have some lively engine options and this 2005 Knaus Sun Ti was constructed on a Renault base vehicle.

This updated version of the traditional VW Camper van was recently being built under licence in Brazil.

Toyota Hiace van and Hilux pickup

The mid-sized Hiace van is a rear-wheel-drive vehicle. The Hilux four-wheel-drive pickup truck is a good base for dismountable motorcaravans.

Volkswagen Transporter and LT

Van conversions have been based on Volkswagen vehicles for a long time – but less frequently as a basis for coachbuilt motorcaravans. Other models in the VW range have included the car-like Caddy and the LT. The latter, however, hasn't been a popular base vehicle due to its truck-like features, including a floor-mounted gear shift.

Historically, the 'split-screen' Transporter of the 1950s and the later 'bay window' model of the 1960s and 1970s undoubtedly popularised motorcaravanning in Europe; many regard it as an 'icon' in its own right.

Compared with the Transporter, VW's LT van has never been a popular base for motorcaravan manufacture. This model finally ran its course around 2006, to be replaced by the VW Crafter. This shares components with the Mercedes Sprinter and exemplifies the continuing links forged between different vehicle manufacturers. Engines, however, are not shared and VW offers the Crafter with its car-type five-cylinder power units. Whether it will

The VW Crafter replaced the VW LT van in 2006, but whether it will be used by many converters remains to be seen.

be used more by van converters remains to be seen, although at the time of writing models have been built in Germany by CS-Reisemobil, Robel and Seitz. Automatic transmission is likely to become an option.

A number of specialists are importing pre-owned Mazda Bongo vehicles from Japan to convert into campervans.

Mazda Bongo Friendee

On account of the strict test regimes in Japan, many vehicles are replaced when comparatively new. This has led to a blossoming import strategy in the UK whereby pre-owned models like the Mazda Bongo are used for converting into motorcaravans. Not only is there a price attraction, but these base vehicles are usually well-equipped with numerous optional extras, including four-wheel drive. Wellhouse Leisure near Huddersfield is one of several specialists which convert these imports to suit customers' individual requirements.

Summary

The base vehicle is undoubtedly an important part of any motorcaravan 'package', and whilst it's often claimed that there are few poor vehicles being manufactured today, that's not to say that there aren't some that suit some owners more than others. That's why it's so important to arrange a test drive before making a purchase.

Many different base vehicles are now available and potential owners should take a test drive before making a purchase.

CHAPTER FOUR

DESIGN AND
CONSTRUCTION

Many potential owners are not particularly interested in the design and construction of motorcaravans and some might skip this chapter. However, that could be a bad mistake; if you acquire a rudimentary knowledge about constructional elements, you'll soon be able to recognise good and bad workmanship. Similarly, if something goes wrong you'll be better informed about remedial work when discussing repairs with a dealer.

51

Designers are faced with the task of fitting a lot into the available space.

If a motorcaravan is to provide comfortable living irrespective of season, good insulation is essential.

Is it really necessary to know how motorcaravans are designed and constructed? Provided everything is working properly, why would you need to know anything about its construction, roof design or choice of components like windows?

Let's compare this with the purchase of a house. Does a potential buyer need to enquire if a property has double glazing? Does it really matter if rain creates large puddles on a flat roof? Is there any need to know the strengths and weaknesses of different types of central heating system and the fuel they use? Of course there is! And such things are equally important when you're purchasing a motorcaravan. Thermal insulation, for example, determines whether a vehicle can provide comfortable accommodation in cold weather. Some motorcaravans are far better insulated than others and this also affects comfort levels in summer. Park a vehicle with poor insulation in direct sunlight and it becomes like an oven inside.

Practical issues such as these need to be taken into account. To give another example, you'd be surprised how many coachbuilt models have poorly designed roofs. This might not be apparent during the first few years of ownership, but when sealants lose their effectiveness, that's when a roof starts to leak.

LEARNING THE ROPES

Although the intention here is to look mainly at structural considerations, let's start with some day-to-day issues. Here are three practical features that should concern a discerning purchaser.

Exotic interiors are impressive but may not be the best answer for families with young children.

Soft furnishings

For a number of years, the majority of British manufacturers equipped their motorcaravans with fitted carpets. This is a homely floor covering, but designers seemed unaware that campsites often get muddy. Accordingly it might not be the best choice for people with active outdoor hobbies, the parents of young children, or dog owners. However, other owners have passive leisure interests and regard carpeting as an essential comfort feature.

When you compare British products with motorhomes manufactured abroad you'll notice that many models from mainland Europe have vinyl floor coverings. This is more practical than carpet, but plasticised sheeting isn't very warm on the feet.

A much better idea is to have a vinyl base layer topped by tailor-made removable carpet sections. This combination was fitted in the author's first self-built van in the mid-1980s and its versatility was soon apparent. Regrettably it took more than a decade for British manufacturers to adopt this alternative arrangement and today you'll still find some models with a fitted carpet.

Light upholstery fabric with suede trims might not be wise for owners with dogs.

 Useful Tip

Consider the floor covering in relationship to your leisure interests. Similarly, look at the upholstery and consider whether it would show dirty marks too easily. Some motorcaravans, though wonderfully exotic inside, are wholly impractical for many people's needs.

Don't be immediately enamoured by the attractiveness of a kitchen. Picture what it would be like to use. Is there sufficient worktop space? What's the draining board like? Where would you temporarily dispose of a tin, a teabag or bacon rinds?

Remember, too, that if you plan to purchase an imported motorcaravan their kitchens are often much smaller than those in British models, for one very good reason: their owners prefer to dine in bars and restaurants. Furthermore, only a few people in mainland Europe have discovered the pleasure of toast, so the fitted hobs seldom include a grill.

Like many German-built kitchens, the facility in this Knaus Sport Ti has very little worktop space.

Kitchen design elements

Practicalities are important, and another oddity of British manufacturers is the fact that for many years they seldom supplied a waste bin in their kitchens. In contrast, this was normally a standard fitment in German and Italian motorhomes. Frankly it's hardly a major design challenge to create a kitchen that includes a compact waste bin, but most UK manufacturers made no such provision.

In consequence a lot of owners dangle a plastic carrier bag from their oven door-handle – hardly a dignified practice in a motorhome purchased for thousands of pounds. One manufacturer even complained that I'd voiced this criticism in magazine reports, because customers were now asking for a bin to be fitted!

Today, thankfully, a bin is usually provided – and in Germany, some models now have three, differentiated by colour to accept different types of waste . . . in accordance with recycling practices.

External omissions

A third oversight noted during live-in tests is the fact that manufacturers of coachbuilt models seldom fit rear mudflaps. In consequence the underside of floor panels behind the rear wheels become bespattered with thick mud. Electric cables to the road lights soon get coated with road dirt, and the mechanisms of waste water drain-down taps may fail prematurely as well.

It's true that manufacturers have to monitor build-costs very closely, but since commercial mudflaps from lorry component suppliers sell for less than £5 apiece there's really no excuse. However, in

Poor kitchen design meant that rubbish had to be put into a plastic bag in this award-winning model.

Left: The lack of mudflaps on this 2006 Swift Kon-Tiki Vogue meant the drain-down tap control was caked in mud.

Below: The 2006 Mobilvetta Top Driver S71 was fitted with mudflaps, as are models from Auto-Sleepers and Auto-Trail.

2005 both Auto-Sleepers and Auto-Trail acted on this complaint and started fitting flaps, but, sadly, numerous other reputable manufacturers haven't responded at all.

These examples draw attention to design and specification shortcomings – matters that can sometimes be resolved retrospectively. However, poor workmanship and instances of bad installation are likely to present considerably greater problems.

Useful Tip

Make a general inspection of external features and remember to look under the floor. Locate the waste water drain-down control, consider its location and check its operation. Also look at pipe runs on the underside. Check there are no uphill sections and downturns in the waste-pipe where water would collect and then freeze in winter.

See if there's a step to assist entry into a high commercial cab and see if it's easy to access the living area from outside. Also check that there's a light near the door so that you can find the keyhole when it's dark.

This Auto Cruise Starmist has a poorly secured drain-down hose and there are better emptying systems.

Check waste pipes under motorcaravans – look for consistent gradients rather than rises and falls in pipe runs.

This Dethleffs Esprit has a useful step created by the converter to improve access to the cab.

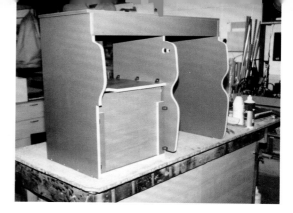

Contoured furniture for Bilbo's van conversions is assembled on a bench and fitted in the 'van later.

VAN CONVERSIONS AND COACHBUILT MODELS

The point was made in the previous chapter that the majority of motorcaravans are constructed by either converting a light van or by constructing a coachbuilt body on a 'chassis cab' vehicle.

When comparing both types of vehicle you'll find that some elements are the same. For example, electricity and gas supply systems are constructed using similar components and in accordance with British Standards (BS) and European Norms (ENs). Appliances like space heaters and refrigerators are similar too. The main differences between conversions and coachbuilt models concern the body structure itself.

Body detailing in van conversions

In a van conversion, the body of the original base vehicle should provide full weather resistance from the outset. When a converter fits additional windows and ventilators, or an elevating roof, their success depends on: a) the quality of the product; and b) the installation itself.

Fitting-out work inside is the real challenge. It's so much harder than fitting furniture and installing domestic appliances in a coachbuilt model, where the living area is normally assembled using flat, preformed wall boards. In contrast a panel van is full of curved panels, composite angles and strengthening members.

Insulation will also need to be added all around the enclosure, whereas the majority of coachbuilt models are created using composite boards that already include a bonded layer of rigid foam in the core. Constructing items of furniture that faithfully match a van's internal shape can also be a time-consuming operation.

As explained in Chapter Two, these issues help to explain why van conversions are often surprisingly costly.

When furniture units are built and installed they're either constructed in situ or assembled on a bench and offered-up for installation later. Larger manufacturers such as Auto-Sleepers, Bilbo's and Murvi normally favour the second approach. Once the standard patterns have been created for a particular layout, items of furniture can then be replicated and assembled on a bench to achieve speedier completion.

In addition the production of modular units away from the assembly area frees-up space inside the van's enclosure, thereby allowing other operations to be carried out. It's only in one-off bespoke conversions that items of furniture are created *inside* a vehicle and not on a bench.

Also be aware that in many van conversions modular furniture is constructed using light, but surprisingly substantial (15mm), plywood. This usually has factory-bonded plastic laminate facings. In coachbuilt models it's more common to see furniture constructed using frameworks that are subsequently clad using 3mm faced plywood. This approach leads to much lighter assemblies than furniture built using 15mm ply, but if the units are well designed rigidity is still assured.

Body detailing in coachbuilt models

The chassis of a coachbuilt model is the key foundation on which the habitation area is built, and the different types were outlined in Chapter Three.

There are also two main types of body construction. Chapter Two made reference to moulded monocoque ('one-piece') shells made with materials such as glass-reinforced plastic (GRP). As was pointed out there, these follow the same practices adopted when building GRP boats and their water-resistance is second to none.

A GRP monocoque 'shell' can also be visually attractive because curving profiles can be made to match those of the cab itself. Aesthetically the end-product is a far cry from the flat-sided boxes that typify so many coachbuilt models. Repairs to

This Mobilvetta Kimu has a single-piece, seam-free monocoque living shell moulded in GRP.

Although there are flat 'slab sides' on this Auto-Sleepers Sandhurst, GRP mouldings enhance its appearance.

damaged sections are much easier to carry out too. But there are snags. To achieve the appropriate strength, for instance, monocoque shells are usually heavy. And fine though the curves are to a critical eye, fitting-out a shapely interior involves the same time-consuming challenges already mentioned in the description of van conversions.

That's why the majority of coachbuilts are constructed instead like touring caravans, using prefabricated, bonded and insulated panels. However, to prevent the finished vehicle from looking too much like a commercial box-van with windows, more expensive versions have a GRP moulded panel over the cab, while the rear section is often made using a full-size moulding and the roof is GRP too.

Bonded panels

'Sandwich construction' using prefabricated bonded panels was first introduced around 1980. Individually the three components forming the 'sandwich' are light and surprisingly weak. However, when the components have been coated with industrial adhesive and bonded in a huge press they assume remarkable strength.

Floor panels

When making a bonded floor, two layers of treated plywood (around 5mm or 3/16in thickness) are bonded on either side of rigid styrofoam insulation panels (around 30mm or 1¼in thick). Timber battens are also bonded into the core of the sandwich to add further strength.

- **Advantage** – The resulting product is light, rigid, and well-insulated.
- **Disadvantage** – If part of the adhesive agent fails, areas of plywood can lose their bond with the foam. This problem, referred to as 'delamination', leads to a huge reduction in a floor panel's strength. If you're purchasing a pre-owned coachbuilt motorcaravan and notice that the floor is creaky in certain places, it's a common sign that

delamination is taking place. For more information on this problem and illustrations showing how a dealer repairs a delaminating panel see pages 39–40 of *The Motorcaravan Manual* (2nd edition) by John Wickersham, published by Haynes.

Composite floors are assembled using styrofoam, battens and ply panels, which are subsequently bonded in a press.

Wall panels

In sandwich-constructed wall panels the components are typically:

1 A 3mm-thick decorative-faced plywood for the interior finish.
2 Block foam insulation such as styrofoam. (Polystyrene foam is occasionally used instead,

ⓘ Technical Tip

The level of insulation in motorcaravans varies and some models only have 25mm boards in the walls. This is often revealed by opening either a window or the entrance door and checking wall thickness at the aperture. Models from Auto-Trail are much better, having been built using 35mm insulation in the walls and floor. At 116mm (4½in) overall the insulation boards in the Italian Genetics 2007 models from GiottiLine are even thicker. Remember that efficient insulation not only retains heat inside during winter trips, it also keeps out excessive heat when a motorhome is parked in direct sunlight.

Some models have an aluminium trim strip along the junction where wall and roof panels meet. This will be bedded on a non-setting

mastic and fastened in place with screws. In time, however, mastics dry out, become brittle and fracture. That's when rain finds its way into a structure via the screw holes. Bearing this in mind, a much better way to finish the junction between adjacent panels is to bond plastic angle trim over it. If trims are secured with adhesive sealant, screws won't be needed and there won't be any holes in the structure.

Some models only have 25mm (1in) bonded side walls, but this Auto-Trail floor sample is considerably thicker.

To cope with the severities of winter, the walls of GiottiLine Genetics A-Class models are incredibly thick.

External corners on this 2005 Pilote Reference have bonded cover sections, which are so much better than screwed trim strips.

All the plastic mouldings around the lighting units on this Dethleffs Esprit are made in acrylic-capped ABS.

which may be as thin as 25mm or 1in.) Wood strengthening battens will be fitted at the perimeters and around apertures for windows and doors.
3 Pre-painted aluminium sheet. (For several years, models from the Swift Group have been finished on the outside using thin GRP sheeting instead of aluminium. Some dealers find this hard to repair, so 2007 models from this manufacturer were once again clad using sheet aluminium.)

Diversity of body materials
Although bonded panels are important components in the construction of a coachbuilt, these are only one of a surprising number of materials used externally. For example, other materials might include:

• Painted steel panels (on the cab)
• GRP mouldings (sometimes installed over the cab)
• ABS mouldings (sometimes used for wheel arch embellishment)
• Moulded aluminium panels (sometimes used for side skirts)
• Pre-painted smooth aluminium sheet (external cladding)
• Pre-painted textured aluminium sheet (external cladding)
• Pigmented (*ie* pre-coloured) layers of thin GRP sheet (alternative external cladding)
• Various types of plastic used for ventilators and grilles (such as refrigerator vents)
• Extruded aluminium strips (for body trim)

An important point here is the difference between mouldings made in GRP as opposed to mouldings made in ABS plastic. Whereas many body repair specialists know how to repair GRP, far fewer are trained in the repair of ABS plastic, even though this is being used more and more on coachbuilt models. In consequence many service centres merely replace damaged ABS mouldings, though obtaining replacements can take several weeks.

Identifying ABS and GRP

- GRP stands for 'glass-reinforced plastic', which is often incorrectly referred to as 'fibreglass'. Some GRP contains a colourising pigment that's added when the polyester resin is being prepared. Other GRP mouldings contain no added pigment and are subsequently sprayed with an etching primer followed by automotive paint.
- ABS stands for 'acrylonitrile-butadiene-styrene'. If it's acrylic-capped ABS it will have a further surface coating in order to give it a high gloss finish. An ABS moulding is usually pre-coloured during manufacture.
- The word 'mould' refers to a master shape in which a component is cast.
- The word 'moulding' refers to the finished product that's been made in the mould.

These distinctive types of moulded plastic body panels are easy to identify. The rear face of a GRP

The moulded section here is made in GRP – the rough surface on the reverse confirms that it isn't ABS plastic.

61

(i) Technical Tip

External damage is an ever-present possibility on *any* vehicle. Some repairs are easy to carry out and are inexpensive; others are extremely costly, and if spare parts are needed they can take a long time to obtain. Sales staff seldom mention 'reparability' issues and you can get a better insight into the reality of repair work by consulting make-specific owners' clubs whose addresses are published in magazines.

On an aluminium-skinned bonded wall, the repair strategy usually involves carrying out structural repairs first and then re-skinning the entire side by bonding a new cladding of aluminium sheet on top of the original. The re-skinning operation is more complicated if a thin GRP sheet has been used for cladding instead of sheet aluminium. That's partly why fewer manufacturers are now using the GRP product.

As regards ABS mouldings, these are usually replaced, but this poses problems on older vehicles because spares aren't held in stock for ever. Fortunately there are companies, such as V&G, which can reassemble cracked components and take a copy mould in GRP. This new mould can then be used to fabricate a GRP moulding that replicates the shape of the original ABS component.

When a replacement ABS bowl was no longer available, V&G staff made this copy mould in order to create a GRP replica.

This rear skirt made from acrylic-capped ABS plastic hit a kerbstone. Although repairs are possible, most repairers would replace this.

moulding is normally rough and you'll often be able to see the strands of glass used as a reinforcing binder to give strength to the polyester resin.

In contrast, the rear face of an ABS moulding is smooth, and this material is often used for vehicle bumpers, albeit with a textured outer face. Acrylic-capped ABS is shiny on both faces and is often used for items such as fairings on motorcycles, wings on cars and external detailing on motor caravans.

Both materials can be repaired when cracked or split, but although the process is similar the chemicals involved are different. That's why you need to establish whether a damaged moulding is made from GRP or ABS. And be warned: though many repair specialists in both automotive and marine workshops successfully repair cracked or split GRP mouldings, motorcaravan service specialists prefer to order replacement components, which are often surprisingly costly.

A new rear lamp housing is being fitted on a Bessacarr after the original one got cracked when it brushed against a wall.

Rainwater that ponded badly on the roof of this Knaus Sun Ti Sport was adjacent to some mastic-filled joining seams.

DESIGN AND CONSTRUCTIONAL POINTS TO CHECK

Keeping all the above in mind, let's consider some specific features.

The roof

Even when there's an access ladder to reach the roof of a motorcaravan, it's evident that few prospective buyers bother to inspect this all-important part of the vehicle. Whereas some products are well-designed and carefully constructed, others reveal disturbing features which could later result in water ingress.

Even a recent award-winning model that impressed the competition judges with its smart upholstery and fine internal fittings had a poorly finished roof. The judges obviously didn't bother to inspect this important constructional element either.

Features to check

Remember that a well-designed roof is no less important than a well-equipped kitchen or a thoughtful interior layout. Look for the following features:

- A design which facilitates the swift discharge of rainwater whenever a vehicle's parked on a level pitch
- Specifically constructed outlets so that water will be released in a planned manner and at appropriate points
- A slope (or slopes) so that puddles don't form on the roof when the vehicle's parked on level ground

The draining outlets are a good feature on the roof of the 2006 Orian Gemini. Some designers don't include this facility.

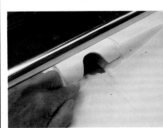

The one-piece GRP roofs on recent Auto-Trail models have well-designed but discreet channels for discharging rainwater.

• A one-piece roof panel. This is more likely to offer better weather resistance than a roof assembled in separate panels with its junctions sealed using flexible mastics.

In an outdoor setting a roof gathers dust and dirt; it's also hard to keep clean. When it rains you don't want accumulated dust dispersing all over the sides. It's better to have a couple of outlets so that any post-rainfall discharge is confined to one or two areas.

It's also important to recognise that a substantial quantity of discharging rainwater shouldn't challenge vulnerable components mounted on the sides. Some lockers, for example, are susceptible to leaks, especially when subjected to torrents of water. Equally you wouldn't want copious quantities of roof water to head towards a 230V mains input socket.

Now let's look at actual examples.

Roofs under scrutiny

One manufacturer that has spent time designing good roofs is Auto-Trail. On recent models you'll notice there's a single-piece GRP roof moulding which means there are neither joins nor gaps through which water might seep when a sealant starts to lose its effectiveness.

Moreover, when a model like the 2004 Auto-Trail Cheyenne was tested it was noted that when the vehicle was parked level, its roof sloped gently to the rear. Less conspicuous – unless you check the roof more closely – are the rainwater channels also found on either side. Good design means that rain drains away and doesn't form in puddles.

More manufacturers are now designing roofs with outlets, but with variable success. It's not unusual to find that when the structure was assembled an

The idea behind this drain-away channel on a Dethleffs Esprit is fine, but having been part-filled with sealant it won't do its job.

outlet point was blocked by excessive sealant. And don't be surprised to find a junction of adjacent panels that introduces a step, thereby impeding the intended outflow of water.

Weaknesses are certainly more evident on vehicles parked outdoors on a dealer's forecourt. An inspection of these may reveal examples of 'ponding', and it's worth looking for dirty patches even if recent rain puddles have dried up. Then check if there's a sealant-filled seam in the vicinity of the spot where water appears to settle.

Roof fittings

If you do have an opportunity to check a roof, also look carefully at the installation of roof windows, vents and fixed roof rails. On a well-designed model, roof windows will be mounted on a raised section of the roof. This means that any rainwater resting on the surface won't threaten the join around the perimeter of the component. On a GRP roof, a good designer will have created raised plinths on which to mount the skylights.

Above: Since a roof takes the worst of the weather, sealant between panels must be good. The join on this new Swift Kon-Tiki was poorly finished.

Below left: When components such as racks are screwed through a roof, sealant is important. It wasn't applied well on this Mobilvetta Kimu.

Below: This roof window is wisely mounted on a raised plinth, and to the right you'll see a diffuser that protects its forward edge.

Not all roofs are meant to be walked on but that's not the case on this TEC Freetec. Note the use of abrasive surface strips.

Also check if there's a deflector on the forward side of skylights. When you're proceeding briskly along a motorway in driving rain, water can easily challenge the forward edge where these fittings are mounted. Bedding sealant around a rooflight flange takes the brunt of the weather and a deflector offers protection.

Structural capacity
Many owners like to use the roof to carry equipment, either by fitting a rack or by installing roof boxes. However, you should check the feasibility of this with the manufacturer. For instance, some A-Class vehicles, such as the 2002 Niesmann+Bischoff Arto 69 GL Lux, are fitted with side roof rack rails and a ladder. However, in response to a critical observation relating to this vehicle's roof published in *Which Motorcaravan (Dec 2002)* a Marketing specialist for the Company advised that, "... the roof is not actually designed to be walked on." His statement came as a surprise and one is left wondering how a canoe or surfboard could be secured to the rack if you're not permitted to walk beyond the top rung of the access ladder.

Clearly you need to seek guidance on such matters prior to purchase, especially if you plan to fit a roof box or purpose-made rack to transport equipment. Remember, too, that some side rails are merely cosmetic appendages. On models where it's acceptable to use a roof for access and storage, abrasive strips are an excellent safety feature.

Windows
In the commercial vehicles used for motorcaravans, single-glazed safety glass is fitted in the cab. If a van with side windows is used for conversion, safety glass will again be in evidence. Double-glazed units

A single glazed panel over the cab of this Knaus model is fine in warm weather, but condensation is bad in some conditions.

are sometimes fitted in high quality coaches but these are extremely heavy and are only installed in very expensive motorcaravans.

Automotive glass is certainly resistant to scratches and that's a great benefit if you brush against a hedge or encounter overhanging brambles. Unfortunately it doesn't offer effective thermal insulation and condensation problems are commonplace.

To reduce heat loss in converted vans and coachbuilt models, manufacturers normally fit double-glazed acrylic plastic windows instead. There are two distinct types of plastic window and, predictably, the costlier version is certainly the better product. The less expensive type doesn't have a frame and weatherproofing is provided by a rubber sealing strip that's fitted around the aperture cut in the motorcaravan's side. Understandably, a frameless

Double-glazed acrylic windows such as this aren't made with a separate frame.

With frameless windows, the seal around apertures is important. It didn't fit well on this 2007 Swift Bolero.

window has to achieve a close register with the rubber strip and its catches need to hold it securely in place. Over time a deteriorating rubber surround or failing catches sometimes lead to the ingress of rain.

The installation of frameless units certainly helps to keep down the price of a finished vehicle. However, it's generally agreed that framed windows, although more expensive, are not only better performers but are also easier to install. Accordingly they're normally fitted in high specification motorcaravans, although you'll find them in many van conversions as well.

Seitz units are the best known and comprise an outer frame that secures the acrylic pane, together with an inner frame complete with blind and fly-screen. When these interlocking frames are fastened together a van's wall panel is sandwiched tightly between their flanges to provide good weather-resistance.

Framed windows fitted on this Auto-Sleepers Sandhurst are smartly finished with matching white frames.

Seitz framed windows comprise an outer frame which houses hinged or sliding plastic panes. An inner frame has a blind and fly screens.

It's inevitable that windows sometimes get scratched or even damaged beyond repair. When it comes to replacing standard automotive glass, main dealers or specialist windscreen companies can usually help. It's seldom a problem if the model's base is a light commercial vehicle.

However, replacing a windscreen or side screen in an A-Class motor caravan sometimes presents a problem: usually it's a job for a dealer specialising in that particular model, or its UK importer. Replacement screens are often very costly too. Not that acrylic double-glazed windows are cheap to replace either. On recent models, the normal way to get a replacement unit is to order it through a dealer-workshop. Awaiting delivery calls for patience, however, because receipt of the component might take more than a month.

 **Useful Tip**

Most vehicle windscreen specialists are able to fit replacement glass in light commercial vehicles, and units are normally obtained without difficulty. However, some owners of A-Class vehicles have reported problems. In some cases a replacement has been extremely costly and there's sometimes a long wait. These may be exceptional cases but it would be wise for anyone planning to purchase an A-Class vehicle to enquire about windscreen costs and delivery dates.

Conclusion

Inevitably this chapter has only focussed on a selection of issues relating to the design and construction of motorcaravans. However, if it has drawn attention to points that many purchasers completely ignore it will have achieved its intended objective.

BUYING **ADVICE**

There are so many contrasting types of motorcaravan being manufactured that deciding which one to buy is far from easy. There are also many different ways to make a purchase, and the advice that follows compares the options. Incidentally, if you've never spent long in a motorcaravan before, then hiring one for several days is a practical way to find out what you need.

71

For first-time buyers, a forecourt offers a bewildering choice of models.

'Just Go' is one of many UK motorcaravan hire specialists.

Preceding chapters drew attention to a number of important issues. Between the extremes of a compact campervan and an American RV are leisure vehicles of all shapes and sizes. The people who use them are different as well. There's no such thing as a 'typical motorcaravanner', and *your* needs are likely to be different from those of other people you'll meet.

That's is why it's so important to look closely at as many motorcaravans as possible before you buy one. You should also talk to some owners, and read the reports in magazines. Hire one for a few days to find what a vehicle's like on both the road and the campsite. Then compile a personal checklist, which will help you focus your needs more clearly.

MODEL CHOICE

Although it's important to choose your preferred layout inside, many people make the mistake of basing a purchase on that factor alone. So check the issues raised in earlier chapters. For instance, the importance of choosing the right base vehicle

Many spare wheels are far harder to reach than this one.

To obtain unusual facilities required by their leisure interests, some owners build DIY models instead.

was discussed in Chapter Three. Then there are practical issues such as how easy it is to get out a spare wheel, to check a leisure battery, or to drain the waste water tank. There are also constructional matters to check, as explained in Chapter Four.

Throughout the search process, don't expect perfection! Unless you have a bespoke vehicle constructed by a specialist builder, or embark on a self-build project, you *won't* find a model that meets all your criteria.

On the subject of layouts and interior detailing, the illustrations here will serve as a reminder of some of the options. Firstly there are practical issues to keep in mind. Secondly there are decisions to be made about things like kitchens, beds and toilets. The following guidelines will help.

General practical issues
• Will your motorcaravan have to be small enough to park outside your house? Are their covenants that restrict the parking of large vehicles? Is there sufficient space and height to manoeuvre it on to its parking place?

Parking space at home determines many owners' choice of vehicle.

Right: Children often spill their food so look for easy-to-clean surfaces.

Far right: Some important switches are harder to reach than this one.

Right: In some models you can erect a portable cot, like this one from Graco.

Far right: When using a motorhome with children, storage facilities are especially important.

- If a family includes children or grandchildren, will surfaces be easy to clean if there's a spillage? Can they operate switches? Is there room for a travel cot? Is there plenty of storage?
- Are the users' leisure interests active or passive? Outdoor sports participants will often track mud inside, so check that floor covering materials can be easily cleaned. Fixed carpet is hardly the best choice.
- With ever-changing legislation regarding seat belt provision in motorcaravans, how many seats in the living space are designated as 'travel seats'? Are the belted bench seats suitable for children's seats and booster bases? Seating units in the living area are often too soft to provide good support to a child-seat; when you're turning a corner their foam can compress, the inertia reel belt pays out more strap and the child-seat sometimes tips over.

Below: Check how many seats in the living area are designated as 'travel seats'.

Below right: Child-seats can be unstable on a soft cushion base, and on corners they sometimes turn over.

- Will you be travelling abroad? The beams on some of the latest high output headlamps can't be redirected merely by applying adhesive tape. Instead, the lights have to be realigned at a workshop for driving on the right, and sometimes the bill is surprisingly high.
- To maximise space, it's always useful if the cab seats can be rotated to provide extra room in the living area. However, with many layouts and cab-seat designs, swivel mechanisms can't be used.
- Don't overlook the fact that some motorcaravans, both van conversions and coachbuilt models, can't be fitted with towing brackets.

Contrasting interior designs

- Cooking facilities vary enormously. Some kitchens have large worktop areas whereas others are desperately small. The kitchen will certainly be an important feature for many owners and a full complement of appliances is often required. Other motorcaravanners are content with more rudimentary facilities.
- A washroom and a shower are often omitted from small camper vans, and if a portable toilet has to be pulled from a drawer for use indoors a

Some headlamps can't be adjusted like this for driving abroad and have to be realigned in a workshop.

These cab seats can be swivelled so that you can make use of the cab when you're parked. That's not possible on some layouts.

A surprising number of motorcaravans can't be fitted with a towing bracket.

There's generous worktop space in this Auto-Trail Miami 740D.

Small van conversions need a privacy curtain for their toilet because there's insufficient space for a fixed cubicle.

temporary privacy curtain is needed. At the other extreme, larger motorcaravans sometimes have grandly appointed dressing rooms complete with washbasin and shower cubicle, duly adorned with opulent fittings.

- Beds come in all shapes and sizes, as the panel alongside shows. Where a couple are to be the sole users of a motorcaravan, fixed double or single beds situated in a purpose-made bedroom has become a popular arrangement. However, that's redundant space during daytime and larger families

Right: The daytime bench seats in the lounge of this Auto-Sleepers Sandhurst convert into beds.

Far right: This Romahome offers two singles, but many small vans have to fold the cab seats flat to achieve a good length.

Right: Not everyone wants to climb a ladder to reach a bed and children need safety-net sides.

Far right: Many owners want a fixed double bed like this example in an Auto-Trail Chieftain.

Right: A recent trend in coachbuilts such as this Cheyenne 840 Lo is to create a bedroom with permanent single beds.

Far right: A-Class motorcaravans have sufficient width in their cabs to accommodate a drop-down double bed.

Erecting beds
Potential purchasers viewing motorcaravans at a dealer's showroom should always ask sales staff to demonstrate how *all* the beds are erected. Experienced sales specialists who know the product should be able to do this in minutes.

Always get a sales person to demonstrate how all the beds are set up.

On this Lunar coachbuilt motorcaravan a clever base provides bed and seat versatility.

prefer sleeping arrangements whereby daytime bench seats are converted to beds at night.

- Tables vary too, and several German manufacturers fit robust units mounted on concertina pillars that cannot be removed. Some rattle when you're driving. Freestanding tables that can be moved outside for picnics are useful. Tables used as bed bases will usually cause damp to form on the underside of bed cushions unless a purpose-made ventilation underlay is used.

Whether or not a layout works well is really only apparent when you put a 'van into use. That's why hiring a motorhome is useful in highlighting some of the issues you need to keep in mind.

A number of German motorcaravans have a fixed table with a rise-and-fall mechanism.

Hiring a motorcaravan
This is an ideal way to evaluate a motorcaravan, and a report in the April 2006 issue of *Which Motorcaravan* included a table listing no fewer than 126 hire specialists located around the UK. Regarding hire prices, these are considerably higher for peak season than in winter. Hiring in winter will show the effectiveness of heating systems and internal lighting during dark evenings, so it's a good time of year to evaluate a vehicle. Insurance can be high, however, and regrettably there are age restrictions that often preclude hiring by people under 25 and over 70 years of age. Penalty points on driving licences may also pose a problem.

Personal checklist

It's impossible to draw up a 'definitive tick list' when everyone's needs and preferences are different. You're therefore advised to create your own list of personal 'must haves'. The contrived one that follows represents the requirements of an imaginary couple with a young child who want to purchase a new van conversion.

Base vehicle

- ☐ Any colour except white, preferably a metallic paint
- ☐ Turbo diesel engine but not one that's underpowered
- ☐ Manual gearbox preferred
- ☐ Front-wheel drive
- ☐ Fitted with a high-top roof
- ☐ Optional higher output alternator if available
- ☐ Headlights that are easy to convert for driving in France
- ☐ Panel van rather than a window van with its single glazing
- ☐ Double-glazed plastic windows installed in the living section
- ☐ Able to be fitted with a towbar
- ☐ Electric windows in the cab preferred
- ☐ Generous payload potential – it's likely to carry heavy gear
- ☐ Mustn't be longer than 5.5m (18ft) in order to park by the house
- ☐ Generous-sized driving mirrors with electric adjustment

External conversion features

- ☐ Easy-operate drain-down valve for waste water tank
- ☐ Good colour matching of GRP high-top roof
- ☐ Colour co-ordinated painted Dometic fridge vents preferred
- ☐ Medium-sized roof window in the high-top
- ☐ Towing bracket with bolt-on towball and 12N socket
- ☐ Reversing camera with integral LED lighting for night use
- ☐ External shower rose in locker for cleaning wellies
- ☐ Small rear rack to stow a toilet/shower tent for external use

Internal conversion features

- ☐ Swivelling cab seats
- ☐ Facility for two small gas cylinders in a sealed locker
- ☐ Easy-to-reach leisure battery; preferably room for a 120Ah unit
- ☐ Bench seat in rear to make into a double bed
- ☐ Occasional bed for child in the high-top
- ☐ Small absorption fridge
- ☐ Provision for stowing a portable toilet
- ☐ Oil-fired compact locker-type space heater
- ☐ Water heater not a high priority item
- ☐ Hob and grill but no need for an oven
- ☐ Roller blinds for windows but no need for curtains
- ☐ LED lighting – generous provision including reading lights
- ☐ Two double and one single mains sockets (minimum)
- ☐ One of the sockets near small table for laptop/phone charging
- ☐ Semi-rigid push-fit plumbing pipe rather than hose and clips
- ☐ Vinyl floor with some edge-bound removable carpet pieces
- ☐ Dark-coloured upholstery that doesn't show dirt easily
- ☐ Combined charger/mains supply and 12V fused control unit
- ☐ 12V socket for TV

Remember that this is a hypothetical checklist for a couple with a young child. Setting this out helps to narrow down the choice of vehicles, but don't expect to find a model that matches everything on your wish-list.

Buyers' tip

Many new motorcaravans bear the National Caravan Council (NCC) approval badge which confirms compliance with: European and UK requirements, national regulations and industry Codes of Practice.

To gain an approval badge, a prototype model is inspected by NCC engineers and the process involves checks on over 400 elements including an evaluation of its Owner's Manual. This onerous task which typically takes up to seven hours gives prospective purchasers sound reassurance about a product's overall integrity and fitness for purpose.

Some imported motorcaravans like this 2007 Adria Twin bear an NCC approval badge.

Magazine tests

A good way to find out more about new or pre-owned motorcaravans is to read magazine reports. Specialist magazines have teams of experienced journalists who put products under the microscope for several days and then compile their candid reports. In some instances manufacturers and importers lend models to magazine editorial staff for six-month periods; reports are then compiled using a number of different user-perspectives.

Design and Drive competition

The Caravan Club conducts an annual 'Design and Drive' competition. In the 2007 event, for example, 41 models were placed in seven different categories. The classification took price into account and three types of vehicle were identified: Van conversions, Coachbuilts, and A-Class models. A rigorous checking schedule included scrutinising vehicle weights, evaluating performance on the road, and appraising a wide range of design elements.

Imports as well as home-built models are put under the judges' critical eyes. The contest was introduced in 1996, and although honours have been widely shared it's noteworthy that Murvi, a small-scale van converter based in Devon, has won 14 Caravan Club Awards in different classes.

Warranty terms and conditions

When comparing new models in a shortlist, don't forget to check the warranties too. These differ in a number of ways, especially with regard to the period over which a motorcaravan's external fabric is insured against leaks attributable to construction faults.

The Marquis branch near Newbury always has a wide stock of models to inspect.

MAKING A PURCHASE

There are obviously many ways to purchase a motorcaravan, irrespective of whether you're buying new or buying one that's had previous owners. Here are some of the options.

Buying new

Choosing a dealer
This isn't quite as simple as you might imagine. For example, an impressive discount from a motorcaravan specialist whose base is a long way

Tip

Pre-delivery inspection (PDI)
A motorcaravan should leave the factory in a clean state and in full working order, although large manufacturers require their dealers to arrange a final PDI. Some dealers carry this out in their own workshops; others commission a nearby service specialist to perform the final cleaning and operational checks. Many dealers take this very seriously and supply vehicles to customers in tip-top condition. Others are less meticulous and owners collecting new vehicles often comment about loose screws rattling in drawers, sawdust left around installed appliances, and faults such as blinds that don't work properly. Small-scale converters who sell direct to customers are seldom the subject of critical reports.

The PDI had been poorly carried out here, with odd screws and sawdust on the floor of some lockers.

from your home carries with it a problem that doesn't arise when you buy a car: in the event of a warranty repair being needed on a conversion element (*eg* a collapsing bed) you usually have to take your motorcaravan back to its original supplier. If the dealer's workshop is a long way from your home and it's a job likely to take more than a day, you may have to arrange overnight accommodation. That isn't the case with the base vehicle, of course, for which warranty work relating to original automotive elements can be carried out at *any* franchise dealership.

Many people order a motorcaravan on a manufacturer's stand at an indoor exhibition.

Buying at an exhibition

Caravan and motorhome exhibitions don't follow the pattern of motorshows, where manufacturers are solely in attendance to display the latest models. By contrast, caravanning exhibitors usually take orders on the stands as well as showing the latest products.

Although some of the larger dealerships have their own stand at indoor exhibitions, a lot of sales take place on the manufacturers' stands as well. This is because major manufacturers share their stands with staff from a selection of their approved dealers from around the country. First-time visitors can find this confusing.

For example, if you start looking at new models, suited sales staff will often offer help and might later endeavour to conduct a sale. Let's say, by way of example, that the factory making the motorcaravans is based in the East Yorkshire/North Lincolnshire area, whereas some sales staff on the stand represent a dealership located in the West Country. If you return to the stand some hours later for a second look you might be made a competing offer from a dealer who comes from Surrey. This can get rather confusing, and if, in this example, your home

Barons had many vehicles on sale at this outdoor show held on Peterborough's Agricultural Showground.

is in Shropshire that's when you need to be careful. Money-saving bargains lose their benefit if warranty work on the conversion itself has to be repaired a long way from your home.

Outdoor shows held at race courses (between meetings) and agricultural showgrounds offer similar buying opportunities, except that they're also attended by some of the direct-selling, small manufacturers because the pitch costs are much cheaper.

In reality, many satisfactory deals are negotiated at indoor and outdoor exhibitions, but letters sent to motorcaravanning magazines also report the ones that go wrong. To reinforce earlier advice, we would emphasise again that magazine letters really *are* helpful to read.

Delivery and sales calendars

Having chosen a motorcaravan in a brochure, there's often a long gap between placing an order and obtaining the vehicle. Magazine reports often relate tales of woe in which promised handover dates are later revised. Some owners order at Easter, book a ferry and campsites for a July holiday and then find delivery is delayed until August.

Experienced motorcaravanners are more familiar with the annual cycle in this seasonal industry. For instance, next year's models are usually unveiled around September. Experience also shows that a motorcaravan ordered in late autumn is likely to be delivered in time for a trip the following Easter. However, the waiting period can by much longer if you place an order in early spring – which is when the season hots up.

Similar time delays occur if you want to purchase a bespoke van conversion built by a small-scale specialist; good manufacturers are never short of work. For example, Young Conversions advises

(i) Tip

Buyers' Guides
Most monthly magazines include 'Buyers' Guides' in which key information is tabulated for easy analysis. This allows you to identify new models which meet your needs using criteria such as price, weight, payload, dimensions, berths, belted seats, heating provision and many other factors. Magazines also give manufacturer/ importer addresses, thereby enabling you to send for brochures. In addition a growing number of manufacturers also have websites.

potential clients that when an order is placed for a new base vehicle with a particular specification of extras, there's usually a wait of at least two to three months, depending on the model. When the van is finally delivered, you then have to arrange a date for the commencement of the conversion itself. Again there are seasonal variations, and Young Conversions' work programme typically involves a wait of three to four months.

On a different seasonal note, bear in mind that from late August onwards, dealers need to clear their forecourts to make way for the following year's models. That's when the Sales period starts with a vengeance, and reductions in price can be stunningly good. Similar reductions arise when a base vehicle manufacturer introduces a new or facelifted model – during the transition period dealers are left with stocks of motorcaravans built on the outgoing model, and these are often sharply reduced in price.

When a new-look Fiat arrived in 2007 previous models were sold with generous discounts.

 Tip

Test drive
When you reach the final stage of making a purchase, you should always request a short test drive. It's amazing that many owners don't arrange a drive prior to purchase and some dealers don't encourage this either. Naturally, a dealer doesn't want to add miles to an odometer on a new vehicle, but if you're intending to purchase a motorcaravan that costs thousands of pounds a brief test drive is really important.

In autumn, dealers offer big discounts to clear their forecourts in readiness for the next year's models.

*Lowdham Leisureworld in
Nottinghamshire always
has a good selection of
pre-owned motorcaravans.*

BUYING SECOND-HAND

Purchasing privately

Specialist magazines contain a classified advertise-ments section devoted to motorcaravans. There are certainly some good products for sale, but never forget the expression *caveat emptor* – 'buyer beware!'

In truth, every transaction has to be evaluated individually and it's quite impossible to give any more than a few guidelines here. Suggestions include the following:

- Establish when a motorcaravan last received vehicle and habitation services and ask to see the signed service schedules. Has the base vehicle got a full service history?
- Ask if there are recent approval certificates to verify that the gas and electrical systems have been checked and deemed to be safe.
- Enquire when the last professional damp check was carried out, and ask to see the workshop certificate.
- Have an HPI check carried out.
- Always inspect a private sale at the vendor's home, and not at a public car park.
- Ask the vendor if they would object to the vehicle being checked at the buyer's expense by a mechanical engineer appointed through the AA or RAC.
- The habitation element can also be checked by an independent specialist such as Autovan Services, Wimborne, Dorset (01202 848414).
- Insist on arranging a test drive – tall drivers sometimes find the top of the screen is too low for their line of

HPI check

Working closely with the UK motorcaravan industry, HPI has created a joint venture called 'Minder' to protect against theft and fraud.

The HPI website states: 'Motorhomes sold since 2001 carry a unique motorhome identification number (MIN), a vehicle identification number (VIN) and their vehicle registration mark (VRM).' Vehicles built in the UK since this date also have a hidden electronic tag and the MIN number is etched on the window.

Requesting an HPI check can establish whether a motorcaravan is stolen, written-off by an insurer or still subject to further payments under a loan agreement. Securing the check involves payment of a fee, but it's a wise measure when buying a motorcaravan of unknown provenance and from an uncertain source. To find out more, contact HPI on 01722 422422 or use the website, www.hpicheck.com, where you can see a sample HPI check report.

vision, and some models are known for a problem in which the vehicle jumps out of fifth gear.

Notwithstanding the points made above, you often find that service documentation is missing and it's then up to you to ascertain whether the motorcaravan has been well looked after. If the price is attractive and you're prepared to get servicing and checking work carried out yourself, that's a gamble you might decide whether or not to take.

Without doubt, there are examples of well-cared-for motorcaravans on sale that have been lovingly cherished and maintained by fastidious owners. Some are advertised with a touch of personal sadness too. Ill health or a bereavement sometimes prompts their sale, and low mileage models are often advertised in motorcaravan magazines. When an owner is no longer in a position to continue motorcaravanning dealers are disinclined to trade-in a vehicle if they won't be selling the client a replacement, and the owner may then endeavour to sell the vehicle privately – often at an attractive price.

Dealer pre-owned models

Obviously there are inherent risks when purchasing privately whereas buying a pre-owned motorcaravan from a dealer generally includes support in the event of subsequent problems. Admittedly the degree of cover offered by a warranty on a second-hand motorcaravan varies from dealer to dealer but there's far more likelihood of after-sale assistance. Whilst the asking price is usually higher than in a private transaction, this secures you additional peace of mind.

Naturally there's more likelihood of redress if you have problems with a 'van bought through a dealer.

Sales of caravans and motorhomes are conducted by British Car Auctions; events are regularly held at BCA's Measham branch in the Midlands.

You might also negotiate for a new MoT test to be arranged (where applicable) as a condition of purchase.

Motorcaravan auctions

British Car Auctions (BCA) organises regular sales of caravans and motorhomes throughout the year, particularly at its centres in Measham and Nottingham. Full advice is given in BCA literature on procedures for bidding and making a purchase. Undercover and outdoor compounds are used and there's plenty of opportunity to check vehicles prior to the start of each sale.

If you want to purchase a light commercial vehicle with a view to having it converted, BCA also conducts auctions of commercial vehicles at many of its centres. Dates of sales and other information is given on the BCA website, www.british-car-auctions. co.uk.

One of the problems buying this way is the fact that you'll be expected to produce the full payment in a day or so. Moreover, you really need to know how to spot a sound vehicle.

Imported models

A growing number of people import motorcaravans themselves, with models coming from both Europe and North America. On the face of it there's a lot of money to be saved, but there are also numerous things that need to be done. For example, a vehicle has to gain a UK registration, which involves completing a V55/5 form issued by the DVLA. And with regard to insurance, companies sometimes set higher premiums for imported models.

Some potential purchasers also overlook the fact that an imported vehicle usually has to be altered in a number of ways before it can be legally used on

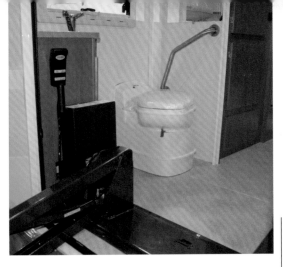

A very substantial wheelchair hoist and a converted toilet room were built on this Benimar coachbuilt.

Britain's roads. For instance, a vehicle has to comply with the UK's Construction and Use regulations as well as legislation relating to road vehicle lighting. In that regard, headlamp units often need to be changed and other road lights might need to be added.

Items such as the mirrors must provide the required field of vision appropriate for driving on the left. Speedometers also have to show speeds in mph rather than kmh.

In the living space, electrical sockets will need changing, and older foreign vehicles often have gas appliances that run at a different pressure from their British counterparts.

Making alterations can be quite involved and it's certainly easier to buy an imported model through a specialist company. A number of dealers import pre-owned vans from Japan, such as the Mazda Bongo; these are popular, and Japanese vehicles are right-hand drive like ours.

Middlesex Motorcaravans runs a similar operation importing and selling pre-owned VW motorcaravans from Germany. Since these are left-hand drive vehicles they might not be to everyone's liking, but with prices starting around £5,000 at the time of writing this is one way to start when you're on a tight budget. Resale of these products might not always be easy but the company also offers a generous buy-back scheme.

VAT concessions for the disabled

HM Revenue & Customs (HMRC) operates VAT relief to assist motorhome owners with disabilities. However, strict criteria have to be met and these are set out in HMRC Notice 701/59. You can also receive guidance by telephoning 0845 3020203, although only general advice is given because

The Motorhome Information Service
www.motorhomeinfo.co.uk

The MIS represents the motorhome industry in the UK and provides potential owners with information on buying, hiring and using a motorcaravan. Its publication *Horizons*, which includes buying advice, is available free of charge. There are also leaflets giving lists of dealers, information on insurance, the dates of shows, and procedures for reclaiming VAT payments for purchasers registered as disabled.

Guidance on construction legislation is published periodically and MIS information service staff attend some of the major exhibitions.

applications are evaluated on an individual basis according to needs.

As a rule, a person who is permanently wheelchair-dependent and who wants to purchase a motorhome with permanent adaptations is normally able to claim full VAT relief on the vehicle. The administrative process is carried out at the supplying dealers and the disabled person has to complete a self-certifying form. At one time this concession was only applicable if the user had to remain seated in the wheelchair within the vehicle, but that's no longer the case. There are other points of detail too. For instance, if a trailer and tow bracket are considered necessary these fall outside the vehicle's VAT-free concession arrangement.

There's also some VAT relief for people with less severe disabilities. This includes owners who aren't wheelchair-bound but who need the benefit of equipment such as support rails and other adaptations. In this instance VAT relief normally only applies to individual fittings and not the vehicle as a whole. Moreover some retrospective alterations, such as having an automatic gearbox fitted, don't qualify for concessionary treatment.

The Motorhome Information Service can provide further guidance. Similarly, *Motorcaravan and Motorhome Monthly* magazine periodically publishes a 'Mobility Supplement' that provides a wealth of information and addresses.

Final handover

When a new owner collects their motorcaravan, the level of attention during the handover will vary from dealer to dealer. Some are extremely busy during the height of the season and don't provide the level of help a buyer deserves. Furthermore, today's motorhomes are sophisticated products and

Conversions by Middlesex Motorcaravans using new or pre-owned vans are popular with new owners.

a complete beginner can be easily bewildered by the technical issues.

However, it's not always like that. At a Marquis branch near Portsmouth many years ago, the author was given an excellent introduction to a Swift motorhome that he had hired for a fortnight. Equally, when a bespoke camper van was handed over to a complete beginner recently, the manufacturer provided three hours of explanation and several mugs of coffee when describing how everything works. That is the sort of service a customer needs.

The co-owner of the company spent three hours giving a thorough explanation of how everything worked.

Although built to suit the purchaser's needs, there was still a lot of equipment to demonstrate at handover time.

Early apprehensions were soon cast aside, thanks to the attention given by this family-owned manufacturer.

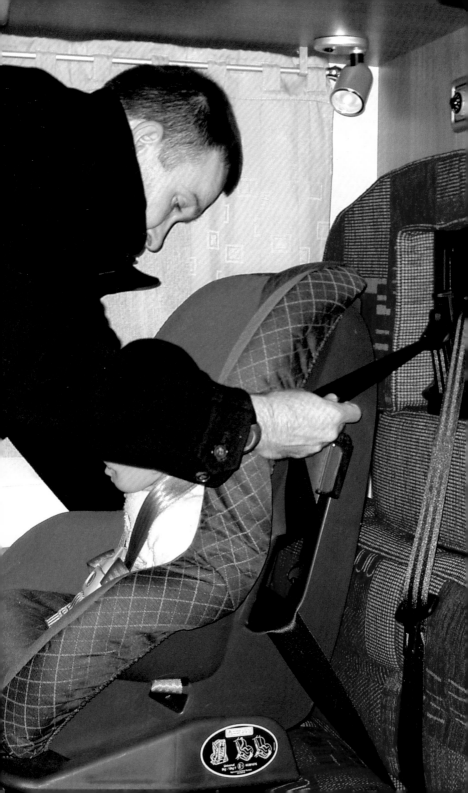

CHAPTER SIX

LEGAL
CONSIDERATIONS

The fact that some motorcaravans are compact 'campervans' whereas others are very much larger inevitably means that legal requirements vary. For instance, dissimilar rulings apply on the basis of motorcaravans' weights; the driver's age and qualifications may also be involved. Then there are matters relating to Vehicle Excise Duty, MoT testing and seat belt requirements, all of which serve to complicate the situation. This chapter provides an introduction to such issues.

91

Seat belts in motorcaravans are a matter of recent concern.

Charges for entry into London's Low Emission Zone might discourage visitors from using the city's caravan and motorhome sites.

 Info

London's Low Emission Zone

1. Vehicle charges are based on their Gross Vehicle Weight (GVW).
2. Collection of tariffs payable on large vehicles (over 12 tonnes GVW) commenced on 4 February 2008; other rates are being enforced in stages, the last of which is scheduled to come into effect in January 2012.
3. For more information see Transport for London website: tfl.gov.uk/lezlondon or phone 0845 607 0009.

Of the seventeen chapters in this book, this is the one that will need updating the most often, since laws relating to the classification of vehicles, Road Tax categories, Driving Licences and seat belt requirements are constantly under review.

To illustrate how things can change, the adjacent panel describes past and pending modifications to the design of approved towbars. This is just one of many motorcaravan-related issues currently being discussed in high places.

So here's the problem. Whilst it's important to describe key issues relating to motorcaravans, laws change with such frequency that you'll need to confirm the latest directives and mandatory issues by checking official literature or website information issued by the appropriate Government agencies. Also bear in mind that these sources sometimes lack explicit guidance concerning commercial vehicles that have been converted into private leisure accommodation vehicles, *ie* motorcaravans.

Some administrators seem to overlook this issue. For example, there has been concern recently about London's Low Emission Zone (LEZ) charge rates. Transport for London (TFL) has published charges payable by drivers of light lorries entering the Zone, but these will also, by definition, apply to most motorcaravans.

Arguably not many motorcaravanners would want to drive directly to attractions situated in the heart of our busy capital, but significant Zone charges still have to be paid if you want to use one of The Caravan Club's excellent sites at Abbey Wood or Crystal Palace. Naturally, these fees will discourage some tourists, many of whom are visitors from mainland Europe. At the time of writing protests are being sent to TFL, whose committee must have been aware that motorcaravans are often built using commercial base vehicles.

With so many congestion problems, issues such as this arise frequently, and whilst the advice given in this chapter is believed to be correct at the time of

(i) Technical tip

Towing brackets and motorcaravans

Laws are continually changing. At the moment, for example, the majority of motorcaravans can be fitted with a bespoke towing bracket, whereas the brackets fitted to virtually all recent cars must be Type Approved products that comply with European Directive 94/20/EC. This became a requirement in the UK for cars first registered on or after 1 August 1998 following an amendment made to the Road Vehicles (Construction and Use) Regulations 1986. It didn't include commercial vehicles at the time, but changes to this ruling are expected in 2008 or shortly thereafter.

Moreover, in anticipation of a time when motorcaravans will be required to obtain 'whole vehicle type approval', recent models in the Swift Group's ranges have already achieved Type Approval status. This is a praiseworthy step and motorhome manufacturers recommend that only Type Approved tow-bars are fitted on Type Approved vehicles. The one made by AL-KO to bolt directly onto an AL-KO chassis is one of the few examples of Type Approved brackets made for motorcaravans.

Specialists have been permitted to design and fit bespoke towing brackets but this will change if it becomes mandatory to fit only tested Type Approved products.

The AL-KO towing bracket designed to couple directly to an AL-KO vehicle chassis is currently one of the few examples of a Type Approved bracket for motorcaravans.

writing you'll need to check for yourself if the rulings have changed.

However, when a vehicle-related law is introduced it is not, as a general principle, applied retrospectively – in other words, existing vehicles seldom have to be altered to comply with new legislation. Hence there are many 'classic cars' still being legally used on our roads that aren't equipped with seat belts. That's because seat belt laws don't carry retrospective enforcement. The position is the same regarding seat belts in motorcaravans.

What is a motorcaravan?

In Chapter One, the definition of a motorcaravan is reported as 'a special purpose M1 category vehicle constructed to include living accommodation'. The same chapter also explains some of the issues that differentiate its status from that of commercial road-going vehicles even when their base units are the same. In addition the definition is normally made explicit on a vehicle's registration certificate.

However, different interpretations occur when it comes to Vehicle Excise Duty (VED). For example, the M1 Status of motorcaravans means that these vehicles normally fall into the same category as cars. Yet in the context of VED, most motorcaravans are paradoxically treated as either Private Light Goods vehicles or Heavy Private Goods vehicles.

Efforts are being made by independent specialist bodies such as The Motorhome Information Service (MIS) to gain a discrete classification for motorcaravans, thereby permitting greater clarity for legislators, owners and the Police. At present it's unhelpfully confusing when in one context a motorcaravan is treated like a car, whereas in another situation it comes under rulings applicable to Goods Vehicles.

The Department of Transport also appears to be experiencing difficulties differentiating between 'motorcaravans', which are fully-equipped leisure vehicles, and 'living vans', which are commercial vehicles equipped with a facility enabling the driver to sleep inside – many long-distance lorries, for instance, have a sleeping compartment over the cab. As explained in the next section, that's why the words 'motor caravan' should be entered in section D.3 (headed 'Body Type') on the V5C Registration Certificate.

The Registration Certificate

This document, once referred to as the 'Log Book', has undergone several changes. For example, the V5 'Registration Document' was replaced by a V5C 'Registration Certificate' so that all Member States of the European Union adopted a common format. A leaflet (INS163/2) from the Driver and Vehicle Licensing Agency (DVLA) published in March 2004 stated that by 'June 2005 all keepers of taxed/ SORNed vehicles will have been issued with a new style Registration Certificate.' (The term SORN is explained in the next section.)

Owners should also note that it's their legal obligation to notify the DVLA if details on a V5C Registration Certificate need alteration. For example, notification must be given of the installation of a different engine, a change of body colour, or alterations that place it in a new revenue category. A change might occur, for example, when a Private/ Light Goods (PLG) vehicle hitherto driven as a panel van for delivering goods is later converted into a motorcaravan. The term 'motor caravan' must then be recorded in section D.3 ('Body Type'). Formal recognition of its status as a leisure vehicle as opposed to a goods-carrying vehicle has implications for matters such as speed limits. Should you find mistakes, the Certificate should be returned to

DVLA, Swansea, SA99 1BA, with an explanatory letter so that the appropriate amendments can be made. This is important when a new vehicle excise licence is due. If, for some reason, you don't receive a V11 Licence Renewal form in the post you have to produce your Registration Certificate at a licence-issuing Post Office or DVLA Local Office. Naturally it should contain up-to-date information.

When a commercial panel van is subsequently converted into a motorcaravan, the change must be recorded in Section D.3 (Body Type) on the Registration Certificate.

Statutory Off Road Notification (SORN)

Like owners of 'Classic Cars' and self-built 'Kit Cars', there are some motorcaravanners who only use their vehicles during the warmer months of the year. In consequence they only pay Road Tax for a six-month period and then provide statutory off road notification (SORN) when the vehicle is removed from public roads and put into storage. Once the declaration has been made, the Driver and Vehicle Licensing Agency (DVLA) sends a notification letter verifying that this request has been officially recorded.

When an owner subsequently wants to re-licence a vehicle for use on the road, it's necessary to complete and then submit Vehicle Licence Application form V10 to a licence-issuing Post Office or DVLA Local Office. This must be accompanied by the V5C Registration Certificate, a Certificate of Insurance, and a valid MoT certificate (if applicable).

Although it's better from a mechanical viewpoint for a vehicle to be used regularly throughout the year, some motorcaravan owners work abroad for long spells and are forced to lay-up their vehicle for an extended period. In this case SORN is something to be aware of. It's no longer permitted to allow payment of Vehicle Excise Duty to lapse – you're legally required to declare SORN and to remove your motorcaravan from public roads.

Detailed guidance on SORN is available from licensing Post Offices, DVLA Local Offices and on the Internet (www.direct.gov.uk/motoring). Note that you can also declare SORN via the Internet, and the website explains the procedure.

Different categories recorded on a driving licence indicate the size and types of vehicle the holder is permitted to drive.

MOTORCARAVAN WEIGHTS

It might seem curious to find a section dealing with vehicle weight in a chapter concerned with legal issues. However, the reason for this is simple: Driving Licence categories and speed limits are related to vehicle weights.

Loading terms

Weight is currently expressed in kilograms (1kg = roughly 2.2lb). An imperial ton is 20cwt, *ie* 2,240lb. A metric ton, properly called a 'tonne', is 1,000kg, or 2,204.62lb.

- **Actual Laden Weight** (ALW): This is the actual weight of a motorcaravan including all its contents, its passengers, and its fuel. A check on a weighbridge will reveal whether the ALW exceeds a vehicle's 'maximum technically permissible laden mass' or MTPLM. (Using a weighbridge is explained on pages 99–100.)
- **Maximum Technically Permissible Laden Mass** (MTPLM): This refers to a vehicle's total allowable legal weight, as defined by the base vehicle manufacturer. It has previously been called the 'Maximum Laden Weight' (MLW), 'Maximum Authorised Mass' (MAM), 'Gross Vehicle Weight' (GVW), and 'Maximum Authorised Weight' (MAW). Incidentally, the DVLA uses the term MAM, whereas the Caravan and Motorhome industries refer to it as MTPLM.
- **Mass in Running Order** (MIRO): This is the unladen ('ex works') weight of a vehicle. It sometimes takes into account a full fuel tank, essential liquids and may include a weight allowance for the driver, often taken as 75kg.

The term Gross Train Weight refers to the maximum permitted weight of a laden towing vehicle, together with its trailer and the load being carried.

- **Maximum User Payload** (MUP): The payload is a vehicle's maximum carrying capacity and is calculated by deducting a vehicle's mass in running order from its maximum technically permissible laden mass.
- **Maximum Axle Weights** (MAW): Front and rear axles have maximum weights too, and these figures must not be exceeded by the load. On vehicles with front and rear axles, their loading can be checked on a weighbridge by driving one axle at a time onto the weighing plate.
- **Gross Train Weight** (GTW): This refers to the maximum weight permitted for the vehicle together with a trailer and the combined loads being carried. It's important to note this when towing heavy items such as a support car. GTW is sometimes referred to as 'Combined Weight'.

Data relating to weights is displayed on a metal information plate that's usually permanently fixed in the engine bay or on a door surround. Since 1999, new motorcaravans have been covered by BS EN 1646-2, which specifies the way that weights and payloads should be expressed.

Unfortunately, manufacturers often express the weight of ex-works vehicles (ie mass in running order, or MIRO) in different ways. Some include a

Below left: Many plates are permanently fixed in engine compartments.

Below: A few plates are mounted on door surrounds.

Payload

Nowadays, this is subdivided into three categories:

1. Essential equipment, such as gas cylinders and toilet chemicals.
2. Optional equipment, such as solar panels, bike rack and air conditioning system.
3. Personal effects, such as clothing, food and holiday gear.

Together, these items add up to the 'payload', and working within the MTPLM limit some motorcaravans can carry much more equipment than others. So ask about the weight of optional equipment that you might want to purchase – particularly heavy products such as an onboard generator. This should be related to your payload potential. Also compare any addition with the equivalent weight of shoes, socks, shirts and cold-weather wear. Adding accessory items will mean that fewer personal effects can be packed.

Personal effects form part of your permitted payload and families with children often carry a surprising variety of holiday items.

hypothetical 75kg driver, fuel tank filled to 90 per cent, tools, and a spare wheel. Also confusing is the fact that some models are sold with a 'de luxe' package that might include a roll-out sunblind, a TV set, and alloy wheels. The addition of accessories such as these inevitably means that a published MIRO figure is often inaccurate and correspondingly reduces the payload that can legally be carried.

However, there's no argument about a vehicle's maximum weight limit, which is shown on its data plate. Not only could it be dangerous to exceed this limit, it's also a serious offence.

The claimed payload of a vehicle can also be misleading. Information published in some manufacturers' brochures is pleasingly accurate; in others it's wide of the mark. For this reason, when the author conducts tests for magazine reports an empty vehicle is filled to the brim with fuel and then checked on a public weighbridge. A calculation duly reveals if a claimed payload figure is accurate or optimistically exaggerated.

Inaccurate claims aren't unusual. This problem has also been noted by The Caravan Club when vehicles are entered for the annual Design and Drive competition. As a matter of routine each model is taken to a weighbridge for checking

The motorhome is driven onto the weighing plate and the driver usually alights before the reading is taken.

before the judges commence their searching evaluations.

Roadside inspections conducted by the Police have also revealed examples of gross overloading, and whereas towed caravans used to be the subject of additional scrutiny, attention is now turning to motorhomes.

As regards 'payload', it has now become customary to divide this into separate categories as shown in the adjacent panel. Moreover, manufacturers are also publishing weights of the 'Optional Extra' items offered in their catalogues, which is particularly helpful.

Using a weighbridge

All motorcaravan owners should get the weight of their vehicle checked, so contact your local authority for a list of nearby public weighbridges. In my County Council offices the information used to be kept in the Weights and Measures Department; now it's available from the Trading Standards Service.

Telephone the weighbridge operators, enquire if an appointment is needed, and ask about fees. As a rough guide, each measured weight costs around £5–£10.

On arrival, the vehicle is driven onto the weighing plate, the driver alights and the weight is recorded. Then you drive forwards to vacate the plate. Having done that you then reverse so that only the rear wheels rest on the platform. Disembark once again, and the rear axle loading is recorded.

You could repeat this operation placing just the front wheels on the plate, but to save money most people simply subtract the rear axle reading from the total vehicle weight to calculate the front axle load.

As part of the service you'll be issued with a dated certificate giving the weights, but you also need to

Driving just the rear wheels onto the plate enables the operator to take a back axle load weight.

Information is recorded on an electronic device that's linked to a printer.

You'll be given a dated printout with the registration details of your vehicle and the weights recorded.

record if your vehicle was carrying gas cylinders, drinking water and items such as a toolkit at the time the weighbridge was used.

Back at home you can then add the combined weight of passengers and driver to find out what payload remains for accessories and personal possessions. Alternatively you could return to the weighbridge with your vehicle loaded-up for a typical holiday, thereby confirming beyond doubt that it's not illegally overweight. Naturally, you shouldn't need to do this prior to every holiday, but be mindful of weight when loading-up for each trip.

With this information you can then confirm that your loaded vehicle isn't exceeding its MTPLM. Also check that individual axle loadings aren't over the limits stated on your vehicle's data plate. For instance, a loaded motorcaravan might fall within its MTPLM, but if too many heavy items are positioned at the back this could exceed the rear axle's limit and lead to prosecution.

Upgrading the MTPLM

Some commercial vehicle specialists, such as TVAC in Leyland, Lancashire, are equipped to upgrade the MTPLM of a vehicle. For example, it's sometimes possible to upgrade and re-plate a light commercial vehicle from 3,500kg to 3,850kg. However, this can be costly, because it may necessitate fitting uprated

The weight limit on the back axle of a vehicle carrying heavy items at the rear might be exceeded. Motorcaravans with twin rear axles are able to carry much greater loads.

MAXIMUM WEIGHTS AT WHICH THIS VEHICLE IS FIT FOR USE

Drinkwater
TEL: 01772 456888

tyres, strengthening the rear axle tube, altering the suspension, improving brake specifications and so on.

There are also disadvantages in running a vehicle that's plated with an MTPLM greater than 3,500kg. For example:

- Since January 1997 new Category B Driving Licence holders in the UK are limited to driving vehicles up to 3,500kg (or 4,250kg with a trailer).
- Many motoring organisations in the UK will not recover motorhomes weighing over 3,500kg.
- In the UK, the minimum age to drive a vehicle over 3,500kg is 18; it is 17 for vehicles weighing less than 3,500kg.
- When a driver over 70 years of age applies to renew a licence, additional eyesight and health tests are required if the applicant wishes to drive a vehicle in the UK with an MTPLM over 3,500kg.
- Drivers with certain medical conditions aren't permitted to drive vehicles plated at more than 3,500kg. This includes diabetics who have to control their condition using insulin injections.
- In some countries, particularly Germany, a vehicle over 3,500kg is classified as a Goods Vehicle and is subject to lower speed limits, different overtaking rules, and restrictions of vehicle use at weekends.
- In Switzerland, a motorhome exceeding 3,500kg has to pay a Heavy Goods Vehicle tax supplement at the border in order to use motorways.

As explained above, keeping the MTPLM at 3,500kg or lower has several points in its favour.

Down-rating strategies

Mindful of restrictions like those mentioned above, some owners adopt the reverse strategy and get an approved specialist to *reduce* the MTPLM of their motorcaravan and to fit an official replacement plate. Several dealers can carry out this service.

It's not a difficult operation and a magazine reader reported recently that having just turned 70, he

This modified motorcaravan bears a revised data plate after its MTPLM was raised from 3,500kg to 3,850kg.

Throughout Europe, it's often apparent that 3,500kg (3.5 tonnes) represents a significant recognised legal break point in respect of weight limits and legal issues applying to vehicles.

decided to have his motorcaravan's MTPLM of 3,850kg down-rated to 3,500kg. The fact that he no longer used a motorcycle previously carried on a rear carrier meant that this wouldn't involve any hardship. Having completed form VTG10, he reported that it took only two weeks for VOSA to verify that the MTPLM had been amended to the lower figure. Of course, this strategy calls for a stricter approach when packing personal gear, but there are several benefits too, particularly in respect of Driving Licence classifications.

DRIVING LICENCES

Drivers under the age of 70
If you passed your test prior to 1 January 1997
A Category B Driving Licence obtained before 1 January 1997 permits you to drive a motorcaravan without a trailer as long as its MTPLM doesn't exceed 7,500kg. Alternatively, if you want to tow a trailer you're permitted to do this as long as the GTW of the trailer *and* the motorcaravan doesn't exceed 8,250kg.

If you gained your Category B licence on or after 1 January 1997
You're permitted to drive vehicles with an MTPLM up to 3,500kg. However, if you successfully pass an LGV test you're then qualified to drive a motorcaravan with an MTPLM up to 7,500kg. If you want to tow a small trailer behind your motorcaravan, no further test has to be passed as long as it doesn't exceed 750kg and the combined MTPLM of the motorcaravan and trailer doesn't exceed 4,250kg.

To tow a trailer which is heavier than 750kg but weighs less than the motorcaravan, and provided the MTPLM of the motorcaravan doesn't exceed 3,500kg, you're required to pass a further E Test.

As regards owners wanting to tow a trailer heavier than 750kg behind a motorcaravan whose MTPLM exceeds 3,500kg, it's then necessary to pass both a C1 Test and an E Test.

If you wish to drive a motorcaravan which exceeds 7,500kg MTPLM you will have to pass a C Test.

Drivers aged 70 or more
If you passed your test prior to 1 January 1997
Provided the MTPLM of your motorcaravan is less

than 3,500kg, the driving entitlement for both Category B and combined Category B+E is normally retained when you reapply for a licence which will run for three years on reaching the age of 70. If the MTPLM of your motorcaravan is greater than 3,500kg you'll also have to submit a D4 medical form completed by your GP. This involves an eyesight test to verify that your vision achieves the required standard at 20.5m (67ft). Further information on medical requirements is given on the DVLA website (www.dvla.gov.uk).

If you passed your test on or after 1 January 1997
As long as your medical condition is sound you're permitted to drive a vehicle on your B licence provided its MTPLM is less than 3,500kg. However, if your motorcaravan's MTPLM exceeds this weight but is no greater than 7,500kg, you'll have to take a further test to gain a C1 licence – this is the qualification needed by drivers of 'medium commercial vehicles'. Alternatively, you can arrange for the MTPLM shown on the vehicle's plate to be down-rated, as explained earlier.

If you wish to drive a motorcaravan that exceeds 7,500kg MTPLM you'll have to pass a C Test.

For further information see DVLA Booklet D100 entitled 'What you need to know about Driving Licences', available from Post Offices. Unfortunately some editions of this booklet appear not to give a great deal of advice on aspects relating to medical certification for the over-70s.

Many motorhome owners enjoy the benefits afforded by large vehicles, but to drive models exceeding 7,500kg MTPLM you have to pass a C Test.

This 2007 Knaus Sport is subject to the same speed limits as cars because its unladen weight of 2,820kg falls well below the 3,050kg defining limit.

Technical Tip

Speed Limiters

Motorcaravans do not have to be fitted with speed limiters provided certain criteria are met. Key issues relating to this topic are explained in the text alongside.

SPEED LIMITS IN THE UK

As stated earlier, it's important that the words 'motor caravan' are entered in section D3 ('Body Type') of the V5C Registration Certificate. This differentiates your vehicle from those first registered after 2001 that have an MTPLM over 3,500kg and carry either passengers or goods for 'hire or reward'. Under recent legislation such vehicles have to be fitted with speed limiters and are restricted to 62mph when carrying passengers, and 56.6mph when carrying goods. Moreover, they aren't permitted to use the outside lane of a motorway with three or more lanes. Clearly, these are *not* motorcaravans, and speed limiters are not required on privately-owned leisure vehicles.

So what speeds are applicable to private motorcaravans? This isn't straightforward, because it's partly governed by the *unladen* weight of the vehicle. This figure isn't normally given in official documents, although it should be recorded in literature supplied by motorcaravan converters.

Motorcaravans with an unladen weight not exceeding 3,050kg

Note that the figure 3,050kg given here (which goes back to the old 3.0 imperial tons) is *not* a misprint and mustn't be confused with the more usually encountered weight 'milestone' of 3,500kg. As long as an unladen motorcaravan doesn't exceed 3,050kg and is listed as a 'motor caravan' in the V5C Registration Certificate it's subject to the same speed limits as cars. As a reminder, these are:
- 60mph on single carriageway roads unless a lower limit is in force
- 70mph on dual carriageway roads unless a lower limit is in force
- 70mph on motorways unless a lower limit is in force.

Motorcaravans less than 12m long with an unladen weight exceeding 3,050kg

This category includes a very large proportion of coachbuilt models. Speed limits are:
- 50mph on single carriageway roads unless a lower limit is in force
- 60mph on dual carriageway roads unless a lower limit is in force
- 70mph on motorways unless a lower limit is in force.

Motorcaravans more than 12m long

- 50mph on single carriageway roads unless a lower limit is in force
- 60mph on dual carriageway roads unless a lower limit is in force
- 60mph on motorways unless a lower limit is in force.

Speed limits when towing a trailer

- 50mph on single carriageway roads unless a lower limit is in force
- 60mph on dual carriageway roads unless a lower limit is in force
- 60mph on motorways unless a lower limit is in force.

In addition, when you're towing you're not permitted to use the right-hand lane of a motorway with three or more lanes unless signs or roadworks indicate otherwise.

It's unfortunate that speed limits given in The Highway Code don't make mention of the limits applicable to motorcaravans. These are given instead in Section 86 (1) and Schedule 6 of The Road Traffic Regulation Act 1984.

Speed limits abroad

There are numerous differences between UK speed limits and those imposed abroad. There are also intriguing rulings such as the autoroute limits applicable in France, where a lower speed is enforced in wet weather. Presumably the driver has to evaluate the situation and decide when a light drizzle calls for adherence to lower limits.

The 3,500kg MTPLM weight is often significant too. For instance, in Germany vehicles that have been upgraded to a higher MTPLM aren't permitted to be driven faster than 100kph (approx 60mph) on an autobahn, while in Austria they have to be fitted with a so-called 'GP-box' – this is available for

An analysis of exhaust emissions forms part of a standard Class IV MoT for cars, and currently many motorcaravans also qualify for Class IV testing.

a small fee from many of the country's service and petrol stations and is used for road-toll charging. Information on the system can be found on www.austria.info.

As these few examples indicate, it's obviously important for any motorcaravanner driving abroad to find out what speed limits and other driving requirements apply in the countries being visited. Books such as *Driving Abroad* by Robert Davies, also published by Haynes, provide useful advice.

MOT TESTING AND MOTORCARAVANS

When your motorcaravan is due for an MoT test, the inspection is referred to as a Class IV test. Although goods vehicles classified between 3,000 and 3,500kg have to be submitted for a Class VII test, this is not the case for motorcaravans. In this instance they fall under the same classification and test procedures as a car, irrespective of their weight.

This is fine, except for the fact that many MoT stations that conduct Class IV tests for car owners

This MoT test station didn't have an elevating ramp but an inspection pit gave alternative access underneath.

simply don't have good enough access or the height to accommodate a large coachbuilt motorcaravan. Equipment such as the elevating ramp might not have the lifting capacity to cope with a very large model either, and the rolling road for brake testing might not be suitable.

For this reasons many owners take their vehicles to a goods vehicle test station, which is fine – provided the management is familiar with car testing protocols.

Matters relating to MoT testing are dealt with by the Vehicle & Operator Services Agency (VOSA), and further information can be obtained from www.vosa.gov.uk. If you want to check the MoT status of a vehicle this can be done by visiting www.motinfo.gov.uk or by telephoning 0870 33 00 444. You will need the vehicle's registration mark and either the reference number on its V5C Registration Certificate or the test number from a new-style VT20 MoT Test Certificate.

Nowadays an MoT test pass result is recorded on VOSA's database and this, rather than a VT20 paper certificate, is used for legal purposes to verify that your vehicle has achieved a valid pass.

VEHICLE EXCISE DUTY

Although terms such as 'Road Fund Licence', 'Tax Disc' and 'Road Tax' are used in everyday conversation, the term currently applicable in official documents is 'Vehicle Excise Duty', or VED for short.

The amount payable for a motorcaravan varies in accordance with its base vehicle. This raises many questions and provokes hostility among owners. For example, some campervans, such as the Starcraft, are converted saloon cars, while others, such as the models from Wheelhome, are converted MPVs. Then there are converted 'window vans', such as Bilbo's models built on Volkswagen T5s. Other

Although the rear axle tube had been extended on this motorcaravan, it just fitted into the rollers used for testing vehicles' brakes.

The words 'motor caravan' should appear in section D.3 of a V5C Registration Certificate, together with the vehicle's taxation class.

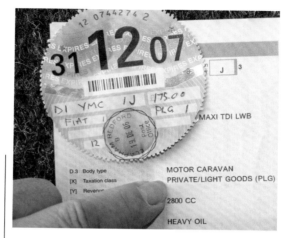

D.3 Body type
[X] Taxation class
[Y] Revenue

MOTOR CARAVAN
PRIVATE/LIGHT GOODS (PLG)

2800 CC

HEAVY OIL

Technical Tip

Vehicle Licensing Classification

An official of the DVLA writing to Motor Caravan Magazine (November 2007), explained the classification process applicable to vehicles registered after 1 March 2001. Since that date, "VED rates for newly registered cars and light vans have been based firmly on the type approval information provided at first registration." Thus a vehicle that is type approved as an M1 Passenger Vehicles is "... treated as a car and taxed according to carbon dioxide emissions and fuel type under the graduated VED provisions. Vans are type approved N1 and are taxed as light goods vehicles." The type approval process for N1 vehicles does not include measurement of carbon dioxide emissions.

Also note that: "Once a vehicle has been first registered and licensed in one of these taxation classes, its status for the purposes of payment of VED will not change irrespective of any subsequent alterations that may then be made to the vehicle."

motorcaravans are constructed on either light or heavy goods vehicles. These dissimilarities have various implications for the amount of VED payable.

Adding to the confusion is the fact that although the words 'motor caravan' should appear in section D.3 of a V5C Registration Certificate, the issued tax disc normally uses the term 'Private/Light Goods' or PLG.

The 2007 Spring Budget introduced radical revisions to the legislation and some window vans converted into motorcaravans are now treated the same as M1 diesel cars. This means that the vehicle is subject to a 'banding' classification, and some VW manual Kombis are classified as Band F, for which the VED is presently £205 per annum, while a Tiptronic Variant registered after 23 March 2007 is placed in the Band G category, for which the VED is currently £300. It would appear, however, that 'panel vans' which have windows added by the motorcaravan converter fall outside these banded ratings, as do motorcaravans built on other commercial base vehicles.

At the time of writing:

- Models with an MTPLM of less than 3,500kg are classified as Private/Light Goods Vehicles and the annual VED is currently set at £180.
- Models with an MTPLM greater than 3,500kg are classified as Private/Heavy Goods Vehicles and the annual VED is currently set at £165

The rationale that governs the VED payable for different types of vehicle may seem obscure. Having said that, the criteria governing VED charges tend to change with surprising frequency.

On the mildest of bends, this child seat depressed the foam of a motorcaravan's bench seat, the recoil strap paid out more slack, and the child was then swinging upside down in the aisle.

SEAT BELTS

Perhaps the most difficult legal area of all for motorcaravanners relates to the use of seat belts. A well-established requirement states that when a seat belt has been fitted it must be worn. That is certainly the case with regard to the cab seats. It's also the case in respect of seats equipped with belts in the living area, these often being described as 'designated travel seats'. That aside, many experts assert that sideways-facing seats equipped with belts may cause their occupants severe injuries to the torso in an accident.

Bearing in mind the point made earlier that laws are not applied retrospectively, *ie* to older vehicles, since October 2007 it has been required that all forward and rearward-facing seats in new motorcaravans must be fitted with belts. These can then be designated and badged as 'travel seats'. Moreover, it is now illegal to use sideways-facing seats on new motorcaravans when a vehicle is being driven.

As regards the use of children's booster cushions and safety seats, the recent laws applicable to cars are also applicable to motorcaravans. The website www.thinkroadsafety.gov.uk gives advice about this, but the author has discovered a serious problem: children's car seats that fit safely and successfully on a standard vehicle seat are often wholly ineffective on the soft cushion bench seats in the rear of many motorcaravans. The accompanying photograph shows what can go wrong.

Stability is also much worse when a booster seat is placed on a motorhome bench seat. Doubtless the safety specialists will convene further debates.

CHAPTER **SEVEN**

OWNERSHIP
ISSUES

Before embarking on your first trip, several products will need to be purchased. For example, only a few models are sold with a complete complement of cutlery and crockery. You will also need bedding, and whereas some owners are content to use sleeping bags, others prefer a duvet and fitted sheets. Finally, you'll want to keep the interior and exterior smart, and that requires some specialist products.

Having purchased a motorcaravan, you'll want to look after it.

Fire Brigade demonstrations at motorcaravan shows reveal the folly of putting water on to a burning chip pan.

When Carlight caravans were introduced more than 50 years ago, the wife of the Company's owner enjoyed living in style and was particularly fond of Gordons Dry Gin. In consequence, these fine touring caravans came equipped with a bone china tea service as standard and a purpose-made cabinet holding a bottle of Gin!

Regrettably this quaint tradition came to an end just a few years ago and today's caravans and motorhomes are seldom sold with portable items. However, there are a few exceptions – Murvi van conversions, for instance, include items such as a First Aid kit, cutlery, crockery, warning triangle, spare bulb kit, gas cylinder and carbon monoxide detector. Models in the Auto-Sleepers and Orion ranges are also often sold with smart crockery.

But this is unusual and new owners will normally have to purchase a variety of items before setting off on their first trip. Inevitably there's no such thing as a standard list of prerequisites, but this chapter provides some helpful reminders.

 Useful tip

Fire extinguishers

When Fire Brigades visit outdoor motorhome shows they sometimes re-create the effect of putting water on a chip-pan fire in a purpose-built display vehicle. The resulting huge flames are a frightening sight.

Fire extinguishers are manufactured to deal with specific types of fire and these have to meet the requirements set out in British Standards and European Norms. However, it would be impracticable to carry a range of extinguishers designed to deal with fires involving liquids, solid materials, flammable gases, electrical products and so on. Since the living area in a motorcaravan is quite small, a dry powder extinguisher is generally recommended for all-round use.

An extinguisher should be located where it is easily reached but shouldn't be situated too close to a likely fire source, such as the hob. Be familiar with its operating mechanism and keep a note of the date on its casing.

For chip-pan fires, a 'fire blanket' complying with EN 1869 is also a recommended purchase. In larger vehicles a smoke alarm is desirable too. A motorcaravan dealer can offer advice on suitable products.

SOME ITEMS TO CONSIDER

☐ Although this 2006 Orian Gemini is supplied with china cups and plates, this provision is rather unusual. Many owners will visit a dealer's accessory shop and choose a set of lightweight Melamine picnic plates.

☐ Coat hangers will be needed but the type shown here doesn't retain clothing for long, and items soon fall off when you're driving. Owners adopt a variety of solutions including pegging clothes in place and using elastic shock cord.

☐ It's wise to have a tyre gauge in your glove box. Dial types are usually preferred, and to achieve optimum accuracy the required pressure reading should fall midway in the range. This one is from the International Tool Co.

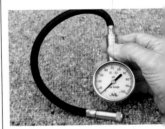

☐ If you are a practical person who would normally fit a spare wheel yourself after a puncture, it's worth buying a telescopic wrench with sockets to suit the fixings used on light commercial vehicles.

☐ High visibility reflectorised jackets or waistcoats aren't expensive to purchase and in some countries it's obligatory to have one with you. It would certainly be unwise to attempt roadside repairs without one.

☐ Some owners fill a fire bucket with water when stopping at a site. This might help in an emergency but you should also have an appropriately mounted dry powder extinguisher and fire-retardant blanket indoors.

Of course, this list isn't claimed to be exhaustive. Furthermore, if you're planning to travel abroad you'll find that different countries have additional requirements, including an obligation to carry spare vehicle bulbs, First Aid kits and one (or sometimes two) breakdown warning triangles.

Among the best sources of information on European requirements are The Caravan Club's *Caravan Europe 1* and *Caravan Europe 2* site guides and touring handbooks, which present detailed general advice as well as country-specific requirements.

You will also need to decide which gas product you want to use. There are many suppliers of portable gas cylinders throughout Europe and some of the more common UK products are described in Chapter Fourteen.

Bedding

Preferences in respect of bedding are very much a personal matter. Some owners, for example, are content to use sleeping bags that they might have used previously on camping trips. Where space is limited – *eg* in small campervans – sleeping bags that can be pushed into compact stuff-sacks are often preferred.

However, when a large motorcaravan is equipped with a fixed double bed many owners prefer to purchase fitted sheets and duvets. Recognising this trend, several specialists are now selling motorhome-specific bedding and the range from Jonic is particularly comprehensive.

Also bear in mind that where a mattress is supported by a solid base there's a tendency for damp to form on the underside. This can be avoided if air is able to circulate beneath the foam, and many motorcaravanners use a thin, fibrous underlay like Ventair 15 which helps retard the incidence of condensation.

Bedding and related products

☐ If you want a mattress protector under your base sheet, Jonic will make one to order – the company already holds information on mattress sizes used in many popular makes of motorhome.

☐ Pillows are another bedding item about which people have strong personal preferences. Some prefer feather pillows; others prefer synthetic

foam. The pillows shown here are made using 'memory foam', which retains its shape.

☐ If a mattress is supported by a solid base as opposed to a slatted surface it's a good idea to purchase a special underlay. Some are made using natural coir, others are synthetic, but both allow air to circulate underneath.

☐ Where young children are assigned a high level bunk or bed it's important that there's no likelihood of them falling out. These safety nets from Seitz are often fitted as standard but they can also be installed later.

CLEANING

Like any vehicle, a motorhome deserves to be cleaned when it's dirty. One of the problems with most models is the fact that there are so many different types of material to be treated. Frankly it's impossible to formulate one product that can clean materials as dissimilar as glass reinforced plastic (GRP) mouldings and acrylic windowpanes, or painted aluminium sheet and rubber tyres. Ideally each needs its own cleaning product, although some do go a long way towards achieving multifunctional effectiveness.

There's also the possibility of damaging some materials through a chemical reaction with the cleaning product. For example, methylated spirits is often put into windscreen washer bottles, since apart from preventing the contents from freezing in moderately cold weather 'meths' also cleans automotive glass. Under no circumstances, however, should it be used on the acrylic 'plastic' windows often fitted in the living area. Initially meths will give them a shining appearance, but after several days the entire surface develops a mass of tiny, hairline cracks. This is a condition called 'crazing', for which there is no cure.

So the careful choice of well-established products is most important, and plastic windows are particularly susceptible to damage. However, scratches *can* be polished out using light abrasive pastes recommended by their manufacturers.

116

Acrylic 'plastic' windows

Double-glazed acrylic windows supplied by specialists such as Polyplastic BV and Seitz are often fitted to the living quarters of motorcaravans – both panel vans and coachbuilt models. Care instructions recommend that they're cleaned using warm, soapy water, followed by clean, fresh water. However, there are several proprietary products that can also be used to good effect. For example, Autoglym 'Fast Glass' is good on both safety glass *and* acrylic plastic windows. You can also use Autoglym's general purpose 'Caravan and Motorhome Cleaner'.

Keeping windows clean

☐ If a window's coated with grime and dry dust, apply fresh water. However, windows aren't often dirty enough to warrant this preliminary dousing. Then spray on 'Caravan and Motorhome Cleaner'.

☐ Agitate the area using a soft sponge. If the windows are hard to reach you can use a very soft brush to activate the cleaner. However, the bristles should first be thoroughly cleansed with water to ensure there's no grit in them.

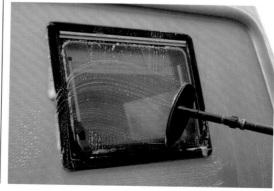

☐ Then remove the suds with clean water before drying the window off using a leather or synthetic cloth. If you choose to use 'Fast Glass', spray on the cleaner and then remove it using a sheet of absorbent kitchen paper.

☐ 'Fast Glass' is good on vehicle windows too. After being sprayed sparingly onto the surface it's polished off using absorbent paper – modern micro-fibre cloth is also very effective.

Cleaning equipment

If you have a high motorhome you'll need some means of access to reach the roof, since few people own the type of mobile platforms that dealers use.

This is why brush and squeegee products mounted on a telescopic pole are so useful. Examples are sold at most major exhibitions but don't buy the cheapest one in the racks. Get one that's robust, because these make light work of cleaning. Of course, there's not a lot of point cleaning the sides of a motorcaravan if you omit to clean the roof – one shower of rain will prove the folly of that misguided strategy – so you'll also need a robust set of steps or trestles together with a telescopic brush to reach the top.

Below: Few owners will have the access equipment used by dealers.

Below left: Soft brushes mounted on telescopic poles are sold at most exhibitions.

High-pressure hoses are used by workshop staff but can cause damage in the hands of inexperienced owners.

As regards high-pressure jet hoses, these can achieve good results in the hands of an experienced user – in fact dealers often use them to clean their forecourt models. However, indiscriminate use without making appropriate reductions in pressure can cause a surprising amount of damage. On coachbuilt models in particular, a high-pressure hose directed at joining seams can soon blast away fragments of hardening sealant. The effect of this might not become apparent immediately, but after a few heavy rain showers the resultant water ingress can start to wreak havoc.

It might seem easy to clean a vehicle using a high-pressure washer and there are certainly some good machines on the market, but, having said that, other approaches might be better in the long run.

Wheels and tyres

When you own a motorcaravan you often find that some types of wheel embellisher have a nasty habit of making a break for freedom. Fortunately, many light commercial vehicles now employ attachment systems that retain their embellishers much more effectively. Alloy wheels have also become a way of enhancing the appearance of a leisure vehicle, but if your model has clip-on embellishers it's worth anchoring them with some cable ties.

Another issue that can be much more serious relates to the availability of tyres. Many coachbuilt motorcaravans are supplied with a 'Camping' grade of tyre that has a ply structure designed to survive the heavy loadings typical on this type of vehicle. Once a motorcaravan conversion is completed, the base vehicle never re-achieves its light state even when all your personal effects are removed. So 'Camping' grade tyres are normally specified from the outset by motorhome converters, and vehicle manufacturers such as Fiat fit them as original equipment.

However, the base vehicle manufacturers'

If your motorcaravan has clip-on embellishers it's worth anchoring them in place using cable ties.

demand for uninterrupted supplies of 'Camping' grade tyres sometimes means that owners find difficulty obtaining replacements. After an irreparable puncture, for example, the author found to his dismay that a six- to eight-week wait for replacement tyres isn't unusual.

A national shortage of particular tyres undoubtedly poses problems when the tread depth gets low, particularly if an MoT test is approaching. Safety and legality are important issues and it's therefore advisable to keep an ongoing check on the availability of your particular size of tyres, especially if they are 'Camping' products. Also ensure that your spare is both in a good state and ready to be brought into commission if it's unexpectedly needed. Anyone can suffer from a puncture and if a sidewall sustains damage, repair work can't be undertaken.

General cleaning

Many parts of a motorcaravan can be treated with products designed for cars, such as dark plastic bumper cleaners, vinyl cleaners, wheel cleaners and tyre cleaners. Shampoo additives are normally fine for a general wash-down and car polishes are often used, Mer and Autoglym Resin polish being popular examples.

However, motorcaravans are also afflicted by black streaks that develop below some of the body fittings. For instance, rainwater discharging past a refrigerator ventilator or window frame often trickles down leaving lines of black deposits that are surprisingly hard to shift.

Mindful of this problem, the chemists at Autoglym's Letchworth laboratories formulated 'Caravan and Motorhome Cleaner'. This fluid is applied directly from the bottle, agitated with a sponge or brush, hosed off, and dried with a leather. Although this is principally intended as a preliminary treatment preceding the application of polish, it's easy to apply and leaves a pleasing

Tyres designated as 'Camping' grade are manufactured to cope with persistently heavy loadings.

Rainwater trickling past external ventilators often leaves black streaks that are hard to shift.

Autoglym 'Caravan and Motorhome Cleaner' is sprayed on to a small area direct from the container.

It is then agitated with a sponge or soft brush before hosing off.

shine. Consequently many owners use it for most cleaning operations and only resort to applying polish when time permits.

Paint sealing products

A different approach to cleaning is to have a sealing product applied to the painted areas and to self-coloured glass-reinforced plastic (GRP). For many years sealing products were used solely on expensive cars, passenger planes, public service vehicles, cabin cruisers and trains, but such products are now being sold for use on caravans and motorhomes too.

The principle behind such systems recognises that a sealant provides body panels with a protective coating. It has to be applied to a pre-cleaned surface and the barrier it provides resists black streaks, bird lime, algae and other marks. Once a motorcaravan has been treated, a quick wash reinstates a shining surface with the minimum of effort. When it rains there's even a self-cleansing effect on vertical panels.

Admittedly it often takes a full day to prepare a motorcaravan and apply a proprietary sealant, but the benefits are subsequently enjoyed for a period of three to five years before re-treatment is needed.

For the DIY enthusiast, A-Glaze is a treatment pack of cleaner and paint sealant that certainly should last for three years or more if applied carefully after painstaking preparation. Paintseal Direct is another specialist that uses a product containing Teflon®. This is professionally applied and the full service includes the application of treatments on upholstery items inside. When a dealer applies the Paintseal 'package' on a new motorcaravan the benefits are claimed to last around five years. If you own an older motorcaravan, Paintseal Direct can also arrange a thorough body refurbishment as a precursor to the application of its sealant system.

Once the body has been treated with a sealant, post-cleaning products make light work of routine washing. The accompanying illustrations show what this entails.

A sealing operation undertaken by Paintseal Direct

☐ On this older motorcaravan being prepared by Paintseal Direct, a full buffing and cleaning regime removes remnants of previous polishing compounds and surface dirt.

☐ Work on a medium-sized coachbuilt model may take around five hours to complete. Obviously an application of the sealant itself can't be carried out on a blemished surface.

☐ A paint sealant compound is sparingly applied on painted surfaces and GRP mouldings using a rag and a microfibre cloth. It isn't applied to some plastic components.

☐ Finally a damp cloth is used to ease the product over the surfaces. If work can't be carried out indoors the operation has to be undertaken in favourable weather conditions.

Indoor fabric cleaning

Many treatments designed for interior car cleaning can be used in motorcaravans. The accompanying illustrations show examples of products in use.

Interior cleaning work

☐ Compounds for reviving the appearance of vinyl and other plastics used inside modern vehicles are sold at most car component retailers.

☐ Foam interior shampoo products are easy to use on vehicle seat fabrics. Many are equally successful on seating in the living area, but check this point carefully.

☐ Several products like this cleaning foam in the Autoglym range can be used on cookers as well as seating fabrics.

☐ Microfibre cloths and pads are a useful addition to the vehicle valet's armoury of products. Avoid using old rags that contain lint, because this is abrasive.

A completely different approach to keeping interior fabrics in good condition is to apply a barrier product. Examples have been used on new household settees and upholstered chairs in the past, and Paintseal Direct has recently introduced similar barrier treatments for the upholstery found in motorhomes.

Treating internal fabrics with a protective finish

☐ Included as part of the Paintseal Direct exterior treatment process is an application of stain repellents on seating and other fabric surfaces.

☐ The treatment product is applied in a mist spray from a pressure container and then gently distributed over the surface with the help of a sponge.

Conclusion

How much you're prepared to pay to keep your motorcaravan in tip-top condition depends on many factors. Suffice it to say, there are more products available now than ever before, and many of them make cleaning much less of a chore.

CHAPTER EIGHT

CHOOSING
PLACES TO STAY

Some motorcaravanners prefer to stay at camping sites that offer home comforts and modern amenities. A holiday might involve dining at restaurants, dancing at discos and using a washroom that's warm. In contrast, others seek places away from the crowds. A modern, well-equipped motorhome is fine in wild country if that's the experience you want. *You* make the choice, and here are some of the options.

125

A French municipal site at Allemont, near Alpes d'Huez.

L'Escale site on the outskirts of Le Grand-Bornand in the French Alps.

When you own a motorcaravan, there's a wide variety of places to stay. For instance, waking up alongside an empty beach on a Scottish island has a magic that's hard to describe. It's a very different experience from stopping at a lively site on the fringe of an Alpine village that's fully encircled by mountains; or sleeping on a remote roadside verge to cheer Tour de France cyclists who'll be tackling a Pyrenean summit. It would be impossible to catalogue the very dissimilar places where motorhome owners spend their nights!

You'll also find different facilities as you travel round Europe. For example, in Britain there are few places, other than campsites, where you can legitimately park to sleep. It's perversely annoying to see motorway signs exhorting motorists not to drive if they're tired when there aren't any places to stop for a snooze. In many towns, height barriers prevent access to car parks as well: others have signs forbidding overnight sleeping in vehicles. The

Wild camping on the Col d'Aubisque, where Tour de France cyclists scale the French Pyrenees.

consumer magazine *Motorcaravan Motorhome Monthly* even runs an ongoing campaign called 'The Height Fight' which draws attention to towns that readers report to be unwelcoming to motorcaravanners. The campaign's objective is 'to persuade authorities to provide dedicated daytime parking, and overnight halts, for motorcaravans'.

Attitudes about impromptu overnight sleeping differ profoundly from one European country to another; types of campsite are different as well. In France, for example, football pitches and adjacent changing rooms are often converted into municipal campsites in summer. So are other spare grassy areas in villages and towns. Meantime in Britain, members of the two major caravanning clubs have access to thousands of five-unit stopovers called Certificated Sites or Certificated Locations. So let's compare these different provisions.

Certificated Sites or CSs (The Camping & Caravanning Club) and Certificated Locations or CLs (The Caravan Club)

The Caravan Sites & Control of Development Act 1960 permits the establishment of these venues, which need neither a site licence nor planning permission. They're privately owned and mustn't accommodate any more than five units, *ie* caravans or motorhomes. Typically located in rural areas, they're usually quiet, informal, and often on farms. Many provide club members no more than a tap, rubbish disposal facility and an emptying point for a chemical closet. However, an increasing number are now offering mains hook-ups as well. Fees are remarkably modest and the two clubs have a total of more than 4,000 examples listed in their members' site directories.

This Alpine municipal site at Allemont is well laid out.

Five 'vans is the limit on Certificated Locations and Certificated Sites.

In France, Aires are strictly for motorcaravans (camping-cars) and can be used for overnight stops.

(i) Tip

Wild camping in the UK (*camping sauvage* in France)

In the UK, contrasting views are held about impromptu overnight sleeping in motorcaravans. It's sometimes claimed, for example, that all land in the United Kingdom is owned by somebody, and overnight parking without a landowner's consent is tantamount to trespass. On the other hand, there are many motorcaravanners who park by the roadside in wilderness locations for short spells and leave *nothing* behind when they leave. No harm is done, and in many instances no one is any the wiser.

Different views are also held throughout mainland Europe, and tolerance of wild camping varies from country to country. However, a policy statement from The Caravan Club, affirms that it 'does not advise or condone so-called "wild camping". We would always recommend that motorcaravanners stay on a recognised site, for their own security, and out of respect for the local area and community.'

Aires de Service

Although the provision of *Aires des Camping-Cars* in France receives frequent approval in magazines, similar parking facilities with a tap and sanitary point are found in other countries, too. In Italy you'll find night halts called *Area Attrezzata*. In Germany there are *Standplatz* complete with stay-and-display machines which issue 24-hour passes. Emptying points in Spain are signposted as *Area de Servicios para Autocaravanas*, and there's often overnight parking as well.

Regrettably this provision is seldom seen in Britain and motorcaravans seem to be regarded with less favour than they often are in mainland Europe. Presumably there's a general feeling abroad that motorcaravanners make significant contributions to local economies. Having said that, *Aires* in France generally don't permit overnight stopovers to be used by touring caravans. Moreover, some people spending the night on motorway stopovers in Europe have been targeted by teams of professional thieves. Though rare, narcotic gas attacks have also been reported as a prelude to break-ins and that's why motorcaravans are often fitted with gas alarms.

Stopovers in rural areas are different and many motorhome owners use them when touring from place to place.

Commercial UK sites

Many kinds of privately-owned sites are distributed throughout the UK. Some are small, others are large. In fact some of the large sites that offer facilities such as a clubhouse, restaurant, takeaway meal service, swimming pool, entertainment programme, crèche and cycle hire operation are often referred to as 'holiday parks'.

Organisational aspects vary as well. On less formal sites pitches might be merely indicated by numbered pegs around a field, whereas in high-quality parks individual pitches are sometimes formally enclosed by low hedges and enhanced by shrubs. Moreover,

an increasing number provide each pitch with its own mains hook-up, tap and drain for waste water. However, not many include a coupling facility for accepting toilet effluent; these are often provided on 'Camping Grounds' in North America, but the idea has yet to gain acceptance in Europe.

Commercial sites in mainland Europe

Commercially owned sites on the Continent also vary in size and style. However, many have a remarkably short season, and after an extremely busy July and August period closures often start in September. During the height of the season, larger sites in the Netherlands, Belgium, France and Germany run activity programmes, especially for children. Playgrounds are often elaborately planned, and near the Alps and Pyrenees artificial climbing walls are sometimes included.

Because of its close proximity France is especially popular with British motorcaravanners, although many retired owners spend their winters further afield in Spain and Portugal. French sites are marketed with great vigour and there are collective organisations like the Castel chain (inaugurated in 1959) and the Sites aux Paysage Group. As their names imply, the former includes sites established in the grounds of historic chateaux, while the latter comprises countryside sites.

Individual pitches shielded with shrubs are found at Pencelli Castle, a high-quality site near Brecon, South Wales.

Below left: Some sites in mainland Europe become exceedingly busy in July and August.

Below: At Luz St Sauveur near Lourdes, climbing courses are held for children on the campsite's climbing wall.

The Camping and Caravanning Club site set within Kingsbury Water Park, south of Tamworth, is justifiably popular.

Club sites

These are owned or managed by The Caravanning and Camping Club and The Caravan Club. Most are purpose-built and have high-quality facilities. A few, however, are 'managed sites': these include racecourse sites that are used for caravanning between meetings, and sites run on behalf of local authorities. Some Club sites are exclusively for members whereas others welcome non-members, although a small extra charge is payable. You can usually join the club on arrival as well.

Sites with restrictions

In the last few years a growing number of 'adults only' sites have been created by private owners. These are usually quiet, football-free places, and one site accepts no one under 30 years of age. Another site accepts children at certain times but requires them to reside in a special compound – which hardly sounds welcoming for future generations of motorcaravan users. Other sites with restrictions include places where dogs aren't allowed, usually on farms that rear livestock. Most sites accept dogs, however, and some have special 'dog walk' routes.

Owners of large motorhomes, especially American RVs, should also check in advance if a chosen site has restrictions applying to large vehicles. For example, if there are narrow, twisting site roads and

Owners of large motorhomes need to check if the site they plan to visit can accommodate this type of vehicle.

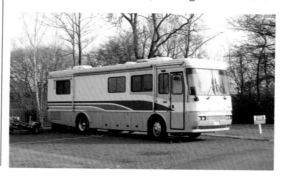

a lack of hard-standings, really large motorhomes couldn't gain access.

131

Through a joint venture, The Camping and Caravanning Club is running Forest Holiday sites for the Forestry Commission.

Forestry Commission sites

These wooded locations can be found all around the UK. Some have fairly extensive facilities whereas others are more limited. If you like woodland and wildlife experiences, these are delightful, sylvan settings. A recent joint venture has led to The Camping and Caravanning Club being entrusted with the management and running of the 20-plus Forest Holidays sites on behalf of their owners, the Forestry Commission.

Year-round sites

Though not usually open for a full 365 days per annum, some sites get extremely close to providing an all-year-round service. A number of these are Club sites but there are also some private owners in the UK who operate for most of the year.

As a general rule year-round sites are able to offer a large number of hard-standing areas, which are essential for owners of heavy motorhomes when grassy pitches are wet. A few site owners also organise Christmas and New Year packages that include a seasonal events programme. Heated marquees are erected and these celebratory occasions are popular, and have to be booked in advance.

A few private and Club sites are open for most of the year, including this Caravan Club site at Wythall near Birmingham.

Pencelli Castle site near Brecon has deservedly won many awards for its high standard of service and facilities.

CHOOSING, BOOKING AND ARRIVAL

Since there are many different types of site, guidebooks are helpful and there are site-searching facilities on the Internet, too. You also need to be aware of the marketing groups made up of independent owners who pay for corporate marketing and inclusion in a site guide booklet. Just as there are groups in France like the Castels chain, the UK's Best of Britain chain comprises sites which fulfil the criteria required for acceptance. These are usually high-quality holiday parks rather than remote rural retreats.

Some guides only contain information on camping sites that have been successfully inspected by specialist assessors. The Alan Rogers' Guides, for example, are compiled with the help of independent assessors who travel all around Europe. Scrutiny of each listed site involves a rigorous inspection and owners are visited, unannounced, on a regular basis.

Awards of excellence

Several organisations, such as Calor Gas, run national competitions to find the best sites of the year in England, Scotland and Wales. There are various sub-categories too – for example, there's even a 'Loo of the Year' award! These competitions carry prestige, and winning sites are undoubtedly impressive. In a similar way, The Caravan Club conducts a contest to find the best Certificated Locations of the year.

In addition to these annual competitions there are 'tick' and 'star' schemes run by tourist boards and motoring organisations, which confer quality indicators on participating venues.

Booking

When it comes to booking, procedures vary. Normally the process starts with a telephone call, and a deposit might be requested. However, more and more

sites are accepting bookings on the Internet and this trend will undoubtedly continue to grow.

Arrival protocol

When booking a site, enquire what time the site reception closes, especially if you're likely to arrive late in the evening. Legislation in the UK has had an effect on working hours and this has led to offices on some small sites closing earlier. Moreover, an increasing need for security measures has prompted many sites to be fitted with a barrier, and reception staff provide a code number or a 'swipe card' to lift the bar. Arriving early is therefore important.

Clients are often invited to walk round the site to choose a pitch. Whether a view over the sea is more important than a pitch close to a toilet block or the clubhouse is a matter for you to decide. However, try to avoid pitches under trees that shed sap, particularly if you use an awning. Removing sticky deposits from fabric can require a lot of work.

Should you decide to use a mains hook-up, remember to ask how many amps are available. Chapter Twelve explains why that's important.

As regards late arrival procedures, some sites offer a small compound near the entrance where you can stay overnight until the reception opens next morning.

Before proceeding on to a site, it's important for visitors to complete the signing-in procedures at the reception.

An increasing number of sites have a security barrier and visitors are given a card or code to lift the bar.

Recognising that some visitors arrive after the reception office has closed, a 'late arrivals' area is sometimes provided for overnight parking.

Most people want clean toilets. Few match the standard of Pencelli Castle's impeccable facilities.

Below: Waste water emptying points differ from site to site. This steel inspection cover on a French site has to be lifted first.

Right: With this system for receiving water from a waste tank, a motorhome has to be positioned with accuracy.

Facilities

Not surprisingly, most people locate the toilet block first. Washrooms and showers will be checked as well, together with fresh water taps, waste disposal points, toilet emptying points, ironing rooms, laundry rooms, and so on. Some sites also provide washing-up sinks and vegetable preparation areas.

Don't forget to confirm where the fire points are situated. Some motorcaravanners place their own fire bucket on their pitch, although this practice is less common now that many motorcaravans are

Below: Emptying points for chemical toilets are often outdoors, although a few are situated in a covered cubicle.

Right: Some motorcaravanners prefer to take dirty dishes to the site's sinks; children can play a part as well.

It's all too easy to overlook a safety check regarding the location of a site's fire-fighting facilities.

Holiday sites at home and abroad often have swimming pools but lifeguards aren't always employed by the owners.

equipped with a fire extinguisher and fire blanket.

If there's a swimming facility, confirm what safety precautions are in place. You won't always find lifeguards on duty and several pools don't mark the deep end. Some countries are strangely lax in these matters.

The rest depends on personal circumstances. Parents may want to inspect the children's' playground; owners of dogs might want to find the dog walk. Others will check the site's restaurant menu before boiling a kettle and making a brew.

Below left: Some owners don't want to cook on holiday, so this Alpine restaurant's popular on L'Escale site at Le Grand Bornand.

Below: On-site play areas are often provided but it's the duty of parents to check on the welfare of their children.

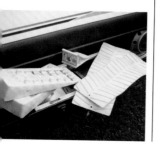

The levelling ramps and wheel-support plastic mats made by Fiamma are carried on board by many owners.

Pitch spacing

A practice followed on Club sites relates to the space required between adjacent units. This is mainly a precautionary measure in case of fire, although it also makes good sense where noise is concerned. For instance, The Caravan Club states: 'At the discretion of the Warden, caravan outfits may be positioned on the pitch in any way, provided that there is not less than six metres (20 feet) spacing between facing walls of adjacent caravans and that there shall be left a minimum clear space of three metres (10 feet) between adjoining outfits in any direction, in order to restrict the spread of fire. An "outfit" for this purpose comprises all mobile and other equipment brought on to the site by visitors.' (*The Caravan Club Magazine*, March 2001.)

No one likes too many rules and regulations, but this proscription makes sense. Occasionally you'll find commercial sites, especially on public holiday weekends, where the close proximity of caravans and motorhomes is neither safe nor satisfactory.

ARRIVAL PROCEDURES

When arriving at your pitch, the following tasks need to be carried out:

- Decide where you want to position your motor-caravan, recognising that some sites give guidelines about orientation, awnings and ancillary equipment.
- Either reverse or drive your motorcaravan on to the pitch.
- On soft ground or during wet weather it's advisable to drive onto non-slip plastic mats to maintain traction. When a heavy motorcaravan remains unmoved for several days it can start to sink, and that makes departure manoeuvres a problem.
- Some owners keep a small spirit level or part-fill a translucent plastic water container to check for slopes. Motorcaravanners also carry portable ramps to use when a pitch has a slope.
- Some motorhomes have rear corner steadies to minimise suspension movement, and these can be lowered once your vehicle is suitably parked.
- On the 12V fused distribution control panel, set the main switch to its ON position as described in Chapter Thirteen.
- To use a mains hook-up, follow the coupling procedures given in Chapter Twelve and leave spare cable loosely unravelled underneath your 'van.
- Turn on the gas supply cylinder to run your

refrigerator as discussed in Chapter Eleven. If coupled to mains, you have a choice whether to run the fridge on gas or 230V.

- If your toilet hasn't been pre-prepared for use, add chemical and one litre of water to the waste tank; top up the flushing water.
- If you use a directional TV aerial, you'll need to get this pointing in the right direction to achieve a good signal.
- Some owners fit a portable security device while staying at sites.

DEPARTURE PROCEDURES

Once you've stowed all your crockery, cutlery and other loose items, consider what else you need to do before leaving your site. Get into a routine and consider creating a check-list like this:

Inside
Close roof lights
Close windows
Secure cupboards
Clear open shelves
Secure the fridge door
Select 12V operation on the fridge controls
Turn off the 12V switch on main panel
Make sure toilet waste is emptied.

Outside
Turn off the gas supply at the cylinder
Disconnect the mains supply as described in Chapter Twelve
Stow the mains hook-up cable
Retrieve any levelling devices.

To secure a pitch when using their motorcaravan to drive off-site, many owners display a small notice confirming its occupancy.

If you'll be returning to the site later in the day, it's often wise to leave a sign that indicates occupancy of your pitch. Some owners erect a notice to this effect; others have an independent awning for storing a barbecue, bicycles or sunbeds.

Another method of showing that your pitch is occupied is to erect a free-standing awning such as this Ventura product.

Leaving the site
Road safety advisers point out that road accidents often occur in the first few moments of a journey. Without doubt, if the exit gate of a site takes you into a country lane that lacks road markings, extra vigilance is needed – especially on the Continent. Some British drivers leaving a foreign campsite have a momentary lapse of concentration and drive away on the left-hand side of the road.

CHAPTER NINE

ACCESSORIES

A motorcaravan has to fulfil our personal needs and interests. Some owners enjoy passive leisure and a TV is very important to them, while others enjoy active pursuits and derive pleasure from outings on their bikes. Everyone's needs are different – which is why so many motorcaravan accessories are available, including satellite TV systems, equipment racks, and products that offer additional storage. There are also utility items such as awnings, support vehicles, levelling devices, solar panels and security equipment.

139

Some owners tow a support vehicle like this Fun Tech Microcar which fits into a Ventura Space Storage 'shed'.

Motorcaravanning magazines provide plenty of in-depth advice about accessories you might want to buy. Apart from convincing claims made by the advertisers, more candid appraisals are provided in the form of independent reviews and editorial advice. Naturally, the amount of editorial space dedicated to accessories is always generous. Readers welcome reports on products that they need to purchase, and comparison tests on competing brands are also popular.

Inevitably, this chapter only focuses on a handful of items and many more could be added. For example, useful products that aren't illustrated include:

■ Reversing aids

Some of the audible warning devices that are used when reversing are helpful, although the author's experiments have shown that not all of them detect small bollards and high kerbs. Rear-mounted cameras are usually more effective, but when monochrome systems were superseded by colour cameras with microphones (and sometimes built-in illumination) fully-installed systems became surprisingly costly.

■ Security products

Remember when considering these that there are several different types, including:

1 Physical deterrents such as wheel clamps and upgraded door locks
2 Electronically activated alarm systems
3 Tracking devices linked to detection centres.

Also be aware of work carried out by the Sold Secure Trust (www.soldsecure.com). This is an independent organisation that conducts laboratory attack tests on products and then publishes lists of successful items for the public's benefit.

As regards motorcaravan security, one of the most notable system providers is Van Bitz, whose sophisticated Strikeback protection systems are installed on both conventional motorcaravans and large American RVs. They are one of the pioneers of a system that can send a warning to an owner's mobile phone whenever a protection device is activated. Many motorhome owners speak highly of Van Bitz products and the installation service.

■ Air conditioners

In small van conversions, a fan is an inexpensive accessory that helps when it's hot. However, owners of larger motorhomes often have air conditioners

Strikeback electronic alarm systems from Van Bitz are very effective but need to be installed professionally.

fitted. Two main types are manufactured: water evaporative cooling units (*eg* the Trav-L-Cool from CAK), and refrigerative air conditioners (*eg* those from Dometic). The former run on a 12V supply, are light and relatively inexpensive, but work poorly in humid conditions. The latter are heavier, costly, require a 230V supply, and are sometimes quite noisy.

The water evaporative principle is experienced if you inhale through a damp cloth stretched over your mouth. Build this system into a unit with a water supply, a pump, an absorbent filter and a 12V fan and you achieve good results, as long as the device is switched on well before an interior gets desperately hot. Refrigerative units work with a compressor pump like domestic refrigerators, and models that run on a 12VDC input have a built-in inverter to boost this up to 230VAC, which places a heavy load on a battery. Before making a purchase, talk to owners who have these different products.

■ Other products

Many other accessories are covered in later chapters, including water purifiers, suspension aids, gas leak detectors, inverters and portable battery chargers.

To find out more about these and other accessories see the list of suppliers' addresses given in the Appendix.

POPULAR ACCESSORY PRODUCTS

Gaining space and carrying gear

Roller blinds and awnings
Many motorcaravans are fitted with a roll-out sunblind, some of which have 'zip-in' optional side

WARNING 141
Before purchasing any heavy accessory, follow the advice given in Chapter Six. Note the vehicle's MTPLM, check its empty weight on a weighbridge and then calculate its payload. Now check the weight of the accessory you're planning to buy, because the more items you install on the vehicle, the less scope there'll be left for carrying your personal gear.

This roll-out Safari sunblind from Omnistor's range has smart side panels and curtains which run freely on tracks.

Above: The Khyam Motor-Dome Classic is a freestanding unit with a wide coupling valance and easy-fit interlocking alloy poles.

Right: This robust Swift Shelter from Pyramid, with concertina frame, guys and extra zip in the sides, is good in the garden as well as on a campsite.

Below: The roller blind on this Auto-Trail Cheyenne was quick to set up.

panels. However, a fully enclosed unit generates extra work if you want to leave your pitch in a hurry. Furthermore, if circumstances dictate that a blind is rolled when it's still wet, make sure you unroll it again as soon as possible to dry out the fabric.

As regards free-standing awnings, it's almost impossible to design a universal shape that suits the profiles of so many dissimilar vehicles. Coupling and uncoupling isn't always straightforward either, and that's partly why gazebos and storage sheds have become popular too. Not only do these indicate that a pitch is occupied when you've driven off-site, but they can also be used in the garden at home.

Storage products

Many motorcaravanners would like to have a bit more space to accommodate all the gear that's often

Several manufacturers supply roof boxes, some of which are suitable on van conversions. Check that access is easy.

Left: Back-boxes are easier to reach, and need secure locks. Check the back axle limit and only pack light items here.

Below: Every Beeny Box is made individually, although Auto-Sleepers and Auto-Trail are now licensed to fit them from new.

carried. Roof boxes are one answer, but if you stow heavy items on top, your vehicle is much more likely to roll on bends; so roof boxes should be reserved for light but bulky items, such as lightweight folding picnic furniture. Don't use them to stow costly things that might easily get stolen.

Back-boxes are another alternative, but don't carry heavy items in them that might overload the back axle limit. There are also low-level Beeny Boxes that are made for coachbuilt motorcaravans. These are painstakingly designed to suit individual vehicles booked in to a workshop in Cambourne, Cornwall. Their sturdy support rails permit heavy items to be carried and the contents seldom get wet in the rain.

Even in its weakest position, which is fully open, a Beeny Box will carry up to 45kg (99lb). These products look smart too.

Rear racks for bikes and scooters

Carrying heavy items at the extreme rear of a motorcaravan can lead to problems, particularly on vans that are built with a pronounced overhang rearwards of the back axle. Before having a rack installed it's important to check the advice given in Chapter Six relating to axle loading limits. So always have your rear axle load checked on a weighbridge before purchasing racks for the back. Also find out what your bicycle, mobility scooter, motor scooter or motorcycle weighs.

In addition you need to be cautious regarding racks designed to be either mounted on a towball or bolted to the tow bracket assembly itself. Since

This smart cycle rack from Thule is designed to clamp on a towball, but check the downforce limit on the towball first.

Above: This rack was correctly installed by bolting it through the panel, inserting spacer tubes and fitting spreader plates inside.

Above right: Rechargeable electric bicycles are becoming popular, but check that the rack is strong enough to bear their weight.

Right: Carrying two motorcycles on the rear of a coachbuilt model is very likely to exceed its rear axle weight limit.

these brackets aren't designed for any task beyond towing, it's not surprising that reports of them breaking are sometimes published. Note, too, that the maximum permitted downforce on a towball is typically around 50–80kg (the limit is often shown on a label or plate). So be cautious of optimistic advertisements and never mount a rack on a towball if the combined weight of rack and cargo exceeds its stated downforce limit.

EXTERNAL ACCESSORY ITEMS

Towing using an A-frame
A safe way to transport a support car is to tow it using a purpose-made braked trailer. However, trailers take up space, both on campsites and at

One of the endearing features of this braked A-frame manufactured by TOWtal is its compact size when folded.

Above left: Equipping a support car with a rugged, bespoke, front-end towing assembly normally takes a day to complete.

Above: With the frame attached, its over-run brake cable is linked to an eyelet that activates the driver's brake pedal.

Left: An A-frame hinges up and down but doesn't articulate from side to side, so coupling needs accurate alignment.

home, so an A-frame is a popular alternative.

When towed with an A-frame, a car is defined as a trailer and subject to the laws applicable to trailers. Since small cars nearly always exceed 750kg, the towed vehicle's brakes must be brought into use when it's towed. Braked A-frames are thus fitted with the type of over-run coupling head that's fitted on heavy trailers and touring caravans.

When an A-frame is used, the castor effect of the car's front wheels means that it follows the course taken by the towing vehicle. Unfortunately this fails if you try to reverse a car coupled by an A-frame. Equally, a car doesn't have the auto-release brake assemblies that come into action when braked trailers and caravans are reversed.

This raises uncertainties about the legality of A-frame towing for anyone other than professional recovery specialists, although no one in the United Kingdom is believed to have been prosecuted. Most people, including the author, who have had small support cars adapted by experienced specialists speak highly of stability and overall towing behaviour when a braked A-frame is used. However, in some countries in mainland Europe the practice isn't always tolerated by the local Police.

In the UK, some people declare that A-frame towing complies with current laws, some declare that it's illegal, and others regard it as a 'grey area'. Without question, A-frames with small cars,

146

Above: After arriving on a campsite where the pitches are uneven, some button-pressing gets your vehicle level.

Above right: If towing a vehicle using an A-frame is a 'grey' area, the use of a braked trailer is free from any doubt.

including the Smart Fortwo coupé (which has a gross vehicle weight of around 990kg), must have over-run brake activation or an electronic device like the American 'Brake Buddy'. Among the few cars weighing less than 750kg are French microcars such as the Aixam, the QPod and the Fun Tech.

Whereas A-frame towing is a contentious area, the legality of towing a car on a braked trailer is free from any doubt.

Levelling jacks

Many large American RVs are fitted with fixed hydraulic jacks that allow a vehicle to be parked level. If there's a small pressure leak these hydraulic units sometimes sink over time, but that doesn't occur with motorised jacks. Electric motors were therefore chosen when the LevelTronic leveller and lifter was introduced in the UK in 2006. It usually takes a day to install the four legs, the electronic 'brain' and the wiring harness.

A high lift range of 150mm (6in) means that a motorhome can be automatically levelled on slopes up to 8 per cent. A remote control pad is used, although operation can also be done manually.

This must be one of the easiest ways to get your motorhome level on a campsite, and the LevelTronic

Below: Once the horizontal legs are lowered into a vertical position by electric motor, they extend to level the vehicle.

Right: When this installation was completed the designer showed the body of the vehicle being lifted clear of the ground.

offers some other benefits too. For instance, if a punctured wheel needs replacing you don't need any other kind of jack. You can also relieve pressure on the tyres if your vehicle is laid-up on its jacks for an extended spell. And finally, an elevated vehicle deters motorhome thieves.

Tyre safety

Anyone can get a puncture, and if you're driving fairly fast a sudden loss of control can give you a rather nasty fright. If it's a complete loss of pressure, a tyre's steel-reinforced beading loses contact with the rim, whereupon parts of the tyre fall into the well of the wheel. That's when control is lost. The exposed rims of the wheel make contact with the road, grip is consequently lost, and the vehicle starts to skid.

To avoid this situation, Tyron manufactures bands that fill the wells of the wheels. Fitting isn't difficult and the benefits are great. If your vehicle has a blowout the collapsing tyre is unable to fall into the well because the Tyron band occupies that space. In consequence parts of the collapsing tyre will remain, like a buffer, between the rim itself and the road surface. The tyre will soon be useless, but in blowouts that happens anyway. The point is that you retain full control while bringing your vehicle to a halt. At special track demonstrations using a motorcaravan fitted with Tyron bands, a tyre is purposely detonated with a charge when the vehicle's at speed, and the driver is still able to negotiate a slalom course of cones with the tyre completely deflated.

Recently the company has added two further features to its product. Firstly, wireless sensors affixed to each Tyron band inform you of tyre pressures on a dashboard-mounted panel. Secondly, the nationwide chain of Kwik-Fit independent mobile fitters can arrange for someone to come to your home to install a Tyron system.

Above left: When the author agreed to drive this demonstration motorhome fitted with Tyron bands, good control was possible after a blowout even at fast speeds.

Above: Kwik-Fit mobile fitters have a simple device to compress a motorcaravan tyre when fitting a band in the well.

Above: Clipped on to the latest bands is a wireless transmitter which is able to measure the tyre's air pressure.

Below: A dashboard-mounted panel has a screen on which the pressure of each tyre can be displayed whenever required.

Above: This compact flat-screen TV from Grade UK has a DVD player and a built-in rechargeable battery with a two- to three-hour life.

Below: A wide range of multi-section support arms are sold by Grade UK to enable a TV to face towards its viewers.

Below: The VESA couplings on the back of many sets will accept a quick-release plate to detach a TV for use indoors.

Right: The Status 530 directional aerials have a long mast that can be adjusted from inside while you monitor the picture.

ELECTRICAL ACCESSORIES

Portable flat-screen TVs and aerials

Aerial manufacturer Grade UK has been supplying products to motorcaravan manufacturers for many years. In fact their familiar 'flying saucer' aerials have become a standard accessory on many UK models. These omni-directional aerials need no adjustment and will pick up signals in the areas where reception's good.

However, a better signal is obtained if you fit a 'directional aerial', which has to be pointed in the right direction to get a good-quality picture. Grade's Status 530 can even be raised from inside the vehicle and rotated while you monitor results on your TV. The company also supplies miniature signal amplifiers that improve the signal.

In the last few years Grade has started to supply flat-screen TVs for leisure vehicles, many of which incorporate a DVD player as well. There's even a range of support arms to position a TV screen wherever the viewer requires.

Many portable televisions also have universal VESA

threaded fittings on the back that allow them to be either coupled permanently on a mounting arm or connected to a quick release clamp that lets you transfer the set for use in your home.

Satellite TV in motorcaravans

This has become a popular choice of system for motorcaravanners who want good pictures, a wide range of channels, the benefits of free satellite stations and the chance to view British programmes when they're miles away in mainland Europe. Key items of equipment normally recommended include:

- Either an inexpensive portable dish or a roof-mounted version
- A cable-connecting socket on the motorcaravan wall or roof
- A satellite receiver box
- A satellite finder
- A standard TV set.

The process of coupling-up a system, locating a satellite and finely tuning the reception is often explained in the booklets provided by the equipment suppliers, but specialists such as Maxview and

Above left: Portable dishes are available for mounting on tripods. Many can be secured to parts of a vehicle using clamps.

Below: Roof-mounted dishes controlled from inside can be operated manually or by motors. Domes are even self-seeking.

Below: Unless you buy automatic satellite-finding products, it's worth buying a satellite finder with LED and audible guidance.

Left: Satellite receivers usually run on 230V and some channels are free, but most require the purchase of a decoding card.

It's usually a case of the bigger the better – this 70W output panel is built in a frame and covered with glass.

RoadPro can also provide helpful advice which is welcomed by people unfamiliar with products and procedures.

Solar power

The idea of 'free' electricity is attractive, and photo-voltaic (PV) panels that use light to create a 12V supply are popular with motorcaravanners. Their function is to keep a leisure battery topped up and they're at their most productive when directly facing the sun in haze-free conditions.

Clarity of light is important and somewhat surprisingly they work better in clear polar skies than in Mediterranean sunshine. That's because heat has little to do with PV panels and can even reduce their effectiveness.

On a good sunny day an average-sized panel can give out 20V and this could ruin a leisure battery. That's why a charge controller, sometimes called a 'solar regulator', must be fitted in the system. These devices prevent a reverse flow of current

The 70W semi-flexible solar panel from GB-SOL weighs only 3.0kg and achieves current outputs up to 3.75 amps.

This GB-SOL panel from AB Butt Ltd is being bonded to a curving GRP roof using Sikaflex 512 Caravan Sealant.

when it's dark (which would flatten a battery) and reduce high voltages created on very bright days to an appropriate level. Some controllers have digital readouts that can even record how many amp-hours have been fed into a battery over several weeks.

The panel itself is the main determinant of power creation and these are often quite costly. In fact it may take several years to recuperate the cost of a system, and the main reason for purchasing one is not so much to save money as to become less dependent on mains hook-ups for recharging your leisure battery.

Traditionally the panels are mounted in a frame and covered with heavy-duty glass. However, these are weighty, and on some vehicles they're an unsightly addition. In contrast, semi-flexible panels are covered in a special coating, and their 14mm thickness coupled with their modest weight appeals to owners of van conversions as well as coachbuilt motorcaravans. Helpful leaflets about solar systems are published by most specialist suppliers.

Solar Control

Batt = 13.2U
Solar = 2.6A

SunWorks

A charge controller must be fitted in a solar power system. The more expensive ones provide digital readouts of battery state and input.

CHAPTER **TEN**

WATER AND SANITATION **SYSTEMS**

Obtaining drinking water and dealing with unwanted waste water is a concern of every motorcaravanner. Designers adopt several approaches for meeting these needs, and a surprising number of variations are found in different motorcaravans. It's much the same with sanitary provision and toilets in motorcaravans, which bear little resemblance to those in our homes.

153

*Well-equipped sites have
water service points for
motorcaravans.*

This Caravan Club site near Birmingham provides good access to service points, even for American RVs.

Water systems in motorcaravans are surprisingly different from the systems usually fitted in UK touring caravans. For instance, caravanners normally use two portable containers that they position outside on the ground – one for fresh water, the other for waste. In contrast, motorcaravans are usually equipped with built-in tanks, duly fitted with water-level indicators. However, this is a broad generalisation.

FRESH WATER SYSTEMS

Tanks and portable containers

Looking more closely at caravans and motorhomes, you find exceptions. For example, a few European touring caravans *are* equipped with on-board tanks. Admittedly this practice is less common in Britain, although some models from Avondale, Bailey and Bessacarr have them.

One advantage of having a fixed fresh-water tank is the fact that there's less likelihood of interference or contamination. After all, an external portable water container is exposed to wind-born dust, inquisitive insects, slugs and leg-lifting dogs. On-board supply tanks eliminate these risks but have disadvantages of their own. The main one becomes apparent when you need to empty a fixed waste tank or replenish your fresh water supply.

Water service points

Hitching-up a caravan to get to a water service facility is a chore and most owners of tourers fitted with tanks purchase a portable carrier for emptying the waste water and a further container for fresh water. The routine is usually less

*Touring caravanners
normally use portable
containers, but some
motorhome owners use
them as well.*

155

onerous for a motorcaravanner and most owners don't
mind driving to a water service facility on a campsite.

On the other hand, owners of large coachbuilt
models occasionally take up more permanent
occupation of a campsite pitch. Some stop for
long periods, erect a coupled awning, lower their
stabilising steadies and use a support vehicle for
driving off-site. So don't be too surprised if you see
some motorcaravanners heading for a service point
with caravan-type portable containers. It's especially
common in winter when the contents of underfloor
tanks are likely to freeze (cold-weather strategies are
discussed later).

Fresh water supply variations

Recognising that portable containers and fixed tanks
both have their disadvantages, some van converters
fit an alternative supply system that embraces the
best of both arrangements.

Instead of having fixed tanks, some conversions
from La Strada and Middlesex Motorcaravans
are fitted with two fresh water containers that

 **Technical tip**

'Food quality' hose and fittings

When coupling-up to a water supply tap, you should always
fill your motorcaravan tank using a 'food quality' approved
hose. Unlike a normal garden hose, these are intended for
use with drinking water, yet there's no doubt that some short
lengths of hose permanently attached to camping site taps
are only garden products. That's less a cause for concern, of
course, if your motorcaravan is fitted with a water-purifying
device. It's also less critical if you drink bottled water and
use the water from your onboard tank exclusively for such
purposes as showering, washing dishes or rinsing swimwear.

Right: Rather than installing a fresh water tank, this campervan has two portable containers.

are housed inside. These are coupled using a submersible pump and are easily disconnected for carrying to the nearest tap. This arrangement avoids the need to drive to a service point, and that's especially useful if a tank runs dry at an inconvenient moment. It can also eliminate the need to carry a large coil of hosepipe in order to reach distant standpipes.

Above: The electric pump needs a 12V supply, which is connected using a cigar lighter socket.

Above right: When one of the twin tanks is empty, the submersible pump is merely switched to the full tank alongside.

Right: The empty tank is now taken to a tap, and the supply pipe also has a disconnection joint.

By altering these controls, Whale's Smartflo pump can perform different supply tasks. (Photo courtesy of Bailey Caravans, Bristol)

Combined systems

A recent innovation is the installation of a combined system that comprises both a fixed fresh water tank *and* a plumbed-in, externally mounted inlet for use with a portable container. This arrangement employs a permanently-mounted diaphragm pump (described later), while the plumbing includes bypass routes which are selected either by manual stopcocks or electrically-activated valves. Operating these controls in different sequences provides the user with these three choices of supply:

1 Enabling the pump to supply the taps or the shower by drawing water from the motorcaravan's fixed tank.
2 Pumping water from an external portable container like an Aquaroll to supply the taps or shower.
3 Using the fixed pump to draw water from an external portable container in order to top up the fixed tank.

Having a choice of three operating modes is clearly a great asset for motorcaravanners, although this relatively new system was first fitted in touring caravans like the Avondale Ranger. The Whale Aquasmart version has also been fitted in Bailey Senator touring caravans. At the time of writing, few motorcaravan manufacturers have recognised the benefits of combined systems.

Direct supplies

More and more UK sites are now offering visitors a pitch with its own tap, which can be permanently connected-up using a special coupling hose. To employ this arrangement with a motorcaravan, it's necessary to fit a new input point on the side and to make a minor plumbing alteration to bypass its

To draw a supply direct from a standpipe, the coupling hose must have a pressure reducer.

tank. Water can be then fed straight into the internal pipes from the mains – just like the system at home. However, one consideration that needs to be taken into account is that pipe couplings in a motorcaravan are seldom suitable for withstanding the higher pressure of water drawn from a rising main, so you'll need to purchase a purpose-made coupling hose fitted with a pressure reduction device. The Aquasource from Whale Pumps is one example.

General issues

In the last few years, an increasing number of motorcaravanners have been purchasing bottled water for drinking purposes. Others consider this strategy expensive and unnecessary.

With regard to water quality, few, if any, brand new motorcaravans are fitted with a water purifier and some owners subsequently decide that it's worth adding one. However, as will be emphasised in a later section, taste filters mustn't be confused with water purifiers, both of which are retrofit items. A taste filter might be useful for improving the palatability of mains water, but it is *not* a purifying device.

Above: The Aqua Source Clear is an inline taste filter from Whale Pumps.

Below: At periodic intervals, fresh water supply components should be treated with a sterilising product such as Milton.

Other motorcaravanners are content to drink tap water but like to collect it as and when needed in a small plastic bottle. Their view is that water from the tank is principally for non-drinking purposes, unless it's boiled. Suffice to say, we all have different views on water safety and you have to decide on your own stance.

Bear in mind that algae can form on the inside surfaces of a fresh water tank. Consequently water purifying products like Milton should be pumped through systems and used for cleaning tanks and portable containers at the start of every season, or even more frequently.

Obviously, motorcaravan owners normally drain off their waste water as soon as possible. However, many owners don't drain off their fresh water tanks after every trip, especially when their motorcaravan is being regularly used for impromptu journeys. Arguably this might lead to an accumulation of stale water,

although the installation of a Nature Pure Ultrafine water purifier at least eliminates the likelihood of contamination.

Stability matters

Driving with full water tanks adds significant weight to a motorcaravan, which affects both its economy and its performance. In some cases full water tanks might be a factor in a vehicle exceeding its Maximum Technically Permissible Laden Mass (MTPLM); and driving an overweight vehicle is potentially dangerous and a serious offence. Roadside checks conducted by the police *do* lead to prosecutions, and in one recent inspection drivers of over-laden motorcaravans were not permitted to resume their journeys. Emptying the water tanks was duly recommended, which brought nearly all of them within their respective MTPLM limits. Water is heavy and weighs about 10lb a gallon, or 1kg per litre.

Also be aware that some motorcaravan tanks lack baffles to reduce water movement, and water 'slurping' around a part-filled tank can pose greater instability problems than a tank which is filled to the brim.

Taking these issues into account, The Caravan Club advises its motorcaravanning members to drain both fresh and waste water tanks before driving. This is a wise recommendation, although some owners might consider it to be erring on the side of safety. In practice many motorcaravanners want to have water available for use when travelling from place to place.

Ultimately the owner has to make an informed decision according to circumstances and the first task is to establish whether a motorcaravan has sufficient unused payload to travel with full water tanks. To find this out, load your motorcaravan with typical holiday gear, leave the tanks empty, and then take it for checking on a public weighbridge. Subtracting its measured weight from the stated MTPLM on its plate will reveal the spare payload. This represents what's available to accommodate the weight of the driver, passengers, any accessories

Nature Pure filters from General Ecology are used in the company's highly effective water purifying system.

Above: In this Dethleffs Esprit, the tank below a bench seat is emptied by pulling out a plug attached to the red cap.

Below: This Knaus Sun Ti has a removable overflow tube in its fresh tank that doubles-up as a drain-down plug.

On this Swift Kon-Tiki Vogue, the fresh water tank extended right across the vehicle and hard against the rear wall.

you might add and extra personal gear, and will determine whether there's still enough leeway to include a full tank of fresh water.

Notwithstanding the laudable recommendation of The Caravan Club, and provided you know that your laden vehicle is well within its weight limit, you might decide not to drain your tanks, toilet flush water and water heater if you merely want to drive offsite to purchase a morning newspaper. Common sense should prevail. You certainly might decide to reduce weight by draining off water prior to embarking on a long climb over a mountain pass or for some determined motorway driving.

When considering strategies, also bear in mind that in clear, calm weather on dry roads the stability of a vehicle is less threatened by a tank containing water than it would be when driving in snow or in high winds.

Also be aware that some motorcaravan manufacturers mount water tanks in positions that might provoke instability. For instance, a part-filled tank mounted low down between the front and rear axles is far less likely to cause problems than a part-filled tank mounted right at the back, especially on a coachbuilt model with a large rear overhang.

 Technical tip

Tanks at the extreme rear

Heavy weights positioned at the extreme ends of a vehicle contribute to a phenomenon commonly referred to as 'the dumb-bell effect'. This is based on principles laid down in Newton's Laws of Motion. In practical terms, if you're negotiating a sharp bend on a wet or icy road surface, a heavy weight situated at the extreme back is disadvantageous, especially if the rear tyres lose their grip. Despite this basic rule of physics, a few manufacturers still mount fresh water tanks right across the back. That's when The Caravan Club's recommendation to drain a tank completely before driving becomes particularly relevant.

WASTE WATER SYSTEMS

A waste water tank normally offers slightly less capacity than its fresh water counterpart. During use it will inevitably get dirty inside, so cleaning access should be provided. Typically this is achieved via a large opening fitted with a removable red cap. It's an important feature and it is regrettable that some manufacturers save money by fitting tanks without an access facility.

Coupling hose

Another poor feature is the use of a convoluted connecting hose which has annular ridges on both the inside and outside surfaces. This is another penny-pinching feature; better quality hose has ridges on the outside but a smooth lining on the inside. Whereas the former product tends to trap food particles that subsequently start rotting inside the pipe, the latter has a more efficient self-cleansing effect.

Also disappointing are the routes sometimes followed by waste water hoses, a few manufacturers even disregarding the fact that water doesn't normally flow uphill. Admittedly it isn't always easy to achieve a constant fall (*ie* slope) in a pipe run, especially when chassis members present barriers, but with good planning and thoughtful design it can be achieved. This is one of many reasons why potential purchasers are advised to look underneath the floor of a vehicle. You'll soon learn which manufacturers adopt slipshod practices.

Fortunately several manufacturers are now starting to fit rigid PVCu pipe, as used in domestic plumbing, and install it to achieve a constant fall whenever the vehicle's parked level. Guidance on installing this retrospectively is given in Chapter Seven of *The Motorcaravan Manual* (2nd edition) by John Wickersham, also published by Haynes.

This convoluted hose has ridges on its inner surface; unfortunately these can trap scraps of food.

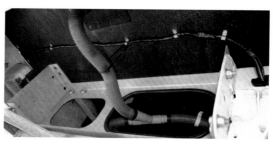

There were disappointing ups and downs in the runs of these convoluted waste pipes.

This water trap complete with removable bowl is now being fitted in some Auto-Sleepers' models.

The use of 30mm plastic pipe achieves an impressive speedy discharge of waste water, whereas on many motorcaravans, regrettably, water discharges from basins and sinks at a disappointing speed.

Installation of traps and interceptors

When comparing motorcaravans enquire whether the manufacturer has fitted water traps under sink, basin and shower tray outlets. Also enquire whether there's a screw cap interceptor, which permits the removal of food scraps *before* they flow into the tank.

To anyone new to motorcaravanning this advice must sound extraordinarily bizarre. One might presume that a professionally-manufactured motorcaravan embraces all the good practices of construction in general, and plumbing in particular. Sadly this isn't always the case, and dreadful drain smells are a potential reality that has spoilt many owners' holidays.

Not that a salesperson always has the knowledge to provide the answers you want. Normally they have to seek the advice of a workshop specialist, but you would be wise to insist that they respond to your queries.

Tank position

A few years ago one of the UK's best-known manufacturers introduced a coachbuilt motorcaravan in which the waste tank was located just to the rear of the shower tray. Purchasers subsequently found that if the waste tank wasn't emptied before driving off, a determined application of the vehicle's brakes caused its contents to surge forward into the shower tray. Thankfully, however, most designers realise that a shower tray needs to be fitted rearwards of a waste tank!

Emptying mechanisms

There are more methods and mechanisms for draining-off a waste water tank than you could ever imagine, and the accompanying pictures illustrate

Above left: This Swift model's lack of rear mudflaps meant its drain-down tap was bespattered with road dirt.

Above: Weak clips prone to rusting and a dangling pipe are a poor arrangement on this Autocruise Starmist.

Left: This TEC system had a sturdy, wide bore pipe, robust clips and a good chance of stretching to a drain.

Left: The tap release lever on this TEC coachbuilt had no protection from rear wheel mud.

Below left: This plastic drain-down valve on an Orian looks fragile and is curiously close to the exhaust pipe.

Below: This sturdy lever and large bore pipe looks good; but the tank didn't drain when this Knaus Sun Ti was tested.

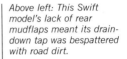

Situated just before the waste tank, this food interceptor on a Swift Sundance is a useful item.

just a few of them. Some drain-off the contents with impressive speed, some get blocked, others seize-up because the release tap gets covered in dirt thrown up from the rear wheels, and a few have poorly secured emptying hoses. Consequently the purchasers of a motorcaravan should always ask a salesperson to demonstrate that the system works properly and is easy to operate.

Unpleasant odours

When a motorcaravan is brand new you won't get any odours coming into the living space via the sink, basin or shower tray. However, the problem may occur once particles of rotting food get trapped in the waste pipe or when water collecting in the tank starts to stagnate.

Drain smells seldom happen in our homes because Building Regulations require odour traps to be mounted under sinks, basins and baths. Typically these traps hold water in a U-shaped pipe so that smells from the public sewer don't get into your home. Similarly, at the foot of a lavatory pan water is retained in a moulding, without which rising odours would be both intolerable and a threat to health.

Water traps to provide a 'smell barrier' have been ignored by motorcaravan manufacturers for far too long. It's only recently that miniature traps have been purpose-made to suit the plumbing systems fitted in motorcaravans. For example, Auto-Sleepers has fitted the DSL Plastics water trap with removable interceptor bowl in a 2006 Sandhurst coachbuilt. But if you look under the sinks of most motorcaravans you'll often find that there's no trap at all.

In contrast, food interceptors situated just before the waste tank aren't unusual and models from Swift have had these for several years. Curiously, though, no mention is made of them in many owners' manuals, so they often don't get cleaned out.

However, there's another contributor to the smell problem. On many waste tanks, the drain-down release pipe is mounted on the side of the

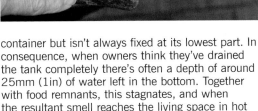

container but isn't always fixed at its lowest part. In consequence, when owners think they've drained the tank completely there's often a depth of around 25mm (1in) of water left in the bottom. Together with food remnants, this stagnates, and when the resultant smell reaches the living space in hot weather it's dreadful.

Recent tanks have been manufactured with a low-level moulded take-off point to ensure that the entire contents are drained off. If you purchase a motorcaravan which has an older tank that lacks this feature, check to see if it has a screw-capped cleaning point on the underside. If so, CAK sells a conversion outlet that can be mounted in this cap. Since the capped outlet normally represents the lowest point of all, it provides a better drain-down facility than a pipe fitted on the side of a tank.

Problems and curative measures aside, several water specialists also supply cleaning compounds such as Wastemaster Superclean for motorhome tanks and portable waste water containers. Their periodic use is certainly recommended, but they're usually unpleasant chemicals so read the instructions with care.

Draining down a waste water tank onsite is usually easy, although you may have to lift the steel cover of an inspection chamber to reveal the drain. Some motorcaravanners carry industrial gloves for this task. Depending on your motorcaravan's water release system, careful driving may be required to get its outlet and the receiving drain in alignment.

Regrettably, a few sites don't have motorcaravan service points. Moreover, one was recently built on a five-star site in France by an owner who'd obviously never used a motorcaravan. To position your vehicle over the intended drain would have involved driving up a flight of five steps! If that sounds ridiculous, a similar mistake was made on a high quality site in Cornwall. Although site owners always provide emptying points for *portable* waste containers, some haven't yet realised that the needs of motorcaravanners are different.

Above left: Recent waste tanks have a drain-down low point – correctly used for the drain-off pipe on this Swift Sundance.

165

Above: On this Bessacarr, the intended outlet fell foul of the chassis so, disappointingly, an outlet was fitted higher up.

Above: Waste Master Superclean from F.L. Hitchman is formulated to clean tanks and waste pipes.

Below: Accurate driving is often required in order to align a waste outlet with a site's drainage point.

Some owners take a bucket because several sites don't provide proper motorcaravan drain-down points.

Potable anti-freeze

Whereas the majority of owners drain down a water system prior to laying-up their vehicle, some adopt a different strategy. They pump a potable anti-freeze such as Camco Winterban into the system and leave it there until the vehicle is recommissioned. Winterban, which is imported from the USA, is often used in American RVs and is available from ABP Accessories of Great Dalby, Leicestershire. But note that its use isn't officially approved by European appliance manufacturers (*eg* Truma) in case it has a detrimental effect on their products' components. Incidentally, the word 'potable' implies that it's fit to drink – though you wouldn't do that by choice.

In frosty weather, some motorcaravanners couple a portable container to the permanently open waste tank.

These problems prompt some motorcaravanners to carry a bucket with them, although this is a laborious method of emptying a large tank. Of course, you should never drain a waste tank onto a public road (which is illegal) or onto a campsite pitch.

PRECAUTIONS IN WINTER

When stopping on a site during frosty weather, it's not unusual for fresh water to freeze in your tank. This can have implications for your water heater, so check its instructions. As regards preparing hot drinks, you'll have to collect water from a tap in a kettle or saucepan – just like in the old days before water pumps were fitted in caravans and motorhomes. It's hardly a great imposition.

A far worse inconvenience is if the contents of your waste tanks freeze solid. This captive tutti-frutti iced lollipop will prevent anything draining from your sink, basin or shower tray, and the only way to empty a full and blocked sink is to bale out the water using a suitable receptacle.

To avoid this problem, experienced winter motorcaravanners copy the touring caravanner and purchase either a portable waste container or a large bucket. Then, before outside temperatures reach freezing point, the tank's drain-down tap is left permanently open so that it never gets filled,

and the receptacle is placed directly under the outlet and linked using a short length of hose. Of course, this could freeze as well, so in severe conditions the screw cap is fitted to the receptacle before bringing it indoors at night. Alternatively, if you use a bucket, this must be emptied with prompt regularity.

Further precautionary measures are needed when your motorcaravan is out of use and parked for an extended spell of storage. Long before the weather gets cold, you must drain down the entire water supply system. The water heater should be emptied too, in accordance with its manufacturer's instructions. The usual tasks are as follows:

- Open all the taps. In the case of mixer taps and shower controls with lift-up levers, you *must* align these in a central position. This acts as an air release point for both hot and cold supply pipes.
- Find the drain-down release cock for your water system and open it fully. Note: *Some manufacturers don't fit a drain-down tap, which*

Above left: As emphasised on the label, tap levers must be centralised and open to prevent frost damage to the hot and cold pipes.

Above: All motorcaravans should have a fresh water drain-down tap at the lowest point, but some models don't have one at all.

 **Technical tip**

Waste water

Whereas most European motorcaravans are fitted with a waste tank to collect unwanted water from a sink, washbasin or shower, the tank isn't made to accept effluent from a toilet. This is normally collected in a portable cassette and emptied separately. Just a few European motorcaravans – eg a few models from the Italian Laika brand – have a separate fixed tank to collect toilet waste.

This is very different from the provision in RVs built in the United States, where sink waste is collected in what is referred to as the 'Grey' tank while the waste from toilets is collected in the 'Black' tank. Furthermore, the camping grounds in North America are regularly equipped with 'dump stations' where both grey and black water can be emptied.

Anyone intending to purchase an imported RV would be advised to seek further guidance about these facilities from one of the UK's RV owners' clubs.

Few models sold in this country have a waste tank for toilet effluent. This Laika is one of the exceptions.

Above: Follow your water heater manufacturer's instructions. This drain-down tap forms part of a Truma Ultrastore.

Below: When residual water in a downturn of pipe froze and expanded, rising pressure in the system split this component.

Below: Stainless steel domestic taps have become popular in motorcaravans, although they're heavy and costly.

Below right: To maximise worktop space, the tap on this Knaus folds down into the sink.

is a gross oversight. In this case you'll have to disconnect the lowest pipe coupling you can find, making sure you choose one where it's possible to catch discharging water in a receptacle.
- Follow the water heater instructions and release its contents as described.
- Check your Owner's Manual for any other advice specific to your particular vehicle.
- Leave the taps open so that any pressure created by freezing water left in pipe downturns can be safely released. Failure to do this can lead to powerful destructive forces that can damage pipe joints and split tap assemblies apart.

WATER COMPONENTS IN MOTORCARAVANS

This section provides a brief pictorial summary of the water supply components installed in modern motorcaravans. It doesn't include information on repair procedures or servicing, which are covered in *The Motorcaravan Manual* (2nd edition).

Taps
Taps made in plastic are light and inexpensive, and good quality examples perform well. Recently, however, it's become fashionable to fit domestic steel taps in many models. These reflect the comforts of

home, although they add both weight and cost to a motorcaravan. Some units fold down into the basin as a space-saving strategy.

Most taps in motorcaravans merely open a valve to release water but occasionally you'll find products that also contain a small switch, referred to as a 'microswitch'. This type is more commonly found in touring caravans and the function of the switch is to activate the electric water pump when you operate the tap. To establish whether a motorcaravan's tap and shower controls contain a microswitch look under the assembly for two cables. You can see these in the accompanying photo, taken in a 2006 Dethleffs Esprit. Provided the damp doesn't get into a microswitch these products work well.

Pumps

Two types of pump are fitted in motorcaravans. You won't often find the submersible units that caravanners lower into the bottom of portable waste containers. These feature a small paddle wheel, called an impeller, which pushes water along the supply pipe. Good ones last a long time but if the casing cracks they have to be replaced. Submersible pumps are not normally repairable.

However, they are suspended permanently in the fixed tanks of several German-built motorcaravans. The accompanying illustration shows one in the bottom of a tank fitted to a recent Dethleffs motorcaravan.

Most European manufacturers, particularly in the UK, prefer to fit inboard diaphragm pumps. These are well-engineered, powerful, efficient, repairable, comparatively costly and sometimes noisy.

Pump switching devices

Fitting a tiny microswitch inside a tap assembly to activate an electric pump has already been mentioned. However, most motorcaravans have a 'pressure sensitive' switch instead, which is either mounted in the supply pipes or within the housing of

Above left: Some taps, particularly those in caravans, embody a tiny switch to activate the water pump motor.

Above: Microswitches are less common in motorcaravans, but wires under this Dethleffs tap reveal that one is fitted here.

Above: Submersible pumps are seldom used in UK motorhomes but this blue and white pump is commonplace in German coachbuilts.

Below: This Mobilvetta Top Driver S71 is fitted with an accessible diaphragm pump, with a filter that's easy to reach.

Pressure sensitive switches are usually fitted; this Whale switch has a pressure adjusting control on the top.

a diaphragm pump. As soon as you open a tap the switch detects that there's a loss of pressure in the pipes and automatically switches on the pump.

Unfortunately, a pressure sensitive switch will also react if there's a small air loss in a pipe connection. Reaction times can also vary according to the state of charge in a battery. Sensitivity is sometimes adjustable but the 'fine tuning' control is often hidden to prevent inexperienced users tampering with the set-up. There's also a tendency for these units to trigger a pump that then gives one or two false 'beats' – which can be distracting at night. Accordingly there's normally a pump override switch on a motorcaravan's main control panel to close it down overnight.

Surge dampers

Sometimes, a diaphragm pump operates in a staccato, throbbing manner, and to cure this condition a surge damper is often fitted in the supply to smooth out its delivery of water. The illustration shows an example.

Types of pipe

As well as the two types of pipe found in waste water systems (the disadvantage of the convoluted variety was outlined earlier) there are also two

Swift sometimes fits underfloor components to which a hatch affords access. The blue surge damper is on the left.

types of fresh water pipe. Of these, the flexible hose coupled-up using worm-driven ('Jubilee') clips is the more primitive system. Poor quality clips can fail and non-reinforced hose soon develops kinks when it passes around tight bends.

Semi-rigid pipe with push-fit couplings is a better product and has been used successfully in domestic installations for around 30 years. Versions are available from Whale Systems and John Guest 'Speedfit'. Many couplings and components are available for domestic installations, and various products are used to good effect in motorcaravans. Channelling to resist kinking is one of many useful components and the couplings are very easy to form.

Filters/treatment: grit, taste and purifiers

You'll come across three main types of filter and treatment products in motorcaravan systems:

- Grit filters: These intercept water-borne particles and are an essential component to fit on the feed pipe supplying a diaphragm pump. If particles of grit aren't intercepted, the tiny pistons and chambers in a pump can be badly damaged.
- Taste filters: Although this type of product normally intercepts grit too, its main purpose is to improve

171

Above left: Hose is coupled with worm-driven clips, and the joints will be suspect if poor quality products are used.

Above: Where hose negotiates a tight bend it often kinks; trying to remedy a deformed section isn't easy.

Below: With JG Speedfit semi-rigid pipe, moulded bend-support channelling prevents kinks from occurring.

Above: When cut accurately, semi-rigid pipe is merely pushed deep into couplings to achieve an airtight joint.

Left: Grit filters mounted on the input side of diaphragm pumps need to be easily accessible for periodic cleaning.

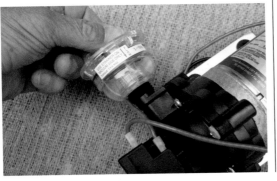

Pump on the left, surge damper on the right, and a Nature Pure water purifier was later added in the middle.

Above: Thetford cassette swivel-bowl toilets can be turned to suit the available space. Bench types have fixed bowls.

Below: Demonstration mock-up of Dometic's vacuum toilet; normally the cassette tank is sited well away from the bowl.

the palatability of water. If a taste filter isn't installed as a standard component it can often be fitted retrospectively. The filter cartridge needs to be changed periodically.

• Water purifiers: Several types are manufactured. The Nature Pure Ultrafine is particularly impressive, though it's not cheap, and as long as a motorcaravan's pump is sufficiently powerful to force water through an Ultrafine filter these American purifiers can usually be fitted retrospectively. The supplier's literature describes the huge array of disease bacteria, toxins, solvents and pesticides that the filter intercepts. Even water drawn from a canal can be converted into clear, pure drinking water. When this product is installed in a motorcaravan the supply from its tank can undoubtedly be considered fit for drinking.

TOILETS AND SANITARY PRODUCTS

A portable flushing toilet with a releasable holding tank is often fitted into small campervans. The advantage of these 'free-standing' products is that if you change your motorcaravan they can easily be transferred. Equally, there are some owners of small van conversions who prefer to erect an outside toilet tent and move their portable appliance into that.

However, most motorcaravans are now equipped with a built-in toilet, of which there are two main types: bench-style fixed units and models that feature a swivelling bowl. Both need flush water, both need chemicals, and both have a cassette that needs emptying when a gauge gives the warning.

More recently vacuum toilets have been introduced, where the holding tank is mounted remotely and the contents of the bowl are removed using what sounds like a powerful suction process. These are a version of the toilets installed in passenger planes and are mainly suitable for large A-Class motorcaravans.

Flushing water

Fixed cassette toilets utilise two distinct flush water arrangements. In some motorcaravans the water is drawn directly from the fresh water tank, but the disadvantage of using this supply is that bowl-cleaning additives can't be mixed into the flush water. Others have their own built-in tank, and are easy to spot because there's an extra filler inlet on the outside wall of the motorcaravan.

Chemicals

The cassette or 'holding tank' is usually 'charged' with a chemical treatment, although some owners fit a ventilated 'SOG' modification kit that relies on natural bacteria to break down solids. Chemicals aren't used in vacuum toilets because the receiving tank is vacuum-sealed.

Examples of chemical treatments include concentrated liquids, granular chemicals and sachets. Always check the dilution requirement of concentrated liquids and remember to put one litre of water into the cassette first of all. Recent Thetford toilets include a measuring facility for chemicals in the cassette cap.

When purchasing chemicals you'll find the blue type is usually based on formaldehyde. Though it breaks down solid matter efficiently, formaldehyde is considered detrimental to the environment, which has led to the introduction of alternative 'environmentally friendly' green treatments. However, some campsite owners discourage the use of green treatments in the belief that they contribute to drain blockages.

User advice

Explaining to adult readers how to use a cassette toilet might seem demeaning, but if it isn't explained here, how will you learn an all-important fact of life on the road? It certainly never gets mentioned in owners' manuals. So here goes.

Many motorcaravanners have 'house rules' which

A filler hatch situated above the cassette compartment indicates that flush water is stored within the toilet.

173

Above: A Thetford cassette being withdrawn. Aqua Kem Green and pink Aqua Rinse are among the popular products.

Below: Recent Thetford caps are marked so they can be used to add the right amount of concentrated chemical.

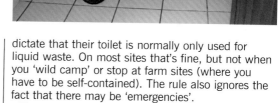

There's a knack to emptying a toilet cassette without an airlock causing splashing.

- When adding a chemical, avoid spilling it inside your motorcaravan; the marks are virtually impossible to remove from carpets.
- It's best to introduce liquid chemical directly into a holding tank rather than via the toilet bowl. If undiluted chemical gets on the rubber seal that keeps the open/close blade watertight, it can cause damage.
- Flushing water additive *does* help to keep a toilet bowl shiny.
- Take note of the manufacturer's recommended cleaners. Thetford's Bathroom Cleaner (sometimes labelled as 'Plastic Cleaner') is both effective and easy to use.

dictate that their toilet is normally only used for liquid waste. On most sites that's fine, but not when you 'wild camp' or stop at farm sites (where you have to be self-contained). The rule also ignores the fact that there may be 'emergencies'.

The time-honoured procedure when using a cassette toilet is to precede a 'performance' by flushing a small amount of water into the pan. Then you carefully place a few pieces of toilet paper to float on the water like flower petals, making sure that they achieve surface contact around the sides of the pan as well. This origami exercise may sound bizarre but it brings its rewards.

Once a 'performance' is complete, you find that when the toilet emptying blade is swung open the solids drop unhindered into the holding tank and the paper encloses them completely with gift-wrapping panache. This means that no stains are left on the pan – or, more importantly, on the blade and its sealing rubber ring. Don't forget that you see this sealing ring every time the cassette is taken for emptying, so you don't want soil marks on it. Though experienced motorcaravanners know that this technique works they aren't always keen to pass on the secret!

Emptying advice

There's a knack to emptying a cassette, and it's not wise to try this out for the first time with a brim-full container. Some points to bear in mind:

- When removing the screw cap, place it well away from the emptying bowl. Site owners aren't happy about retrieving lost screw caps for butter-fingered guests.
- As you point the cassette's outlet to the receiving pan, gently press the air release button. This can sometimes be difficult to reach, depending on how you hold the cassette. However, if you ignore this button the contents tend to glug into the pan and you might get splashed.

Travel advice

Carefully read the instructions provided by the manufacturer of the toilet fitted in your motorcaravan. In the case of fixed cassettes fitted with integral flush water facilities, you're advised to drain this down. Thetford explains that in the pitch-and-toss of driving, water can leak out and cause internal damage. Since en-route 'emergencies' aren't unusual, especially with young children, I queried this and Thetford conceded that putting in a litre or so of water was unlikely to cause problems, even when driving on bumpy roads.

Above: You can use the yellow button to operate the blade, but return it to this position before re-inserting the cassette into its locker.

Below: To ensure the rubber seal stays supple and works well with the blade, Thetford sells a maintenance spray.

- Add some fresh water to swill the last remnants of paper out, but don't shake the water around too vigorously. This can damage the internal float mechanism that warns when a cassette is ready for emptying. Do it *gently*.
- It's often helpful if a new owner carries out their first-ever emptying session using a cassette full of fresh water rather than effluent. The operation isn't quite as straightforward as you might imagine.
- Remember that you must realign the opening knob so that it's parallel with the long sides of the cassette before sliding it back into the motorcaravan.

Lay-up procedure

Obviously it's catastrophic to leave a toilet un-emptied all winter, even though cassettes are fitted with a pressure-relief valve. But you won't make this mistake if you always remember to leave the blade in its open position. Apart from acting as an emptying reminder, this prevents the blade sticking to the rubber valve – which often happens during an extended storage period.

Below: The blade should be closed to reinstate a cassette; then open it again indoors and leave it open during long storage spells.

What's even better is to lubricate the valve prior to laying-up. Do this as follows:

1. Clean the rubber seal using Thetford Bathroom Cleaner or a lukewarm diluted solution of washing-up liquid; never use a household cleaner, which can damage the seal.
2. Dry thoroughly then spray with Thetford's Toilet Seal lubricant or use olive oil. Never use Vaseline or any other form of grease or lubricant.
3. Close the blade, return the cassette into your motorcaravan, then open the blade once again and leave it like that until you recommence using the vehicle.

CHAPTER ELEVEN

REFRIGERATORS

Two types of refrigerator are fitted in motorcaravans and their operating principles are different. It's important to know which type has been installed because this affects the independence you can expect when using your vehicle. This chapter explains their respective merits and gives advice on how to get the best from them. Without doubt, a fridge is an important asset, and only very small campervans use portable cool boxes instead.

A refrigerator is one of the most useful appliances in a motorcaravan.

A cooling unit on the rear of the casing withdraws heat from the food compartment via these metal fins.

Cooling appliances normally have a chemical refrigeration unit designed to reduce the temperature in their food storage compartment. Typically this unit is mounted on the rear of the cabinet, and metal fins (which can be seen in the back of the food compartment) draw heat from the enclosure.

To achieve cooling, chemicals sealed within the unit have to be circulated around a series of pipes – and here lies the key difference between the two types of refrigerator fitted in motorcaravans. In those appliances referred to as 'compressor fridges', the chemicals are circulated by an electrically-driven pump. In contrast, the chemicals in 'absorption fridges' are circulated by the application of heat.

COMPRESSOR REFRIGERATORS

In our homes we use compressor fridges, and it's not unusual to hear the pump start humming when the thermostat registers that the temperature in the food compartment needs to be lowered. It's seldom an intrusive noise in a large room, but when this type of appliance is fitted in the confined space of a motorcaravan some people find the intermittent hum of the compressor pump rather annoying – especially at night.

Compressor fridges also rely on having a well-charged 12V leisure battery to drive the pump. That's hardly a problem if you drive around a lot because an alternator will help to keep a leisure battery charged. Similarly, if you frequently use sites with mains hook-ups, your motorcaravan charger will also keep the leisure battery in a good state of charge. Of course, its condition will also be governed by how many other 12V accessories are drawing current.

For reasons given later, a number of van conversions are equipped with compressor fridges, but this type of appliance is seldom fitted in large coach-built motorcaravans.

Among the manufacturers of compressor fridges is Waeco, whose range includes an impressive variety of medium and compact models. Its smaller units are often fitted in the cabs of long-distance lorries.

Several 'van converters prefer to fit compressor refrigerators in their products.

ABSORPTION REFRIGERATORS

This type of refrigerator is virtually silent in operation and examples fitted in motorcaravans operate using one of three built-in heating systems: a gas burner, a 12V DV heating element, or a 230V AC heating element. This facility is called 'three-way operation', and having a choice of systems is valuable because it lets you keep your fridge running in a wide range of overnight venues. Its versatility is one reason why the majority of motorcaravans are fitted with absorption-type refrigerators.

Absorption fridges work efficiently as long as they're installed correctly, serviced regularly, and used in accordance with the manufacturer's recommendations. When these requirements are met, specialists from Dometic state that their products will perform well in ambient temperatures up to 38°C (100°F). Dometic's products were formerly part of the Electrolux Leisure brand, while

This three-way Norcold absorption refrigerator is fitted in a Hymer Exsis.

The Mobilvetta Top Driver S71 is fitted with a large Dometic fridge-freezer, which is a heavy item of equipment.

A compressor fridge can be mounted away from a side wall – as Bilbo's showed in the Cyclone van conversion.

Some compressor fridges are designed with access lids for installation in confined spaces.

fridges from Norcold are sold as part of the Thetford range of appliances.

Product ranges include portable cool boxes that operate using the absorption refrigeration principle. However, these shouldn't be confused with portable units that have an electric fan and employ what's known as the Peltier cooling process.

Large fridge-freezers fitted in coachbuilt motorcaravans also employ three-way absorption cooling systems.

PROS AND CONS

On the face of it, the case for purchasing a motorcaravan fitted with an absorption fridge might sound wholly convincing. But there are some situations where compressor fridges offer advantages of their own. The pros and cons listed below will help to clarify the respective merits of these two types of refrigerator.

Compressor refrigerators

Advantages
- Normally less expensive than absorption models
- Little routine servicing needed
- Installation is usually easier
- No need to fit an appliance against a side wall
- Available in unusual designs, eg with top access doors

- Compressor fridges are more likely to work when they're not in a level plane, *eg* if you're parked on a slope.

Disadvantages
- Wholly reliant on a 12V supply
- Cannot be run on gas
- Some models are surprisingly noisy
- Not convenient if you camp in the wilds and have no means of recharging the leisure battery.

Absorption refrigerators

Advantages
- No need to depend on having a well-charged leisure battery
- When stopping in remote locations, you can run the fridge on gas
- You can remain parked for extended periods on pitches that aren't equipped with mains hook-ups
- Large fridge-freezer versions are available.

Disadvantages
- Efficiency sometimes compromised because the unit hasn't been installed correctly by the motorcaravan manufacturer
- Regular servicing is needed as defined by the appliance manufacturer
- Normally have to be installed against an external wall because of the flue outlet and cooling ventilators
- External ventilation is essential and grilles might spoil external appearances, especially on the contoured sides of an MPV
- Costly products, and a three-way operation facility often makes motorhome fridges more expensive than household appliances
- Operation is dependent on a vehicle being parked fairly level, though recent models have better 'tilt tolerance'.

Most absorption fridges have two ventilators and a flue outlet that might look unattractive on some vehicles.

181

This Dometic refrigerator offers three-way operation and a setting system that selects the operating mode automatically.

Being aware of these differences is important when purchasing a motorcaravan or having one built to order. Whereas most manufacturers of coachbuilts fit absorption models, some van converters prefer to install compressor appliances.

Manufacturers' preferences

Van conversions from Bilbo's are normally fitted with compressor appliances, whereas models from Murvi usually have absorption fridges.

In some instances van converters give customers a choice, and Murvi will fit a compressor model as a special order.

To give other examples, Wheelhome exclusively fits compressor products, Auto-Sleepers exclusively installs absorption fridges, and small-scale manufacturers such as Middlesex Motorcaravans fits whatever type the customer wants.

Suffice it to say that if you have a strong preference one way or the other, keep this in mind when comparing different motorcaravans.

THREE-WAY OPERATION

There's no doubt that the versatility of a three-way absorption fridge is a very popular feature. However, if you haven't used a three-way appliance before it can be difficult to decide which operating mode you should be using. Earlier models also had fascia controls that sometimes challenged newcomers to motorcaravanning. Fortunately, the controls are now simplified and some of the more expensive appliances even incorporate Automatic Energy Selection (AES). These appliances are built with a 'computerised brain' that chooses the most appropriate heat source on your behalf.

AES models employ a programme that will always select mains operating mode first when you're hooked up to a 230V supply. If there isn't a mains supply, it chooses gas – provided the cylinder is switched for action and isn't empty. Alternatively, when you're driving it selects 12V battery operation. This facility obviously adds to the cost of an appliance and most motorcaravans are fitted with manual selection models.

Here are some points to remember:

Operation on gas

Applying heat from a small burner is a very effective way to circulate refrigerants in the cooling unit and you can alter the degree of cooling by adjusting a control on the front panel. Incidentally, absorption fridges are made to run on either butane or propane gas without any need for alteration.

Several different systems to ignite the gas burner have been fitted over the years. When leisure fridges first became popular around 35 years ago you had to light the burner with a match. However, this was inconvenient, and spark ignition was later developed using a Piezo crystal. Plenty of fridges still have spark ignition and a red push-button on the fascia is a familiar feature. However, an electronic system is even better. Provided the appliance is switched on at the fascia, the electronic circuits will generate a spark automatically whenever the burner isn't alight.

Operation on 12V

You should never run your fridge on gas when the motorcaravan is being driven. It's also both illegal and extremely dangerous to enter a filling station forecourt with an exposed gas flame. To avoid a potentially dangerous situation, fridge manufacturers fit a heating element that runs on 12 volts as an alternative heat source. This means you can keep your fridge working while driving without using the gas system.

However, a refrigerator takes a lot of current to heat the refrigerants (around 8 amps) and this would discharge a 12V battery very quickly. So it's entirely impracticable to run this appliance from a leisure battery when you're staying on a site. Consequently a motorcaravan's wiring doesn't include a circuit that permanently connects this type of fridge to its batteries.

Nevertheless, as long as a motorcaravan has been correctly wired a refrigerator can be switched to operate on 12V when the engine is running. Current for the 12V heating element is drawn from the vehicle by taking advantage of its alternator charging system. In other words the alternator keeps the vehicle and leisure batteries charged even though there's a power hungry appliance calling for current.

Ignition

Ignition systems only work if the spark gap is correctly set at the burner. Moreover, soot is created when a fridge runs on gas and this coats a burner assembly and hinders ignition. That's one reason why a motorcaravan fridge has to be serviced, and the electrode will then be checked and realigned.

Cooling on 12V operation

When you've set a Dometic three-way refrigerator to operate on a 12V supply, you can't control the cooling level as you would when the appliance is running on gas or a 230V supply. On 12V operation the refrigerator runs at a steady level and the fascia controls aren't able to alter the cooling performance. However, don't be misled into thinking that 12V operation is any less efficient than gas or 230V operating modes. This isn't the case.

If you accidentally run a caravan fridge on more than one supply simultaneously, it might damage the system. This can happen on pre-1992 Electrolux appliances – especially when the user has been running the fridge on gas and then selects the 12V option in readiness for driving off-site. Even though the user turns the gas control knob to its lowest setting, this will NOT extinguish the flame on older appliances. The only way to extinguish the flame is to close the supply at the gas cylinder – and that's a safety practice that you're normally advised to adopt before driving.

The misunderstanding has caused some motorcaravanners to find, to their horror, that the refrigerator has continued to run on a low gas flame – as well as 12V – while they've been driving. Entering a filling station with a fridge in this mode could have horrifying consequences. Consequently the fascia gas control on Electrolux refrigerators made after 1992 *does* incorporate a shut-off valve.

184

Poor performance on mains

On crowded sites in summer, especially in popular parts of mainland Europe, the draw on a mains system is considerable. This becomes acute in hot weather when fridges and air conditioning units are running flat out. In some cases there's a significant loss of power, and tests on sites have shown that it can even drop below 195V. When this occurs your fridge's performance can be badly affected. If you can't get satisfactory cooling when running on mains, switch over to gas operation. This often improves fridge performance when a site is very busy.

Operation on 230V

If you select the 230V option, a mains heating element comes into use for circulating the chemicals. On earlier types of refrigerator there was a specific control knob for altering the level of cooling when using a mains supply. This was similar to a second control knob intended for adjusting cooling when running on gas. However, recent models have a combined control instead.

Operating on a mains supply is not only useful on a campsite, it's also useful if the motorcaravan is parked on your drive and you're packing it ready for a holiday. It allows you to pre-cool the fridge before setting off, which is recommended practice.

Finally, when arriving at a site whose pitches have hook-ups you'll naturally prefer the 230V operating option, particularly if you've paid to use the mains supply.

HOW TO OPERATE A THREE-WAY FRIDGE

It has been mentioned already that it's best to run a fridge for a couple of hours or more before leaving home. However, don't leave it empty while you do this. Put several non-perishable products into the food compartment, such as bottles of water and other drinks, before coupling to a mains supply.

Running on mains

If you choose to save your gas and pre-cool the fridge using a mains supply, make sure you run the appliance using your normal hook-up lead so that the RCD and MCB safety protection devices in the 'van are employed. (These are described in Chapter Twelve.)

If pre-cooling a fridge at home using your hook-up lead, purchase an adaptor and an RCD to fit the 13-amp supply socket.

Flame-failure devices (FFDs)

An FFD uses a probe (called a thermocouple) which is angled into the gas flame; when it gets hot it creates a small electric current which automatically opens a gas valve in the supply pipe. However, when you start a fridge from cold you have to hold down the main control for several seconds to manually open this valve while the probe is warming up. If the flame goes out when you release the control knob, the FFD needs attention. Cleaning and realigning the probe are jobs included in a refrigerator servicing operation; so is a check of its electrical connections. Never be tempted to jam a control knob open, because this overrides the protection afforded by an FFD.

The bronze coloured tube (centre right of photograph) brings current from the FFD probe to an electro-magnetic gas valve behind the fascia.

When using a standard hook-up cable you'll also need a plug adaptor to connect the coupling lead to a domestic 13-amp socket. Moreover, to extend protection to cover your supply hook-up lead as well, remember to fit an RCD device in your home socket. These are often sold in DIY stores. RCDs are strongly recommended whenever running mains power tools and appliances outdoors.

Running on gas

If you haven't used your motorcaravan for some time, it often takes several attempts to get a burner to light. Air in the gas supply pipe is the usual cause of problems and it may take repeated ignition attempts before the air is finally purged.

If the problem persists, poor ignition may result from a weak spark, dirty electrodes and an incorrect spark gap. This is a sure sign that a service is needed.

On some appliances, you're able to confirm when the burner is alight by looking through a small inspection port in the bottom left-hand side of the food compartment. Recent models don't have this inspection facility, although on appliances which have electronic ignition (as opposed to a push-button Piezo igniter) you'll hear the unit clicking while it tries to light the burner. In addition, there's often a flashing red lamp on the fascia that confirms it's still not managing to ignite the gas.

Like most gas appliances, absorption refrigerators have a flame-failure device (FFD). This means that if the flame blows out in a wind, the gas supply to the burner will shut off automatically. Information on this device is given in the accompanying panel.

Technical tip

Operating angles

For refrigerant chemicals to circulate correctly, it's important that your vehicle is parked level. Indeed, on motorcaravans built before 1986 this is critical since refrigerators dating to this period seldom achieve cooling if they're 2°–3° degrees from level. After that date, Electrolux introduced 'tilt-tolerant' refrigerators. For example, models like the RM122 and RM4206 operate correctly as long as the degree of tilt doesn't exceed 3°, while models like the RM4217, RM4237 and RM4271 operate at angles up to 6°.

As a point of interest, when you're on the road the pitch and toss of driving isn't a problem for fridge operation. As long as the refrigerator passes through a level plane now and again the cooling unit works effectively.

Running on 12V

Unless a motorcaravan is fitted with an AES refrigerator, it's the owner's responsibility to select 12V operation before taking to the road. And as long as the installer has correctly wired the vehicle to the appliance, a 12V supply will keep the fridge in operation while the engine is running. Since there are no naked flames involved in this heating mode, there's no danger entering a filling station.

Efficiency

As long as a refrigerator has been installed in accordance with its manufacturer's instructions, and provided user-recommendations are followed, a Dometic appliance is claimed to operate efficiently in air temperatures as high as 38°C (100°F). Unfortunately, some motorcaravan manufacturers don't install these appliances as well as they should and cooling efficiency is impaired as a result. For the benefit of owners with a technical interest, this is discussed in more detail at the end of the chapter.

If your fridge doesn't work on gas, check that the supply is switched on at the cylinder and its gas control valve.

SOLVING SIMPLE PROBLEMS

As a rule, an absorption refrigerator that's been serviced regularly and installed correctly will work efficiently. Check these points if you experience problems:

If your refrigerator doesn't work on gas

- Check that the gas cylinder isn't empty
- Confirm that the gas control valve serving your refrigerator is open

- If the burner doesn't ignite after repeated attempts, has your appliance had its annual service?
- If the flame doesn't stay alight when you release the gas control knob, the flame-failure device needs attention.

If your refrigerator doesn't work on 12V

- Check that the fuse in your motorcaravan serving the refrigerator is intact
- Check that the 12V selector switch is in the correct position on the refrigerator fascia
- Ensure the motorcaravan's engine is running – the 12V option is unavailable when the engine is switched off.

If your refrigerator doesn't work on 230V

- Check that the 230V fascia switch is on
- If the fridge is coupled to the motorcaravan's mains circuits by a 13 amp plug, check that the fuse in the plug is intact
- Check that the miniature circuit breaker that controls the fridge supply hasn't 'tripped out' on the motorcaravan's 230V consumer unit (details in Chapter Twelve)
- If cooling is poor and the campsite is crowded, turn over to gas operation – busy sites often experience a mains voltage drop.

In the event of continuing problems consult your motorcaravan dealer.

GETTING THE BEST FROM A REFRIGERATOR

Refrigerators fitted in motorcaravans are obviously different from the appliances we use in our homes. For instance, when you've parked a vehicle in direct sunshine it can get extremely hot inside. In recognition of this, you certainly don't want to open the fridge door with the same casual frequency that you might at home.

Here are some pieces of advice that will help ensure you get the best from your motorcaravan fridge:

Normal use

To reduce the chance of condensation forming on the fridge's cooling fins, wrap anything wet – such as a lettuce – in plastic or cellophane. Also wrap strong-smelling items.

A common mistake is to place packs of drink cans hard up against the cooling fins. The fins draw heat out of the food compartment, so they mustn't be covered up.

Avoid packing food tightly in the fridge and try to position items so that air can circulate around them. This improves the efficiency of heat withdrawal from the compartment.

Apply safety catches before taking to the road. Failure to do this may result in the door flying open and the contents spilling over the floor. Yes, it can happen!

Cleaning

At the end of a holiday it's an important discipline to empty the contents of your fridge. If milk has been spilt, it doesn't take long before mould starts to form.

Keep the interior clean, but be warned that some household detergents damage plastic. Dometic recommends a teaspoonful of bicarbonate of soda added to a litre of warm water.

To clean the inside of Norcold fridges, Thetford (UK) now recommends the use of Thetford Bathroom Cleaner. This is marketed as a specially formulated cleaner for plastics.

To remove resistant marks on the plastic lining of a cabinet, Dometic recommends using a fine wire wool pad lubricated liberally with water to reduce its abrasiveness.

Airing a fridge during storage by leaving the door ajar is important, but some manufacturers fail to fit a securing system to override the magnetic door closer.

Fitting a hinged wooden door might improve appearances, but on this Swift motorcaravan the manufacturer hadn't included a catch to hold it ajar during storage periods.

Winter covers prevent over-cooling in low ambient temperatures and are attached to the grilles with turn buttons.

COLD-WEATHER MOTORCARAVANNING

Many owners take their main holidays in the summer, and poor cooling is sometimes reported. However, if you use a motorcaravan when the outside temperatures are low, you can instead experience *over-cooling*.

Models prone to over-cooling

This problem is only likely to occur on older Electrolux models fitted with a gas valve, such as the RM212, RM4206, RM4230 and RM4200. It doesn't normally happen on models fitted with a gas thermostat, such as the RM2260, RM4237, RM4271 and more recent appliances.

Winter covers

Becoming aware of the over-cooling problem, Electrolux introduced accessories referred to as 'winter covers'. If your motorcaravan has Electrolux or Dometic ventilators, you can purchase suitable winter covers from your dealer. These reduce the flow of air across the rear of the appliance and should be fitted over the ventilators when outside temperatures fall below 10°C (50°F).

Unfortunately some of the cheaper vents used on motorcaravans have a different pattern and you can't buy covers that fit.

Draughts

If a refrigerator has been installed in accordance with the manufacturer's instructions, the cooling unit at the rear of the appliance will be completely sealed-off from the motorcaravan's living quarters. Consequently if a strong wind blows towards the

external ventilators it can't reach the occupants of the 'van.

In reality some motorcaravan manufacturers fail to seal off the rear section as required. Not only does this impair the cooling unit's performance in summer, but it also leads to draughtiness inside during windy weather. Some owners wrongly presume that winter covers are intended to overcome this. Although they might ease the problem, winter covers weren't designed to act as draught excluders.

After removing a cutlery drawer above a fridge, you still shouldn't be able to see the wall ventilators from indoors.

CHECKING AN INSTALLATION

If you're buying a motorcaravan – whether brand new or second-hand – it's often possible to find out if the cooling unit has been sealed off correctly. For instance, if you look through the external ventilators you should *not* be able to see into the living space. On some models you can remove the grille by using a coin to undo the retaining catch, which makes it easy to check this detail.

Alternatively if you remove drawers in the kitchen adjacent to a fridge and peer outwards towards the vents, you shouldn't be able to see any light from outside.

A further test to establish whether the cooling unit has been correctly sealed off is possible when an appliance is operating on gas. If there's a worktop or draining board directly over the appliance, put your hand on it. If it's warm, it's almost certain that the installer failed to fit an effectively sealed diffuser to direct heat out of the upper wall vent. Creating a sealed ventilation duct creates good cooling, and it's particularly important on large fridge-

If a shelf or worktop over a fridge gets warm, the ventilation ducting may not have been effectively sealed.

freezers because the flue also discharges into this routeway. On smaller refrigerators, exhaust gases are sent outside via a separate purpose-made flue.

If you carry out these checks and decide that the ventilation pathway isn't effectively sealed from the living space, the performance of the fridge in hot weather may not be as good as you'd expect.

REFRIGERATOR SERVICING

To ensure that their absorption refrigerators continue to perform well, Dometic recommend that they're serviced every 12–18 months, depending on frequency of use. However, even with spasmodic operation rust can form in the flue and fall on to the burner. Dead moths and spiders also upset the fine operation of gas appliances.

Be aware that if you book your motorcaravan for an annual habitation service, only cursory attention is given to individual appliances. For instance, a refrigerator's cooling will be checked and its gas flame inspected, but the appliance won't be given the full service recommended by its manufacturer.

Refrigerator servicing is usually an additional 'extra', and although the operation itself only takes an hour to complete, transferring the appliance to a bench may take a further hour. On most fridges, service jobs are virtually impossible to complete if the appliance is left in situ, so it's regrettable that the fridge in one well-known Italian motorcaravan takes a full day to remove and reinstall! Many fridges, however, can be disconnected and removed in less than an hour.

Servicing a fridge is not a DIY job. One of the tasks is to fit a new gas jet, because an old one should never be cleaned.

Service jobs include:

- Fitting a new gas jet
- Cleaning the burner, flue, FFD probe and ignition assembly
- Checking spark gaps and realigning the contact unit
- Checking operation of the flame-failure system.

These tasks must be carried out by a qualified engineer. Further information on servicing, operation and installation are given in *The Motorcaravan Manual* (2nd Edition), also published by Haynes.

It's no secret that some owners don't have their refrigerators serviced as recommended and then become annoyed when it lets them down. If that happens, it often occurs during the hottest spell of the year!

A service engineer will clean the gas burner, flame failure probe and check the ignition system.

CHAPTER TWELVE

MAINS
ELECTRICITY

When The Caravan Club decided to fit 12 experimental mains sockets on one of its sites in 1977 it could scarcely have predicted the outcome. Today, mains 'hook-ups' are available on all major sites throughout Europe. Having a supply of 230V electricity is a great asset to a motorcaravanner, but observing safety standards is crucially important.

195

These hook-up pillars are often seen in Britain. This one also houses TV sockets linked to a large site aerial.

In a technical guide published by The Camping and Caravanning Club, it states: 'Electricity is a very good friend but an even worse enemy.' This view is endorsed here and the safety advice which follows is clearly explained, and important to follow.

Just because we have mains electricity in our homes doesn't mean we'll know how to use it in a motorcaravan. Installations in houses and leisure vehicles are surprisingly different. For instance, there are hook-up supply pillars to understand, limits to the amount of current you can use, and wiring procedures not used in a house.

When early trials on campsites found that many caravanners and motorhome users liked having a 230V mains supply, matters of health and safety concerning temporary supplies were given careful thought. For example, a site's supply points – often called 'hook-up pillars' – have to comply with strict regulations. So, too, does the link cable that brings power to your 'van. Then there's a motorcaravan's rather special wiring system that differs from a domestic installation. The mains installation in a house doesn't get bounced about like the ones in vehicles driven on roads!

Even when suitable equipment has been installed it's necessary to learn how to use it correctly. This chapter therefore gives attention to four specific areas:

• The supply source
• Components fitted in a 230V installation
• Putting a system into operation safely
• An overview of popular accessories.

THE SUPPLY SOURCE

Hook-up pillars

A site supply is drawn from a hook-up point, and the voltage in EU member countries has now been standardised. However, supply pillars don't follow a universal pattern and differ both in structure and the sockets they offer.

The accompanying photographs illustrate these dissimilarities, and the one shown at the beginning of the chapter includes sockets for TV aerial cables too. At the base of this pillar there's also a locked door, and if the user overloads the supply a trip-switch is activated and the site manager has to be notified. A member of staff will subsequently unlock the enclosure door and switch the system back on. Other types of hook-up point are shown alongside.

Technical Tip

Loss of power

Throughout this book, 'mains electricity' refers to a 230V supply. However, on very busy caravan sites, particularly abroad, a high demand for mains electricity sometimes results in hook-up pillars only yielding 190V. That ought not to happen, of course, and it's why refrigerators sometimes run poorly on their mains setting, as described in the previous chapter.

Left: On this site in Wales, overload resetting switches are easily accessible, although it isn't intended that clients will operate them.

Above: A few hook-up pillars have 'pay-as-you-go' credit card swipe systems, but they're expensive to install and you won't see them very often.

Left: Newly-built sites in France are fitted with the industrial sockets that we use in the UK. This older site still has traditional French sockets, for which British visitors need an adaptor.

Left: This French site offers different levels of supply (in amps) and the user-fee varies accordingly. The site warden inserts one of the switch blocks shown here to activate a visitor's chosen supply.

Quality of hook-up cable

The girth of the required three-core flexible cable is conspicuously substantial. For the technically-minded, each of the three individual cables within the cover sheath (usually orange) should have a cross-sectional area of 2.5mm² and comply with British Standard/European Norm (BS EN) 60309-2. On the ends of the cable, industrial connections compliant with this BS EN standard include one that has brass pins for coupling to the site pillar, while the other has deeply recessed brass tubes for coupling to your motorcaravan.

Although these connectors are weather-resistant, they're not intended for submersion in puddles. Summer downpours occasionally take us by surprise, which is why extra lengths of cable should never be linked together.

Note: Thinner cable must NOT be used for hook-up purposes. If you see connecting lead being sold at an unusually low price, it might be sub-standard. It has also been alleged that some orange-sheathed products sold in the past have enclosed non-compliant 2.0mm² cable inside.

Mains hook-up cable is sold in 25m lengths with a plug and socket pre-fitted on either end. It has to comply with British Standards/European Norms.

COMPONENTS FITTED IN A 230V INSTALLATION

Hook-up cable

Visitors using a site, people driving vehicles and children at play may all get close to your hook-up cable, which is why it has to comply with British Standard/European Norm regulations. When sites first started offering mains supplies, wholly unsuitable cables were often used, especially on popular sites abroad. Twisted wire joined with insulation tape wasn't unusual and was clearly hazardous. Fortunately these dreadful practices are seldom seen nowadays and safety standards are strictly implemented.

Hook-up cable is sold in most motorcaravan accessory shops complete with a pre-fitted blue plug and socket that adopt an industrial pattern. The 'Technical tip' panel above adds further points of detail.

Note that the supply pillars on a site should always be situated so that any pitch offering a mains supply is close enough to a hook-up point to be reached by a 25m length of approved cable. For safety reasons, lengths of cable should never be joined together.

Input sockets

There are several variations in the type of socket installed by motorcaravan manufacturers. At one time sockets were fitted on the underside of floor panels but that's no longer considered acceptable, since grit and water spray pose a threat to electrical connections.

As shown alongside, some sockets are mounted on the side wall whereas others are located inside a locker. Also be aware that some sockets have a clip that secures the hook-up plug and a détente lever has to be depressed in order to withdraw it.

Above left: This type of motorcaravan inlet has a détente lever that holds the connector firmly in place.

Above: The coupling here forms part of a purpose-made battery box and the socket is well protected.

Below: The socket on this TEC motorhome is fitted in a rear 'garage' and cable entry is via a floor aperture.

 Technical tip

Amps, volts and watts

Expressed simply, the word 'voltage' refers to electrical 'pressure', and in Britain a mains supply traditionally provided 240 volts (V) alternating current (AC). Lower voltages were often used in other countries in mainland Europe. However, as a result of European standardisation supplies are now 230V AC, albeit with a permitted variation between plus 10 per cent and minus 6 per cent.

'Volts' relates to electrical pressure and isn't a measure of *quantity*. The *amount* of power consumed by different electrical appliances is measured in amperes (amps or A), and the word 'current' is used in this context. That's important, because the electrical power available from site hook-up pillars is also expressed in amps and the provision varies from site to site. This has a profound implication for the number of mains appliances you can use – as explained later.

The term 'watts' (W) is the *rate* of electrical consumption and is a combination of both amps and volts (watts = amps x volts). It's generally understood, too, that a mains light bulb rated at 100W is brighter than a 60W bulb, although it's also more costly to run. Electrical appliances are usually rated in watts as well and to find out how many amps they consume, you divide their wattage by the volts. So a domestic 2,000W fan heater consumes nearly 9 amps (2,000 divided by 230 = 8.78), and that's much more than the current supplied by many hook-up pillars.

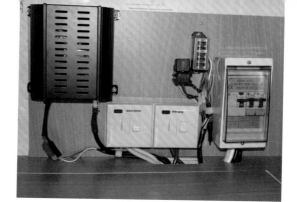

Above: Installing a consumer unit in the bottom of a wardrobe is a curious arrangement but it's not uncommon.

Right: Sargent Electronic Control units are often installed in British motorcaravans and include controls for the 230V system.

Consumer unit

Perhaps the most important component in a motorcaravan's mains system is the 'consumer unit'. It is both a safety item and a master control.

Consumer units are either 'stand-alone' products fitted in a variety of odd places, including the back of wardrobes, or are fitted in a casing that also houses control switches and fuses for the 12V system and a battery charger.

As soon as power arrives at the 230V input socket of a motorcaravan, a short cable (that mustn't exceed 2m) conveys it to a consumer unit. This has two main controls (a later section provides guidance on how to use them correctly), each with a different function:

1 A residual current device (RCD) is fitted with an isolating switch. In 40 milliseconds or less, this automatically breaks the flow of current in all live

In this integrated Power Management unit, the 12V fuses are in the right-hand section; the mains consumer unit is on the left.

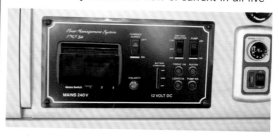

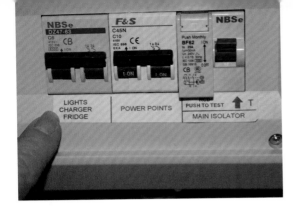

conductors, if, for example, someone accidentally touches a live connection. Essentially an RCD is a life-saving device, and there's a test button so that owners can check its trip-switch is working correctly.

2 Miniature Circuit Breakers (MCBs) are a modern version of old-fashioned rewirable fuses. Usually there are at least two of these. An MCB rated at 5 amps typically protects a motorcaravan's battery charger, its lighting circuits, a TV socket, and the refrigerator. An MCB rated at 10 (or sometimes 16) amps protects sockets likely to be used by higher wattage appliances, *eg* an electric kettle. Their function is to protect a motorcaravan's wiring circuits from overload damage.

A consumer unit also has an earth connection, and BS/ENs require that extraneous conducting components such as the chassis, the gas piping, and such items as steel sinks are bonded using 4mm² cable and permanently labelled with a warning tag.

Supply sockets

On British-built motorcaravans, sockets fitted internally are 13-amp, three-pin products, and on imported models these have usually been fitted in place of the original sockets intended for users abroad. Sometimes 'switched' sockets are specified, but as a penny-pinching measure the switching facility is sometimes omitted. Of course, when a socket is used to run a low wattage appliance such

Above: Miniature circuit breakers (MCBs) protect different types of mains appliances, and these should be marked on the casing.

Below: An earth cable from the consumer unit is bonded to the gas pipes, with a label stating 'SAFETY ELECTRICAL CONNECTION – DO NOT REMOVE'.

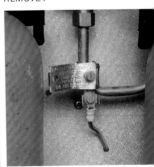

Two 13-amp three-pin sockets are usefully positioned on this worktop but it's a pity they lack switches.

System safety checks

All recent British-built motorcaravans will be correctly wired to British and European Standards. However, if you purchase a second-hand motorcaravan you're strongly recommended to get a dealer or qualified electrician, knowledgeable about motorcaravan wiring, to:

1. Inspect and test the installation
2. Verify that it's safe
3. Make any necessary alterations
4. Issue a signed and dated approval certificate.

Details about approved contractors are given in Chapter Sixteen.

as a table lamp a 3-amp fuse should be fitted in its plug – just as it should when running table lamps at home.

Typically the number of sockets installed in motorcaravans is insufficient for many people's needs, especially when we now want to keep batteries charged for our telephones, laptop computers and other electronic gizmos. In fact many owners get further sockets added retrospectively, and if you entrust this to an electrician it's important to check that they're aware that a different type of cable is used for motorcaravan wiring.

The reason for this is quite simple. In buildings, sockets are normally connected-up using cable manufactured with a solid copper core, but this shouldn't be used in motorcaravans because solid copper wire tends to shake loose in a socket's screw-fit connectors. Instead, 1.5mm^2 flexible mains cable is used because the array of copper strands in the live, neutral and earth wires gives better flexibility and achieves more secure attachments in screw-fit connectors.

PUTTING A SYSTEM INTO OPERATION SAFELY

Before coupling-up to a hook-up pillar you should check at the reception office regarding how many amps are available (supply variations were explained earlier). For example, some site hook-up pillars offer no more than 4 amps whereas others offer 16 amps. To find out what this means in practical terms you have to carry out some simple calculations.

To calculate how many electrical items you can run from a site hook-up, find the wattage of all your appliances.

Calculating which appliances will operate within your limit

To establish what appliances you can and can't run on your pitch, you have to check the wattage of all of them. Here are some typical ratings.

• Mains light bulb: 60 or 100 watts
• Small colour LCD-screen TV: 50 watts
• Built-in battery chargers vary, but 250 watts is not unusual
• Truma Frostair 1700 Air Conditioner: 650 watts
• Truma Ultrastore water-heater running on mains: 850 watts
• Dometic medium capacity RGE 2000 refrigerator: 135 watts
• Dometic large RGE 400 fridge-freezer: 325 watts
• Typical domestic pop-up toaster: 1,000 watts
• Typical fast-boil domestic kettle: 2,500 watts (often called 2.5kW).

Then you need to decide which appliances will often be running at the same time in order to add up their respective wattages. When doing this calculation don't forget that a fixed battery charger is usually working in the background and doesn't have ON/OFF switches, so include this item in your sums.

Once the combined wattage of your working appliances is calculated, dividing the result by 230 establishes how many amps you'll draw when they're running. On some small rural sites offering only 5 amps you'll probably have to reduce the number of items that are running, whereas on Club sites offering 16 amps there's much more scope.

Having to undertake these calculations might sound onerous, so for a quick check you can work on the basis that a site offering 5 amps will allow

A hook-up might offer 16 amps, but on a full site on a dark winter evening you're asked to draw as little current as possible.

you to run a selection of appliances provided their combined power requirement doesn't exceed 1,000 watts. In practice that's not particularly generous and it's fortunate that appliances such as a 'three-way' refrigerator will also run on gas. Similarly, you can avoid using an electric kettle by boiling water on the hob. Your supply of electricity can then be reserved for keeping the 12V leisure battery in a good state of charge, for running lights, and for operating a colour TV.

Another way to ensure that you don't 'trip' the supply limit of your hook-up is to have a device called a 'Fuse Control' fitted in your 'van. This useful component, which eliminates the need for calculations, is covered in the final section of this chapter describing optional accessories.

Note: On cold, dark, winter nights a site's supply will be placed under heavy pressure, especially when all the pitches equipped with hook-ups are occupied. Although an individual pitch might be able to receive a 16-amp maximum supply, a site's mains installation isn't designed so that every pitch occupant can draw 16 amps at the same time. Consequently posters are often displayed advising visitors to be sparing in their use of electricity. Disregarding this request may result in a site being plunged into darkness.

Coupling-up procedures

This is a step-by-step tick list that enables you to couple-up to a mains supply safely and in the correct order of operations.

☐ Inspect the hook-up pillar nearest to your pitch. If you find a multitude of dodgy-looking cables around it, or have doubts about its safety, you might decide not to couple up. Fortunately, there are few examples of inappropriate products on most sites today.

Check that all appliances in your motorcaravan are switched off and move the RCD switch to its OFF position.

Unravel your hook-up cable, and don't be tempted to leave the surplus in tightly wound coils. If left tightly coiled, especially on a drum, cable can overheat when high-consumption appliances are in use. In severe cases its insulation might even start to melt. The correct procedure is to place the unravelled hook-up lead in loose coils underneath your motorcaravan and away from any places where puddles might form during a downpour.

Always insert the cable's 'female' connector (that's the one with the recessed brass tubes) into the motorcaravan's inlet first.

Next insert the cable's 'male' coupling into the socket on the hook-up pillar. This is the one that has three brass pins within its moulded casing.

On some systems the connection has now been completed. However, on others the power doesn't

Above left: It might look more tidy, but don't put surplus hook-up cable into tight coils.

Above: Don't leave surplus cable tightly wound on a drum – tight coils sometimes generate heat.

Below: When there's spare cable, leave it in loose, open coils under your motorcaravan.

Left: This is dreadful! When laying out cable bear in mind that downpours often leave puddles.

Above: Some hook-up sockets don't provide a supply of current until the plug is twisted clockwise.

Above right: To release a plug from this type of socket, you have to depress the red button first.

This isolation switch forms part of the residual current device which cuts off the power.

Below: Two miniature circuit breakers protect individual circuits and are a modern type of fuse.

Below right: To check an RCD trips-out correctly, pressing a button recreates the effect of someone touching a live wire.

start to flow until you rotate the hook-up pillar's coupling clockwise and hear a 'click'. On couplings where this is necessary you'll also see a red button. This is part of a retaining system that locks the plug in place and prevents it from being pulled out accidentally.

Note: There's usually a label that explains this twisting requirement, though in many instances you'll find that the instructions have been obliterated by constant exposure to sunlight.

☐ Check that the cable is laid out in a tidy fashion between the supply point and your caravan. Projecting loops might trip passers-by.

☐ Now go to the consumer unit (described earlier) and move the RCD main control switch to its ON position. Check, too, that the MCB switches are in the ON position.

☐ To confirm your RCD is working correctly, press the small 'check button' to confirm that the emergency trip-switch comes into operation instantaneously. Provided that it does, reset the RCD switch to its ON position once again, secure in the knowledge that your all-important safety device is operating correctly.

☐ Use a test device in one of the 13-amp sockets to confirm that the supply is correctly wired. If this

confirms that the system is sound, you can now run your appliances.

Uncoupling procedures

When leaving your pitch, disconnecting a mains hook-up is principally a reversal of the above sequence. In particular, it involves:

1 Switching off your appliances and the RCD switch on the consumer unit
2 Withdrawing the plug from the site pillar to terminate the supply (on some sites you have to release it by depressing a red button)
3 Withdrawing the plug from the caravan input socket (on some models this involves depressing a release lever).

On damp mornings you'll then want to dry off the hook-up lead before stowing it away.

Reverse polarity

In Britain, switches for wall sockets, lights and appliances or lights are wired to the live cable. This means that when a switch is moved to its OFF position, power can't reach the appliance at all. This enables you to safely change a light bulb at home without having to switch off the incoming supply by means of the main master switch that isolates the entire house.

Unfortunately the safety of the British system is lost if the live and neutral cables are wired up the other way round. For example, a switch that controls the flow of current on the way *out* of an appliance certainly prevents the appliance from working, but in such an arrangement an appliance or light socket remains live, even though it isn't operating. This could be dangerous.

The problem doesn't arise in mainland Europe because the usual practice abroad is to fit switches which operate on both the live *and* neutral cables. These are referred to as 'double-pole' switches and

Above left: Socket testers are available from electrical dealers and show when a system is wired correctly.

Above: The display on this socket reveals that its earth connection has become detached.

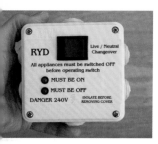

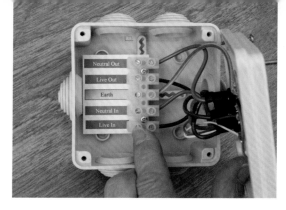

Above: If you find that the polarity of a site supply is reversed, this device fitted inside your 'van rectifies the problem.

Above right: Inside this device, the connecting block is clearly labelled and an electrician could quickly wire it up.

Technical Tip

Double-pole switching

Motorcaravans manufactured since 1994 have a double-pole switched RCD and double-pole MCBs, so the level of protection is improved. It's a pity that 13-amp double-pole switched sockets aren't fitted too, even though these can be purchased in Britain. Their installation would add the final protection to motorcaravanners stopping on sites where the supply polarity's reversed.

Adaptors for use on traditional French hook-up sockets. The one with red/white tape is reverse-wired to correct polarity reversal at the hook-up connection.

ensure that an appliance still doesn't become live even if the live and neutral feeds are wired-up in reverse. In fact on campsites abroad it's not unusual to find that the supply at hook-up pillars has been connected the other way round. This is referred to as 'reverse polarity'.

As a result, British tourists abroad need to check mains polarity as soon as they couple-up at a site. Sometimes reverse polarity is indicated by a red warning light fitted to a consumer unit. Alternatively it can be revealed by means of one of the testers shown on page 207. So what should you do in this situation?

• Many motorcaravanners acknowledge the potential danger and decide not to use the mains supply
• Some recognise the fact that polarity-sensitive appliances may receive damage and that their appliances will remain live, even when switched off, but decide to use the supply in spite of the inherent risks involved
• A few motorcaravanners have a pole-reversal component fitted retrospectively in their vehicles
• Many owners get an electrician to prepare a reversal adaptor using a short length of hook-up cable complete with a plug that's wired the other way round and *boldly marked*; you can't purchase

these, but when one is fitted into a site pillar that's wired in reverse the supply is duly rectified at source and your normal hook-up cable can then be connected

Adaptors

Nowadays the industrial-style couplings used on site hook-up pillars in Britain are being fitted on new installations in many European countries. In fact on some sites abroad you occasionally find hook-up pillars offering traditional national sockets alongside the new ones. But that's unusual and British motorcaravanners touring abroad normally take adaptors to suit the countries they're planning to visit.

In addition you may want to couple your motorcaravan to a supply at home when it's parked in the drive. For example, it was recommended in the previous chapter that a refrigerator should be pre-cooled before you leave home. To save gas, many owners prefer to do this using mains electricity so they purchase an adaptor that fits a household 13-amp socket. In addition they purchase a small RCD unit to fit the supply socket so that the cable running from the house to the motorcaravan is protected. One of these is shown above.

ADDITIONAL POPULAR PRODUCTS

Fuse Control

Earlier in this chapter reference was made to a device manufactured by Reich called the 'Fuse Control'. This eliminates the need for an owner to embark on calculations relating to the consumption of their 230V appliances. When set appropriately, it also ensures that a motorcaravanner doesn't trip the supply switch in a hook-up pillar.

An additional facility is its indication of the

Above left: This adaptor allows your hook-up cable with its blue industrial plug to be coupled to a 13-amp three-pin socket at home.

Above: To protect a hook-up cable running from house to motorhome, put a portable RCD into the domestic socket.

When fitted to your incoming supply, a Fuse Control unit has to be set by using these two buttons.

amps being consumed whenever a mains supply is coupled-up and your appliances are in operation.

A Fuse Control is fitted in the mains supply just before it reaches a consumer unit. Now, let's imagine that the site office has informed you that the hook-up pillars will supply up to 7 amps of mains current. As soon as you've coupled your hook-up cable, you set the Fuse Control to a slightly lower level such as 6 amps. Then you complete the usual coupling-up checks, such as RCD operation, before running your appliances.

The consumption is shown on the Fuse Control panel and the reading will alter when you add or reduce the number of appliances. However, as soon as your complement of appliances calls for more than 6 amps the Fuse Control trips out and starts flashing. You won't trip the site's 7-amp supply because you've set your device to react when 6 amps is exceeded.

Your next task is to switch off the appliance you started running last, since this is the one that led to the overload problem. Then you reset the Fuse Control once again to run on a 6-amp limit and resume your consumption of power.

Naturally, you can set other limits to suit different

On a site providing a 7-amp supply of current, this Fuse Control is set to 'trip-out' when more than 6 amps is drawn.

outputs from other sites and you soon learn from
the display which appliances have a modest
consumption and which ones are greedy.

*Once set and with a 230V
supply being used, the
Fuse Control shown here
reveals that 1.2 amps is
being drawn from the site.*

Petrol generators

Modern portable leisure generators are smartly
designed, compact in size and much quieter
than their industrial counterparts. On the other
hand, they're surprisingly heavy; so, too, are
models designed to be permanently installed in
motorcaravans. This means they take up a significant
amount of your payload allowance.

   You should also be aware that the output from a
leisure generator is usually far less than you get from
an average hook-up point. To achieve a high output
you'd need to purchase an industrial model and
these are both noisier and heavier.

   The output from portable leisure machines is
typically from 650W (around 2.8 amps) to 2,000W
(around 8.5 amps). Also be aware that generators
often have two settings – 60Hz and 50Hz. To
achieve a claimed 650W output you have to select
the 60Hz setting, which provides a less stable
supply that may not be suitable for operating
sensitive appliances.

   And a final warning. As the mains appliances
in a motorcaravan are switched on and off you'll
often hear the generator engine altering its note and
on many models this is accompanied by a brief
irregularity in the output. A similar change of note
can occur when a generator is first started-up and is
running on its choke. Only a few recent models, such
as the Honda EU10i and EU20i generators, feature
electronic systems that eliminate power irregularities.

   Brief surges upset some types of electrical
appliance, especially if you couple a generator to a
motorcaravan's mains inlet to run its battery charger.
Most built-in battery chargers now feature 'switch
mode' circuits, and supply irregularities can easily
damage their electronic components. On account
of this problem some generators have a 12V outlet

Above: There's a 13-amp 230V mains socket on a Honda EU 10i, but there's also this 12V DC socket for battery charging.

Right: The Honda EU 20i is a much sought-after high quality product, so make sure it's protected against theft.

for battery recharging that will completely bypass the built-in charger in your 'van. You merely have to purchase a suitable coupling lead to fit the generator's 12V outlet and take this directly to the terminals on your battery.

Good quality generators are costly and there are often reports of them being stolen, so make sure you're able to secure the product you plan to purchase. There has also been a recent influx of very cheap products imported from China. If you intend to buy one of these, check that it's supported by a reliable after-sales, repair and spare parts service.

Inverters

When an inverter is connected to a 12V battery it will convert its 12V DC input into a 230V AC output. This can be useful, and even low-rated 100W inverters will enable you to run a mains light bulb from a 12V battery.

However, the more you run through an inverter, the

Above: This inexpensive Mobitronic inverter is rated at 100W and has no trouble running a 230V 60W light bulb.

Left: The owner of this 300W inverter uses it to run a 17in flat-screen TV, but the picture is better on a normal mains supply.

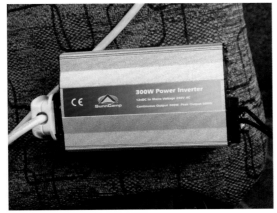

sooner your leisure battery will reach a state of total discharge. To give an example of this, if you were to run a 250W inverter it typically draws more than 20 amps from a leisure battery (250 watts divided by 12 volts = 20.8 amps). In other words, a 60 amp-hour motorcaravan battery running only the inverter would be 'flat' in under three hours. Moreover, inverters often have low-voltage sensors that shut them down before a battery gets too low.

Of course, a larger 90 amp-hour battery would work longer between recharges; the situation is also less acute when using an appliance that operates intermittently, such as an electric shaver. Similarly, if a compact 230V colour TV is used to watch a half-hour episode of a favourite serial, a pure sine wave inverter might be the answer when using a site that's not equipped with hook-ups. On the other hand, long evenings of TV watching would soon leave you with a completely discharged battery. That's why mains hook-ups are so popular.

Technical Tip

Inverter limitations

For sensitive equipment like TV sets, a 'pure sine wave inverter' is recommended, and these cost around three times the price of a 'modified sine wave' inverter. They are complex products and one of the best explanatory guides is a leaflet supplied by Road Pro (Tel 01327 312233; www.roadpro.co.uk).

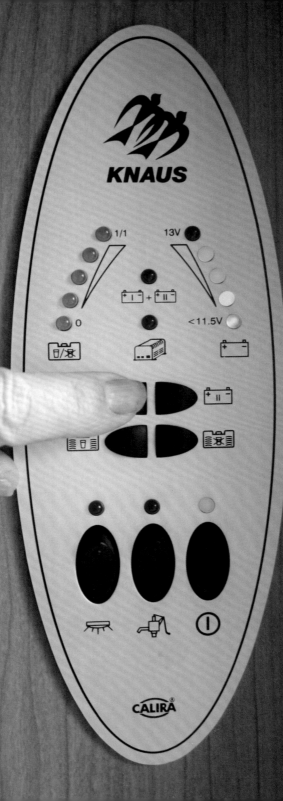

CHAPTER **THIRTEEN**

THE 12-VOLT
SYSTEM

To ensure that a vehicle's battery is kept sufficiently charged to start its engine, 12V appliances in the living area are run from an additional power source described as a 'leisure battery'. However, some motorcaravans are fitted with a surprising number of 12V products and this means that a leisure battery needs charging quite often.

The 12V control panel on this Knaus Sport is clearly marked.

On this TEC motorhome, an ON/OFF master-switch is conspicuously located on the left of the panel.

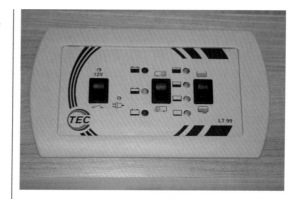

Some Murvi 'van conversions have panels with helpful pictograms accompanied by red LED indicators.

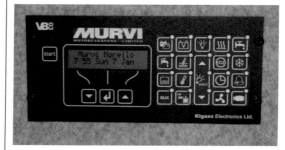

Marked switches and a meter are easy to understand on the Sargent panel fitted in this Swift Sundance.

This Sargent panel on an Auto-Sleepers Sandhurst is full of information, but you need to learn how to use the display.

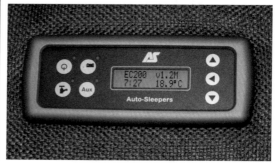

Operating a 12V supply system is usually quite simple. Provided your leisure battery is in a good state of charge, you merely go to a control panel and flick a few switches. Having said that, control panels are often surprisingly different and the accompanying photographs show several examples.

CONTROL PANEL INFORMATION

Fortunately motorcaravan manufacturers have moved away from the idea of fitting complex panels with a galaxy of light emitting diodes (LEDs) reminiscent of flight decks on aircraft. Although some owners like exuberant displays, they don't always suit a motorhome lounge.

When comparing panels, look for the following switches and indicator displays:

- A battery selection switch: These often employ a rocker-type switch that can be set in one of three positions. In the middle, the 12V supply is switched OFF, while the two side positions allow you to draw current from either the base vehicle battery or the leisure battery. However, it's best to regard the base vehicle's battery as an emergency supply for brief use only.
- Accessory controls: Normally a control panel has ON/OFF isolation switches for the water pump, interior lighting, and auxiliary 12V accessories such as a TV socket.
- There are also indication systems that show (a) water levels in fresh and waste water tanks, and (b) charge levels in both the vehicle and leisure batteries. This information is displayed in different ways. Sometimes there's a series of LEDs, as shown at the start of this chapter. Alternatively there's either an analogue meter or a digital display; the merits of the different displays are explained in the adjacent 'Technical tip' panel.

Left: There's an analogue meter on this Pilote Reference to show both water levels and battery charge condition.

Above: In this Auto-Trail coachbuilt, the 12V control panel provides a digital display that gives voltage readings.

ⓘ Technical Tip

Level condition indication

Water levels in fresh and waste tanks are often shown by a series of light emitting diodes (LEDs), and this achieves its objective. However, the indication of a battery's charge condition is less helpfully shown using lights. For instance the appearance of a red light might warn that a battery is getting low, but how low? In the later section on batteries you'll see that a reading of 12.7V indicates that a leisure battery is fully charged, whereas 12.4V shows that it's 50 per cent discharged. This level of precision is more accurately shown by a needle on a graduated meter scale or by a digital readout.

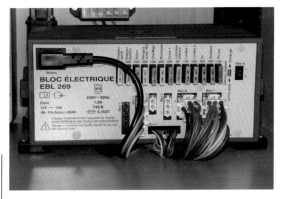

Above: On this 2006 Mobilvetta Top Driver S71, fuses on the driver's seat base are marked with pictograms.

Above right: Fuses in this Pilote are found under the double-bed, and their designations are marked in French.

Above: It's good to see a battery master-switch on a cab-seat base in the 2006 Mobilvetta Kimu.

Below: Fuses on the positive cable coming from the battery in this Auto-Sleeper Sandhurst are enclosed in a tight case.

FUSES AND CUT-OFF SWITCHES

Sometimes control panels are also fitted with fuses to control individual 12V circuits in the living area. Of course, these are completely different from the fuse box that's solely concerned with a base vehicle's 12V systems.

However, on most motorcaravans the fuses protecting 12V circuits serving domestic appliances are located elsewhere. These are sometimes found in odd places, such as underneath a double-bed or even under the driver's seat in the cab. Fortunately the designation for each fuse is clearly labelled, although on imported vehicles it might not be printed in English. Amp ratings on fuses are also marked, and it's prudent to purchase some spares from an auto accessory shop to keep in your 'van.

A few motorcaravans are also fitted with a master shut-off switch adjacent to the leisure battery. This is a good safety feature and it's not too involved to have one of these fitted retrospectively.

There should also be a 12V master fuse fitted on the live cable coming from a leisure battery's positive (+) pillar. Since a battery sometimes emits an explosive gas when it's being charged, and since fuses often spark when breaking, the master fuse should be mounted in a purpose-made airtight case. Alternatively, if the battery is installed in an enclosed box a fuse in a standard holder can be safely situated outside the container.

LEISURE BATTERIES

The main function of a leisure battery is to supply power to 12V appliances in your living area. However, its secondary function is to act as a buffer (*ie* an adjusting component) to absorb any power

Lead-acid batteries such as this 90Ah Elecsol use carbon fibre in the construction of the plates and carry a five-year guarantee.

surges that might come from a motorcaravan's built-in battery charger.

To explain this further, when you've connected your motorcaravan to a mains supply its built-in charger will provide 12V DC electricity. This supply not only charges the battery but also helps run the 12V appliances. However, it isn't always a smooth output, and even a small surge can damage sensitive 12V accessories. However, running a charger's output through the circuit's leisure battery ensures that the supply achieves better stability.

Vehicle and leisure batteries compared

These products are not only constructed differently; they also don't perform each other's job very well.

- Vehicle batteries have to produce a lot of power to start an engine. That's a tough challenge, but as soon as the engine fires up, its alternator immediately replenishes the battery and it doesn't discharge any further. This instant response is important, because if you frequently draw power from a starter battery until it's nearly flat, then apply a recharge, it won't last for long, because it hasn't been constructed to work like that.
- A leisure battery is made to perform a completely different job. Its task is to supply an array of 12V accessories until its condition is pretty low. Then you recharge the battery and it returns to its full state. The constant discharge/recharge cycle is repeated throughout its life, and leisure batteries are built to cope with this pattern of use. In fact they're often referred to as 'deep cycle' batteries. If you want to know more about the construction and characteristics of leisure batteries, refer to Chapter Five of *The Motorcaravan Manual* (2nd edition), also published by Haynes.

Traction batteries are deep cycle units often fitted on forklift trucks. This one has a noteworthy 220Ah rating.

• Traction batteries have a similar discharge/recharge pattern of use. However, they're larger and usually run for longer periods between charges because they have to drive forklift trucks and electric vehicles such as golf buggies. Some motorcaravanners have even started to fit traction batteries in their 'vans, but space is needed to accommodate these larger and heavier products.

Lead-acid or gel leisure batteries?

A leisure battery is already installed when you purchase a motorcaravan, and these are most commonly of the 'wet' lead-acid type. They have removable screw caps on the top and inside each cell is a fluid (called the electrolyte) consisting of a dilute solution of sulphuric acid. This type of battery also has a ventilator tube so that if any gas is created during a heavy charge it can be safely dispersed outside.

Below: The explosive gas produced when charging over 14.4V is not detrimental to a battery but it has to be safely vented outside.

Below right: Gel batteries are being fitted on German models and there's no acid to spill. There's no need for a ventilation facility either.

The alternative is a gel battery in which the electrolyte is an acidic paste. Each cell is sealed and nothing leaks if you turn the casing upside down. Since this type of battery has to be charged at a lower voltage than a 'wet' battery (14.4V max.), it won't produce gas and therefore doesn't need a ventilation tube.

Gel batteries are ideal on jet skis and quad bikes, which occasionally roll over. For safety

reasons they're now being fitted on many German motorcaravans as well. However, most battery specialists point out that from an electrical viewpoint, a lead-acid product is a better performer than its gel counterpart.

Battery capacity

The external dimensions of batteries differ and this is often related to their capacity, which is rated in amp hours (Ah). The greater an Ah rating – marked on the side – the longer a leisure battery will provide power before it needs recharging.

Owners who spend most of their time on sites which offer mains hook-up points often find that a battery with a 60Ah capacity is adequate. At the other extreme there are owners who want as much self-sufficiency as possible and prefer to stop at remote locations or on farm sites, where mains power is seldom supplied. Equally, if you are winter touring, when daylight hours are short and fan-driven heat is essential, a battery offering a higher Ah capacity is strongly recommended.

In practice, many owners of modern motorhomes find that their leisure battery becomes discharged after only a couple of days. If that's the case, a 120Ah battery would be better, although the greater the Ah capacity the longer it takes to recharge from flat. Some owners embarking on visits to remote locations even use two batteries of this size.

The speed of discharge is also influenced by the number and type of appliances fitted in a motorcaravan. It was explained in Chapter Eleven, for example, that a compressor refrigerator places a heavier demand on a 12V supply than a three-way absorption fridge that can be switched to run on gas. Similarly, diesel-driven heaters usually consume more 12V power than gas heaters. Halogen lights are quite greedy as well. None of which matters one jot if you only stop at sites equipped with mains hook-ups.

Battery location

A strange feature of the caravanning industry is that touring caravans are built with purpose-made lockers for housing leisure batteries, complete with an external access door. Splendid! In complete contrast, motorcaravan manufacturers seldom fit purpose-made lockers and leisure batteries are installed in all sorts of strange places.

In small van conversions there's obviously limited space and this necessitates fitting batteries in tight spaces where routine inspections of cells are often a challenging task. However, there's hardly a problem

It's hard to find a space to install leisure batteries in small 'van conversions but this one is pleasingly accessible.

finding a good location for a leisure battery in a coachbuilt motorcaravan. That said, pretty odd places get chosen.

For instance, the battery on a 2002 Buccaneer Cruiser 760 is exposed to the elements at the extreme rear of the chassis, where it's mounted on an elaborate hinged support structure. This poses considerable problems if a tow bracket is later required. Equally, accessing the leisure battery on a 2003 Bessacarr E745 necessitates removing the driver's seat – designated as a job to be done 'by your Dealer'. But that's not unusual; having to remove a seat to fit a battery is surprisingly common.

Fortunately, manufacturers are now adopting better practices. In some models, for example, specially-made boxes are being mounted in the floor of coachbuilt models complete with a useful access hatch. Sadly, however, the storage boxes don't usually include space to add a second battery. Only a few motorcaravan manufacturers, *eg* Knaus, have had the foresight to provide room for a spare, as is evident in the 2005 Knaus Sun Ti.

Of course, some owners who are desperate for more battery power make improvements themselves. In the DIY book *Build Your Own Motorcaravan*, also published by Haynes, the following advice is given:

Good locations for a leisure battery are:
• Where cells can be easily checked and topped-up
• In a compartment sealed-off from the living space
• Where there's warmth, to achieve optimum Ah capacity

Below: The battery in this Auto-Sleepers Sandhurst is mounted in a box under the floor but there's no space to add a second one.

Below right: The locker in this 2005 Knaus Sun Ti is pleasing because there's space to fit a second battery if required.

- As near to an alternator as possible to minimise voltage drop
- Where battery weight suits overall weight distribution
- In a position where it's easy to fit a ventilation tube.

NEVER fit a battery in a gas cylinder locker (cylinder valves can leak; battery terminals can spark).

Incidentally, if you do need to carry a spare battery on special expeditions (either wired-up or ready to swap over), portable battery boxes are sold by accessory specialists such as Towsure. Beeny Boxes can also be installed in most sideskirts of coachbuilt models and these are strong enough to carry a battery or two.

Above left: If you want to purchase a second battery, purpose-made boxes like this are available from Towsure.

Above: Beeny Boxes are bespoke sliding units fitted to motorhomes at the Cornish HQ. They're strong enough to carry batteries.

Ventilation

The panel below explains why a lead-acid 'wet' battery sometimes emits an explosive gas when it's being charged. That's why a ventilation facility is so

---

(i) Technical Tip

Emission of explosive gas

When a battery is charged at a high rate it creates an explosive gas that often lingers around the cells, even after charging ceases. Make certain that no one nearby is smoking when a charger is disconnected from the terminals. When batteries do explode, the casing often disintegrates and acid can easily get splashed on your face. Explosions also occur if there's a flame nearby, such as a pilot light on a gas appliance.

The gas normally only forms when a charging voltage exceeds 14.4V but it can be emitted at lower voltages if a battery cell is faulty. For this reason always ensure there are *no* naked flames or sources of sparks near a battery when it's being charged or its cells are being checked.

Also note that this gas is lighter than air – so if a battery is fitted in a sealed compartment there must be a high-level outlet to allow escaping gas to discharge and disperse outdoors. Alternatively, if a leak-proof tube and connecting elbow can be coupled to a battery this may be routed down through the floor, since gas will be forced downwards under pressure.

The gas relief pipe from a battery installed in an underfloor compartment is correctly fitted here to give external ventilation.

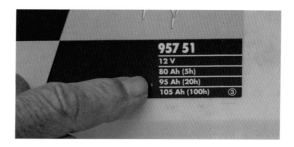

The faster a battery is discharged, the lower its capacity – this Exide label reveals Ah differences over three time periods.

important on such batteries, though it's not needed on gel batteries for the reasons outlined above. Of course, both gel and wet batteries have to be firmly secured using clamps or straps, since damage can be caused if they break free on a journey.

Life between charges

Battery manufacturers emphasise that you should never run a leisure battery until it's absolutely flat. In addition, a battery is claimed to last for many more years if you start recharging it as soon as its charge level drops to 50 per cent. Whether the majority of owners heed this advice is anyone's guess.

The output period is also determined by its amp hour (Ah) rating and this is often quoted by manufacturers for batteries operating in an ambient temperature of 25°C (77°F). The accompanying panel indicates how lower temperatures significantly reduce the Ah performance shown on a battery's label.

Lastly, if you use a battery to run a lot of appliances at once this obviously hastens the time when a recharge is needed. But it's worse than that because a high demand in a short space of time also reduces an Ah rating, and some battery manufacturers quote different figures on the label to reflect this.

Checking battery condition

When you've been charging a battery – including charging via the alternator while you've been driving – a misleadingly high voltage figure will be shown when charging first ceases. To get an accurate indication of charge condition, a battery should be left to settle for at least four hours before a voltage reading is taken. An even truer picture is obtained if you wait 12–24 hours. This is because the condition of any battery appears impressively good when charging is first terminated. Some hours later, however, the voltage reading for an older battery has usually fallen, whereas a newer battery is able to hold its charge.

Keep this in mind when using your motorcaravan's control panel, and if you want more information

---

ⓘ Technical Tip

Temperature effect on a battery's output

A stated Ah capacity presumes an ambient temperature of 25°C (77°F); one well-respected battery manufacturer states that for every drop of 1°C there's a 1 per cent reduction in capacity. So at 0°C, *ie* freezing point, the nominal Ah capacity is reduced by 25 per cent. This means that a battery nominally rated at 60Ah effectively becomes a 45Ah battery at 0°C. Bearing this in mind, a battery mounted externally performs less well in cold conditions than an identical one that's fitted indoors.

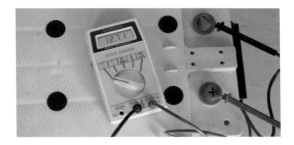

than is provided by a warning light system, a good multi-meter is an inexpensive purchase; even digital models are now available for less than £20.

The voltage reading you've obtained should be interpreted as follows:

Though called a '12V battery', there needs to be a reading of 12.7V to show that it's charged to the full.

Voltmeter reading	Approx charge state
12.7V or over	100%
12.5V	75%
12.4V	50%
12.2V	25%
12V or under	Discharged

Notes
1. Some electrical specialists assert that these percentage indications should be regarded only as an approximate guide.
2. Remember to take the reading four hours or more *after* charging has been terminated.
3. Make sure 12V appliances are switched OFF when the reading is taken. For complete accuracy this should include a clock, although in practice this item doesn't make a great deal of difference.

Looking after a leisure battery

When new a leisure battery is unlikely to need a lot of attention, although it must never be regarded as a 'fit and forget' accessory. For example, the electrolyte in a lead-acid battery should be checked periodically by removing the cell caps. The dilute sulphuric acid should just cover the lead plates. If its level has dropped, top it up using deionised water which is sold at auto accessory stores. DO NOT SMOKE AND DO NOT USE A NAKED FLAME TO SEE INSIDE THE CELLS.

Other points to remember:

• If a leisure battery is left in a totally discharged state for a day or more it will often be irreparably damaged

The individual cells on a lead-acid battery should be checked periodically and topped up using deionised water.

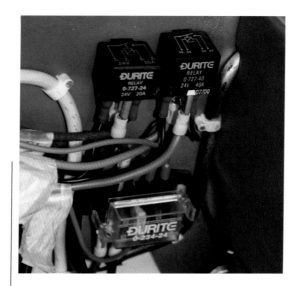

The black cubes in the upper part of this illustration are 'relays', which is the name for electrically-operated switches.

- Avoid running a battery until it's completely flat – whenever possible, it's recommended to start recharging a battery when it's around 50 per cent discharged
- If your motorcaravan is not in use and you want to transfer a battery to a bench for charging, always disconnect the negative terminal first; and when reinstalling a battery, connect the negative terminal last
- To prevent the terminals getting covered with a white powdery substance, lightly smear them with petroleum jelly ('Vaseline').

CHARGING A LEISURE BATTERY

Alternator charging

When driving a motorcaravan, the charge coming from the base vehicle's alternator will be fed into its starter battery. However, some of the charge can also be fed into the leisure battery. To achieve this, motorcaravan manufacturers fit an electrically-operated switch called a 'relay' which is activated as soon as the engine is running. This arrangement links the two batteries and they remain in this coupled state until the engine is switched off. At that point their independence is re-established.

An alternator can play a useful part in charging a leisure battery but you may have to drive for several hours if it's heavily discharged at the time of departure. Equally, if a leisure battery is fitted at the rear of a vehicle – as it sometimes is – the cable

Technical Tip

System shutdown

When a motorcaravan is being driven, an automatic switch called a relay enables a leisure battery to receive a charge from the vehicle's alternator. However, a second relay automatically cuts off the 12V supply to all other services in the living area apart from a three-way refrigerator: if its 12V operating mode has been selected, an absorption refrigerator continues to operate whereas other 12V items like interior lights are all disabled.

This restriction was introduced in the late 1990s when more and more electronic systems were being fitted in motor vehicles. Essentially it's a precautionary measure concerned with 'electromagnetic compatibility' – described in more detail in Chapter Five of *The Motor Caravan Manual*. Suffice it to say, recent engine management systems, braking systems and stability programmes are electronically controlled, and the disabling of 12V supplies in a motorcaravan's living quarters is intended to minimise the likelihood of electrical activity upsetting these control systems.

linking it to the alternator is so long that there's likely to be a drop in voltage before it reaches the battery. To minimise voltage loss it's better to install a leisure battery close to the alternator.

Several other factors also play a part. For instance, some motorcaravan manufacturers don't purchase base vehicles fitted with high output alternators even though these are often 'optional extra' items. In addition, if you park your motorhome for an extended period on a pitch that isn't served by a 230V hook-up and you then use a support car, scooter or bicycle for all local trips, no charge is drawn from the alternator either. To recharge a battery in these circumstances is when owning a generator is useful.

Fixed battery charger

Chargers fitted in motorcaravans as standard items start to operate when the vehicle is coupled to a mains supply. Some have an ON/OFF switch but many start operating automatically as soon as a 230V supply is connected.

Not only does the output from one of these devices charge the leisure battery, it provides a 12V supply to run domestic appliances as well. These two functions operate simultaneously and that's why built-in chargers are designed not to yield more than 13.8V. This restriction means a battery won't start 'gassing' either and it's well within the 14.4V limit for charging gel batteries. Of course, it will make your 12V lights glow more brightly, but it's unlikely to cause them to fail.

Above right: When a battery's removed from a motorhome you can charge it with an initial boost of 15V, which is good for its plates.

Below: The CTEK Multi XS 7000 charger can be switched to give higher voltage charge regimes as well as a 13.6V supply.

The Carcoon trickle charger is a popular unit among classic car owners for keeping a battery sound during long lay-up periods.

Portable stepped chargers

Unfortunately, lead-acid batteries respond better when recharged with an initial input around 15V or more, followed by a gradually reducing charge. This causes an emission of gas and a battery's cells need topping-up more often. However, 'gassing' extends the life of a battery.

In response to this, portable chargers are now available which offer 'stepped charging' working in concert with electronic circuits that monitor the battery's progress. For example, a charging regime might start with a boost voltage which then tapers off as the battery responds.

Some technically-minded owners even disconnect the leisure battery from the 12V circuits in their motorhome, and might transfer it to a bench. Using portable chargers from manufacturers like CTEK, they can then provide the charge regime that suits the battery best. More information on technical issues like this are dealt with in *The Motorcaravan Manual* (2nd edition).

Trickle chargers

These are designed to keep a battery that is already in a good charge condition fully maintained by providing an occasional input of power. Trickle chargers are used by many owners of vehicles that are parked for extended spells, such as classic cars, motorcycles in winter – and motorcaravans. Most can be left permanently connected to both the mains supply and the battery because their electronic circuits monitor voltage and activate charging only when it's needed.

Solar and wind generators

Neither of these products are cheap to buy and purchasers don't necessarily have them fitted in the hope of saving money. When conditions are right, however, both are able to provide a battery with a trickle charge, thereby helping to extend its output before it needs a renovating recharge.

Wind generators are often fitted on boats and work

best in exposed places where prevailing winds are strong. Solar panels only need light but undoubtedly work best in bright sun and clear skies.

To give an example of performance, a 70W Solar Kit that typically costs around £450 (plus fitting charges) can yield around 3 amps in a sunny position on a clear day. The output might be higher at midday but would be considerably less when it's raining and dull. In an hour of favourable light, your battery might receive 3 amps, which represents only a small fraction of the capacity of a 65Ah battery.

So there aren't dramatic daily achievements, but during an eight-week test conducted in the Midlands between mid-July and mid-September 2007 a roof-mounted 70W panel produced a logged total of 540 amps. The yield would be considerably less in the shorter daylights hours of winter, but solar panels do make a contribution, as the author has found.

Sharing excess power

Since the starter and leisure batteries in a motor-caravan are normally kept separate, built-in chargers are normally only wired to recharge the leisure battery. Only a few motorcaravans include a switching facility to recharge a starter battery instead. However, there's another strategy that many owners adopt.

Inexpensive 'power-sharing' products such as the Battery Master Balancer from Van Bitz or the EuroE848 charger are easy to fit and monitor voltage in both batteries. When the voltage in a leisure battery becomes significantly higher than the voltage in the engine battery, a controlled transfer of current automatically takes place. This similarly occurs when you're using a mains hook-up or if a solar panel is permanently feeding the leisure battery.

If there isn't any charging taking place, the battery on a parked vehicle still has to run its clock and items like an electronic alarm. A power-sharing product then ensures that the discharge load won't be drawn from the starter battery alone.

It's a pity these products aren't fitted as standard.

The GB-SOL Flexible 35W solar panel is easily bonded to the roof of a campervan and weighs only 2kg.

The Euro E848 device monitors voltage in both batteries and creates a transfer of current if the starter battery drops a lot lower than the leisure one.

CHAPTER FOURTEEN

UNDERSTANDING
GAS

The most popular fuel used in motorcaravans for cooking and heating is liquefied petroleum gas – or LPG, as it's normally called. However, LPG is also highly flammable and it's crucially important that all users treat it with care, respect and understanding.

In winter conditions, propane performs better than butane.

(i) Technical Tip

Installed gas tanks

Although some motorcaravans are fitted with a supply tank to provide gas for domestic needs, these products mustn't be confused with tanks installed to run LPG-adapted engines. In the automotive context, gas has to be injected in its liquefied state into an engine compartment and changed to vapour prior to injection into the engine. That can't be achieved using a domestic supply tank.

Some motorcaravanners have a refillable gas tank fitted to run their domestic appliances.

Liquefied petroleum gas is readily available in purpose-made cylinders, although some motorcaravanners prefer to have a fixed tank installed to supply their domestic needs. It is also used as an alternative fuel for vehicle propulsion, and in both contexts matters of safety must be fully understood and always observed.

(i) Useful Tip

Terminology

Terms which are ambiguous or inaccurate should be avoided when dealing with LPG. For example:

1. Some people wrongly refer to LPG as 'liquid' petroleum gas, and that's a contradiction: gas engineers correctly refer to it as 'liquefied petroleum gas'.
2. You'll often hear motorcaravanners state that they need another gas 'bottle' and that can certainly confuse a new owner – beer might be sold in bottles, but LPG is sold in 'cylinders'.

For the sake of clarity, the terminologies preferred by gas specialists will be used throughout this chapter.

CHARACTERISTICS OF LPG

A rudimentary understanding of LPG's characteristics will help to reinforce why precautionary measures must never be treated lightly. Note the following points:

- In its natural state, LPG is not poisonous
- LPG does *not* have a smell, which means that leaks might not be noticed
- To warn of leaks, distributors add what is called a 'stenching agent'
- LPG is heavier than air, and if a leak occurs the gas sinks to the lowest point
- The gas escape outlets in a motorcaravan are called 'drop-out holes' and must never be covered up
- Motorcaravanners use two types of LPG – butane and propane
- When an appropriate regulator is fitted, the gas appliances installed in British motorcaravans will run on either butane or propane
- Since LPG is highly flammable it must be stored in accordance with the LP Gas Association Codes of Practice.

 **Safety Tip**

Leak detectors

As a safety precaution many owners have a leak
detector fitted, of which several types are available.
Devices which react to smell run on a 12V supply
and emit a loud noise if a leak is detected. Carbon
monoxide detectors work in a similar way, and these
are often fitted too.

It's useful having a safety device installed but it
shouldn't be regarded as a substitute for periodic
servicing checks conducted by a qualified gas
engineer.

*The 12V alarm from Van Bitz reacts
to many kinds of escaping gas.*

233

STORAGE

At point of sale

Retailers and site operators supplying gas have to
comply with strict rules when storing and handling
LPG cylinders. For example, on rare occasions
cylinder valves have become faulty and leakage
occurs. Noting the earlier point that the gas is
heavier than air and sinks to the lowest point,
storage facilities must allow leaking gas to disperse
safely. That's why mesh cages are normally used and
are situated outdoors, well away from any potential
source of ignition.

In your motorcaravan

Manufacturers have to comply with strict
specifications, and gas cylinder lockers must have
low-level drop-out holes. In fact recent Auto-Sleepers'
coachbuilt models have a base fabricated in steel
mesh that affords a particularly good means of
gas escape.

A storage locker should also offer a minimum of
30 minutes' fire resistance. However, in view of
a motorcaravan's structure some experts regard

*Strict regulations apply to
the storage facilities used
by the suppliers of gas
cylinders.*

Although situated inside this van conversion, the gas locker has low escape holes and a fully sealed door.

compliance with this expectation as unreasonably hard to achieve.

External access is required too, although small van conversions sometimes have an interior door that's totally sealed from the living area. Either way, a gas cylinder locker must never be used to accommodate a battery, contain fuses, include a light or be used as a routeway for electrical cabling unless it's wholly sealed in a conduit. Anything that could create a spark is considered dangerous, although a few models now have recessed, sealed and covered niches containing light emitting diodes (LEDs).

Also required is a means of effectively securing cylinders in an upright position, in recognition of the fact that bumpy roads pose a challenge to any fixing system.

 Technical Tip

Always keep cylinders in their upright position

It's not unknown for valves on cylinders to develop a small leak. For instance, if grit or grass gets caught in the spring-loaded steel ball that forms the seal on a Campingaz cylinder, the obstruction may lead to a seepage of gas. Sometimes you can even hear a faint hiss.

The problem is usually solved by taking a Campingaz cylinder outdoors, checking that there's no flame nearby and then depressing the ball very briefly with a small screwdriver. A sharp blast of escaping gas occurs instantaneously and usually dislodges the obstruction, whereupon the steel ball then reseats itself correctly.

DON'T DO THIS! Even when collecting a replacement cylinder, never lay it on its side – valves can sometimes leak.

The valves on other types of cylinders can also develop leaks and it's therefore extremely dangerous to lay a cylinder on its side. A tiny drop of liquefied butane gas trickling from a cylinder resting on its side will multiply in volume around 230 times as it converts into gas. The increase in volume of propane is approximately 274 times greater. The potential hazard of this is readily apparent.

Butane has a higher calorific value than propane, burns at a slightly slower rate, and is a more efficient heat producer.

At home

Some owners remove their cylinders during a long lay-up period, but it's usually unsafe to store them in a house. In fact the worst place of all is in a cellar, since this is normally devoid of low-level ventilation outlets. In the event of a cylinder valve developing a leak, the heavier-than-air gas then has nowhere to escape so it accumulates around the lowest parts of the floor.

A garage is often unsafe too, especially if it's used for a car, to store a petrol can and to charge a battery. It's better to store a cylinder externally in a weather-protected and well-ventilated position.

TYPES OF LPG

Two distinct types of LPG are used by motorcaravanners in Britain. One is called butane, the other is propane, and their respective characteristics need to be recognised.

Butane

Key points about butane:

- It is widely sold throughout Europe and there are many suppliers, most of whom use different sizes of cylinder and dissimilar connecting systems.
- It has a higher calorific value than propane and since it burns at a slightly slower rate it's a more efficient heat producer.
- It presents problems in extremely cold conditions because it doesn't change from its liquefied state into a gas. This occurs when temperatures fall to minus 2°C (around 29°F) at atmospheric pressure. Accordingly, butane is *not* the preferred gas for winter use or for visits to cold regions.

When the temperature falls, the rate at which liquefied butane changes to gas decreases progressively. So, even though the temperature in a gas cylinder locker might still be above freezing point, a significant reduction in the output of gas might become apparent if you're cooking a meal and trying to run a space heater and water heater *at the same time*. On noting a lower-than-normal flame on the hob, many motorcaravanners wrongly presume that the cylinder is nearly empty and prepare to fit a replacement.

Propane is the preferred winter fuel because it vaporises in temperatures as low as minus 45°C.

• It is heavier than propane. Taking the smallest cylinder sold by Calor Gas as an example, the propane version holds 3.9kg (8.6lb) of liquefied gas, whereas an identically-sized cylinder filled with butane holds 4.5kg (10lb).

In Britain, butane is usually sold in BLUE cylinders.

Propane

Key points about propane:
• This is the preferred winter fuel because it changes from a liquefied state into a gas in temperatures as low as minus 45°C.
• Outside the United Kingdom it's harder to find propane in portable cylinders for leisure activities, although 11kg and 13kg cylinders are available in France, Italy and Spain.
• Some processing companies add a small amount of propane to their butane cylinders in order to improve cold weather performance.
• Propane is lighter than butane in its liquefied state. If you check two cylinders of identical size, you'll see from markings on the side that the propane one holds less in weight than the butane.
• It has a vapour pressure approximately four times that of butane. Note how this affects the type of gas regulator required as described in the accompanying panel.

In Britain, propane used to be sold in RED cylinders but now other colours are used as well.

Which gas should you use?

Taking note of the differences between butane and propane, motorcaravanners who only use their vehicles during warmer times of year often prefer butane. In contrast, year-round owners who tour mostly in Britain generally use propane. However, propane in portable cylinders is less easy to purchase in some parts of mainland Europe.

In this country, Calor is the most popular gas

Technical Tip

Prior to the introduction of universal butane/propane 30mbar regulators (autumn 2003), gas-specific regulators were needed for the two types of LPG. Accordingly when changing from one gas to the other, owners of motorcaravans built prior to 1 September 2003 have to change the regulator as well. More detailed information on regulators is given later in this chapter.

supplier for motorcaravanners and you get a choice of cylinder sizes and the type of gas they contain – *ie* butane or propane. Many Calor Gas dealers even allow you to trade-in an empty butane cylinder for a full propane one, and vice versa. It's not like this in many parts of mainland Europe.

Unfortunately you can't purchase Calor Gas cylinders or Calor-approved refills abroad either. The most common product sold in Europe is Campingaz, which is butane. However, it's generally believed that Campingaz cylinders contain a small quantity of propane mixed with the butane thereby making the product reasonably satisfactory if you visit a cold place like the Alps in winter.

If you don't want to purchase a purpose-made regulator to fit the unique Campingaz coupling, you can buy an adaptor. These fit directly on to the Campingaz cylinder and have a turn-tap on the top. Their outlet connection, however, has a thread which accepts the screw-nut coupling used on regulators made for Calor's 4.5kg butane cylinders.

This coupling-up versatility is fine, but there's still the disadvantage that the largest Campingaz cylinder (called a Type 907) only holds 2.72 kg (6lb) of butane. This is a very modest amount compared with Calor cylinders' capacities, as the table on page 239 shows. Many British tourists consequently take a full Calor cylinder abroad (even though it can't be replaced on the Continent when empty) and a Campingaz 907 unit as well. Unfortunately, that doesn't solve all the problems. Although Campingaz is quite widely available there are some European countries where it's unobtainable.

The supply difficulties that face motorcaravanners visiting different countries prompted revisions to the European Norms applicable to gas systems, which many manufacturers implemented in 2003. The acute need for standardisation led to the introduction of new gas regulators and cylinder coupling methods. The revised components are now being fitted on more recent motorcaravans as described later in this chapter.

Above left: A Campingaz 907 cylinder has a coupling that's unique. The regulator here is made to fit all Campingaz cylinders.

Above: Adaptors for Campingaz cylinders offer a threaded coupling to match the regulators used on Calor Gas 4.5kg cylinders.

(i) Useful Tip

Campingaz cylinders are seldom available in Finland, Norway and Sweden. If you visit these countries for longer than the normal output life of your Calor cylinders, you may have to switch to the countries' own products. That would entail purchasing the appropriate regulators and couplings – though Gaslow can supply these before you leave the UK.

To find the list of countries where Campingaz, is available, contact Coleman UK Inc (see Campingaz in Appendix).

Useful Tip

Obtaining your preferred type of gas cylinder

If you decide to use Campingaz, you start by purchasing a cylinder full of gas. When it's empty, you exchange it for another and merely pay the price for the LPG. The charges are reasonable and in Spain the costs are remarkably low because the product is government-subsidised. In the case of Campingaz use, *you own the cylinder*.

The situation is different, however, if you want to use Calor Gas in your motorcaravan. To obtain a cylinder of gas you have to enter into a cylinder-hire arrangement which entails completing a form and leaving a deposit. Thus when you exchange an empty cylinder for a full one, you only pay for the LPG. Strictly speaking you never have ownership of the cylinder, even if you use a motorcaravan for years and years. In fact if you cease motorcaravanning you can get the deposit back by taking your Calor cylinders to an approved specialist – as long as you can produce the original hire contract papers!

Above: BP Gas Light cylinders are large in diameter, light, and you can see the gas level through their semi-transparent sides.

Below: The hope of finding universal couplings is a long way off but the BP Gas Light clip-on adaptors are easy to connect.

Finally, the dissimilar sizes of cylinders and the many types of motorcaravan being sold make it difficult to give definitive guidance on the cylinders that would fit your own motorcaravan's gas locker. So before purchasing a cylinder, check this with the supplier; some lockers are too small to accommodate several products included in the tables on pages 238, 239 and 240.

Cylinders often used by motorcaravanners

The weights quoted here relate to the gas content and don't include the weight of an empty cylinder (known as its 'tare weight').

The dimensions of cylinders vary a great deal: so do the sizes of gas lockers. Check with your dealer regarding the suitability of cylinders for your gas locker before making a purchase.

BP Gas Light

5kg (11.02lb) propane
10kg (22.04lb) propane

BP Gas Light cylinders are duo-coloured green and white.

Note – Introduced in 2006 by BP in partnership with Truma UK, these light, composite cylinders are around half the weight of similar steel cylinders. Their semi-transparent material lets you check the gas level inside and the 27mm clip-on valve is easy to connect. Cylinders are supplied under a hire arrangement, although a 50 per cent reimbursement fee is only available on returned cylinders that are less than six years old. The success of this new venture will depend on whether a large chain of Gas Light suppliers becomes established.

238

Calor

Left: Propane 'Patio Gas', marketed by Calor in distinctive cylinders, is intended for use at home as well as in motorcaravans.

Above: The weight of an empty Calor Gas cylinder is marked on its metal collar in pounds and ounces.

3.9kg (8.6lb) propane 4.5kg (10lb) butane)	Same external size of cylinder
5kg (11.02lb) propane	Patio Gas with Gas Trac level indicator
6kg (13.2lb) propane 7kg (15.4lb) butane)	Same external size of cylinder
13kg (28.7lb) propane	Patio Gas with Gas Trac level indicator
13kg (28.7lb) propane 15kg (33lb) butane	Same external size of cylinder

The Calor 19kg (41.9lb) propane cylinder is too large for motorcaravan lockers.

Calor Gas butane cylinders are blue; Calor Gas propane cylinders are red; Calor Patio Gas propane cylinders are green with red handles.

Notes
The weight of an empty Calor cylinder is marked on a silver disc attached to the top near the connector. Perversely, it is expressed in pounds and ounces.

Some of the smallest micro van conversions can't accommodate any of Calor's products. Similarly, you'll find that only the larger coachbuilt motorcaravans have room in their gas lockers to accommodate a pair of 13kg propane or 15kg butane Calor cylinders. Calor Patio Gas cylinders are also large in diameter and are often sold at Garden Centres. In spite of their useful level-gauge indicator, they haven't yet achieved popularity among motorcaravan users.

The largest and smallest Campingaz cylinders: only the 907 on the left holds sufficient gas (2.72kg) for motorhome use.

Above: Gaslow offers refillable cylinders in two sizes; these are fixed in a locker and have to be exchanged after 15 years.

Below: A cylinder in a Gaslow system is coupled to an autogas filler permanently mounted on the motorcaravan.

Below right: The link between a Gaslow refillable cylinder and the autogas filler is made using a fixed, stainless steel pipe.

Campingaz

0.45kg (1lb) butane
1.81kg (4lb) butane
2.72kg (6lb) butane

Campingaz cylinders are blue.

Note – Only the Type 907 Campingaz 2.72kg butane cylinder is a practical proposition for the motorcaravanner. The two smaller cylinders are really intended for camping use only.

Gaslow refillable cylinders

6kg (13.2lb) propane 11kg (24.22lb) propane	Normally fillable at autogas stations

Note – Designed for permanent installation in a gas locker, these cylinders have to be permanently connected to an autogas filling point mounted on the side of a motorcaravan. This must be achieved by installing Gaslow's stainless steel pipe.

The cylinders have European Pi approved filler valves that automatically shut off when the container is 80 per cent full. Coupling-up a cylinder to the motorcaravan supply pipework is via the same type of screw connection used on 4.5kg Calor butane cylinders. The cost of gas supplied at autogas stations is significantly cheaper, and once Gaslow's components are purchased both the cylinders and the stainless steel connecting pipe carry a 15-year warranty.

Safety precautions when fitting and removing gas cylinders

When changing a cylinder, make sure there's nothing nearby that could ignite escaping gas. Check that no one is smoking and ensure that the area is nowhere near electric fan heaters, gas heaters, pilot lights on a gas appliance, a fridge running on gas, an outside barbecue, a gas-operated portable awning lamp and so on. Equally, check there's no battery nearby because sparks can sometimes occur at a terminal.

TURN OFF THE CYLINDER YOU WANT TO CHANGE. If you have an approved twin-cylinder coupling device with a manual or automatic changeover valve, it *is* permissible to let the active supplying cylinder remain connected and switched on. But always turn off the cylinder you want to change – it may still contain a small amount of gas, even if it's insufficient to run a motorcaravan's appliances properly.

HOW FULL IS YOUR CYLINDER?

Keeping a check on the amount of gas left in a cylinder can be difficult. However, the recently-introduced BP Gas Light product with its semi-transparent casing makes it delightfully easy. The introduction of the Gas Trac float-activated level indicator on Calor Patio Gas cylinders is helpful too. This starts to operate when the level falls below halfway.

Inexpensive gauges from Gaslow that measure cylinder pressure are also useful, but they only give an indication of a cylinder's contents when it's coupled to an appliance and in use.

The more costly Sonatic system from Truma uses ultrasonics to check a cylinder's 'state of fill' and its findings are relayed to a liquid crystal display mounted inside the motorcaravan. At present the Sonatic is available for operation with Calor 7kg butane or 6kg propane cylinders and its accuracy is notably good. However, some gas engineers point out that its measuring mechanism requires an electrical supply and normally you're not permitted to have cable running in a gas locker without full conduit protection.

Although numerous other devices are also on sale, you can actually work out a cylinder's content using an accurate set of bathroom scales and a calculator. Here's how:

1 As soon as you've collected a full cylinder from a supplier, put it on the scales and take a note of its total weight.
2 You'll know the weight of gas contained in the cylinder from its supplier's information – Calor always displays this on the side.

The two propane cylinders in Calor's 'Patio Gas' range are fitted with a level indicator that uses a float system.

It's possible to monitor gas consumption if you weigh a new cylinder on some accurate scales.

Procedure when fitting and removing gas cylinders

1. *Campingaz cylinders*
Since there's a screw thread on top of a Campingaz cylinder, it means that when the regulator or adaptor finally loosens a small quantity of gas usually hisses out while the valve ball reseats itself. So act promptly to complete the disconnection. The same thing occurs very briefly when connecting a new cylinder.

In view of this brief moment of leakage, you might prefer to lift a Campingaz cylinder out of the locker while making the connections. It also helps to hold the regulator and to rotate the cylinder itself, rather than the other way round which merely twists the connecting hose.

2. *Screw-thread Calor cylinders*
1. When connecting and disconnecting a cylinder, always make sure first that the cylinder's handwheel is OFF – *ie* turned fully clockwise (this has a conventional right-hand thread).
2. When a new Calor butane cylinder is supplied, it normally has a small black cap over the threaded outlet. Remove this by turning it CLOCKWISE when looking at its dome (the coupling has a left-hand thread). Keep it for when you return the empty cylinder.
3. When a new propane cylinder is supplied, it has a small black plug in the coupling. Remove this with a large slotted screwdriver, turning it CLOCKWISE when looking at the slot (the coupling has a left-hand thread).
4. Check the connection surfaces (whether it's a butane or propane cylinder) to confirm they're clean and unobstructed. Then offer-up the threaded coupling. Hand-tighten it first, turning it ANTI-CLOCKWISE, and complete the job using an open-ended spanner. Since they don't have a washer, propane couplings have to be tight.
5. Turn on the gas cylinder's hand-wheel, checking immediately for a hiss or smell. For a more thorough DIY test, apply a proprietary leak-detecting fluid or a prepared mix of soapy water to the coupling areas. Then look closely for bubbles, which signify an escape of gas.
6. When returning an empty cylinder to a supplier, the plastic cap (butane) or plastic plug (propane) should be refitted.

3 If you want to establish the weight of the empty cylinder subtract the weight of the gas from the total.
4 After a period of use, rechecking the total weight of the cylinder will reveal the amount of gas remaining.

Note – On a newly-filled Calor cylinder you don't need scales to establish the cylinder weight because it's marked on the collar plate in pounds and ounces. Firstly, convert this to ounces (there are 16 ounces in one pound). Secondly, take a calculator and convert the ounces into kilograms by multiplying your result by 0.0283495.

For example, the collar plate on the Calor 6kg propane cylinder illustrated on page 236 shows a tare (cylinder weight) of 17lb 6oz, *ie* 278oz. When converted to kg (278 x 0.0283495) this equals 7.88kg. Since the freshly filled cylinder contains 6kg of propane, the total weight of the cylinder plus its gas content should be around 13.88kg.

3. Clip-on Calor cylinders

No tools are needed to connect or disconnect this type of coupling. Furthermore, there isn't an ON/OFF turn-wheel; instead, the ON/OFF control is an integral part of the regulator. As a safety feature the regulator's detachment mechanism won't operate until you've turned the tap to OFF.

Preparing a new cylinder – Rotate the orange cap so that its arrow points towards the opening in the cylinder shroud. Remove the cap by pulling on the plastic strap and lifting as you do so.

Attaching a clip-on regulator – The retaining collar is lifted up with the thumb while the regulator is pushed down onto the cylinder connection.

Switching on the gas – Once the regulator is seated properly and the retaining collar has been lowered you can rotate the operating tap to the vertical ON position.

Disconnecting a clip-on regulator – The design of a clip-on regulator intentionally ensures that the release collar can only be pushed upwards when the turn-tap is in its OFF position.

When a cylinder is exhausted the orange cap is pushed back onto the coupling.

Refillable cylinders

The sale of refillable cylinders has become a contentious issue on safety grounds. For example, liquefied gas is delivered from an autogas pump at some force and any spillage on your hands leaves painful injuries. There are other safety issues too, just as there are when petrol is dispensed by a member of the public into a portable can.

In addition, it's most important that a gas vessel is never filled more than 85/87 per cent, which is why it must have a European Pi approved filler valve that automatically shuts off the gas as soon as a tank or cylinder reaches its 80 per cent limit. Some refillable portable cylinders do incorporate an approved automatic cut-off device; others don't.

Gas specialists became very concerned when refillable gas cylinders were introduced that didn't have an automatic cut-off valve. This placed the onus on the customer to ascertain when to cease the filling process, and that can be difficult – some pumps dispense LPG at surprising speed. Exceeding the 85/87 per cent fill level can have serious

Fuel stations in Australia often have staff able to refill portable cylinders for motorcaravanners.

repercussions and some suppliers strictly forbid the refilling of portable cylinders on a forecourt.

That's not the case in Australia, where refilling caravanners' portable cylinders is a normal practice at fuel stations. However, the staff who refill your special cylinder draw the LPG from a small tank and it would be wrong to compare this service with an autogas forecourt facility in Europe.

Regarding safety issues in the UK, a statement published by the LP Gas Association or LPGA (IS24, June 2007) makes the position clear. This document clarifies that permanently fixed gas 'vessels' related to heating and cooking

'may be permitted to be refilled at autogas refuelling sites provided they:
• remain in situ for refilling; and
• are fitted with a device to physically prevent filling beyond 80%; and
• are connected to a fixed filling connector which is not part of the vessel.'

In other words, appropriately installed tanks are deemed acceptable. So, too, are the specially-made cylinders sold by Gaslow provided they're permanently installed and coupled with Gaslow's stainless steel fill-up pipe to an autogas filler point mounted on the vehicle. The components in this system carry a 15-year warranty, at which point the cylinder (which is marked with a date) must be exchanged.

Of course, not everyone wants to spend a three-figure sum to have a tank or a fixed-cylinder system installed, but safe and easy-to-use systems are available. Moreover, a Gaslow system can often be uninstalled, transferred, and re-fixed in another motorcaravan without requiring major alterations to either vehicle.

Some coachbuilts are fitted with Gaslow's refillable 11kg cylinders; this one also has an automatic changeover

Refillable tanks

With an increasing number of autogas stations opening for vehicles which run on LPG, many motorcaravanners have wanted to use these facilities to refill their domestic supply. You can't refill a standard portable cylinder yourself, of course, and having a refillable tank installed is costly. It's also a heavy component. However, a refillable tank does offer benefits:

- For heavy gas users such as motorcaravanners touring in Europe, having a domestic tank installed can eliminate worries about finding suitable portable cylinders
- Winter users who rely heavily on gas for their heating needs often have a tank installed
- Some owners find it tiresome carrying heavy portable cylinders to a supplier when replacements are needed
- Once a tank has been installed, the cost of gas purchased at autogas stations is certainly less expensive.

Using prices applicable at the time of writing, a 6kg propane refill cylinder costs around £15. Acknowledging that 6kg of gas is the rough equivalent of 11 litres, and with present LPG prices at autogas stations around 42p per litre, the cost of 6kg of gas amounts to £4.62. Naturally, these quoted prices will quickly become dated but you can see that there's more than a 50 per cent price differential.

REGULATORS

A regulator is an essential component in a motorcaravan's gas supply system. Its function is to ensure that gas is supplied to appliances at a consistent and appropriate pressure regardless

Owners who have a heavy consumption of LPG often get a refillable tank installed on their motorhome.

For the diaphragm to work properly, the tiny breather hole on a regulator's casing mustn't get blocked.

 Technical Tip

If you ever get a frightening tall flame on a stove burner, this is 'over-gassing', which is usually caused by a faulty regulator. The condition typically occurs when the tiny breather hole on a regulator gets blocked.

of whether the supply cylinder or tank is full or approaching exhaustion. The pressure of gas in a cylinder is also affected by changing temperatures, which is another reason why regulators are important.

A regulator has a diaphragm inside which stabilises the flow of gas and delivers it at the pressure required by the installed gas appliances. It must be wholly weather-protected, and for the diaphragm to work a tiny breather hole in the casing must not get blocked. Rain entering this hole during winter can soon freeze, and the diaphragm's operation then promptly fails.

Apart from this need for vigilance there's nothing in a motorcaravan regulator to service or adjust. Accordingly its casing is sealed, and a regulator normally gives unfailing service for several years. Opinion is divided in respect of routine replacement. Some specialists recommend every five years, others quote ten years.

Changes to systems

For many years it's been necessary for anyone buying a motorcaravan to also purchase a regulator that matches the type of gas cylinder they want to use. This is the case when regulators are 'cylinder-mounted' because their coupling has to match the type of coupling on the cylinder. Similarly a different regulator is required for a cylinder containing butane as opposed to a cylinder containing propane.

Unfortunately for those motorcaravanners who tour widely throughout Europe, the huge variety of cylinder connections means that an array of regulators might be needed. There have also been problems for companies importing and exporting motorcaravans. In Germany, for example, gas appliances installed in caravans and motorhomes used to be manufactured to run at the higher pressure of 50mbar. In Britain, however, appliances were fitted to run on both 28mbar (butane) and 37mbar (propane) without needing adjustment.

Quite simply there was a desperate need for standardisation among European Union member states. New European Norms were therefore published in 2001 (BS EN 12864) and 2002 (BS EN 1949) and these made radical changes affecting both regulators and cylinder coupling arrangements. The new standards were implemented by UK manufacturers on 1 September 2003; a few German motorcaravan manufacturers were fitting the revised components a month or two earlier.

Recognising the fact that some readers own or intend to purchase a motorcaravan built before Autumn 2003, the earlier systems need to be explained. So, too, do the gas systems installed in post-2003 models.

Systems in motorcaravans built before 1 September 2003

Mounting a regulator directly on top of a supply cylinder has been customary practice for many years, and such cylinder-mounted regulators have to match the type of gas and the style of coupling. To avoid errors, a propane cylinder always has a different coupling from a butane one.

On some butane cylinders there's a push-fit arrangement; on others there's a threaded coupling and you need to tighten this using a spanner. Remember, too, that Calor Gas screw-type couplings have a *reverse thread*. So forget the usual convention for threaded fixings. In this instance you have to rotate the nut *anti*-clockwise to tighten your regulator and vice versa if you want to remove it.

One of the implications of fitting a regulator directly to a cylinder is the fact that gas pressure is immediately reduced and it can then be fed to a motorcaravan's fixed copper pipes with a short length of approved *low pressure* hose. This will be marked on the side, together with the date when it left the factory. It can also be coupled satisfactorily to the main supply pipe and the regulator using good quality hose clips.

The Calor Gas 4.5kg butane cylinder has a threaded coupling, and a spanner is needed when making a connection.

Technical Tip

Since the gas appliances fitted in a motorcaravan are matched to its installed gas supply system, gas specialists have strongly asserted that anyone owning a pre-2003 motorcaravan must not attempt to install the regulators and supply arrangements used for post-2003 models.

Further technical information on this subject can be found in Chapter Six of *The Motorcaravan Manual* (2nd edition), also published by Haynes.

ⓘ Technical Tip

Regulator spanner

Coupling a regulator to a Campingaz cylinder doesn't need
a spanner; a regulator to suit Calor's clip-on system doesn't
require special tools either. However, all the Calor Gas propane
cylinders, together with Calor's 4.5kg butane cylinders, require
a spanner to tighten the regulators' couplings. Accordingly, open-
ended spanners are sold at motorcaravan accessory shops.

But be warned. If someone else coupled your regulator
using a plumber's wrench and unnecessary zeal, a Calor
spanner isn't likely to be tough enough to loosen it when the cylinder needs changing. That's
not something you want to discover when it's dark, cold, and pouring with rain.

During an annual habitation service, this short
length of flexible coupling hose will be replaced.
A replacement needs to be fitted and tested even
sooner – by someone competent – if premature
wear or distortion is noted, particularly near the
clipping points.

This coupling system, which has been used
successfully for many years, has much to commend
it, apart from the fact that regulators have to be
cylinder-specific. Even then, regulators for cylinder-
mounting aren't unduly expensive and are often sold
for well under £10 at the time of writing.

Systems in motorcaravans built after 1 September 2003

The publication of new European Norms/British
Standards prompted changes in gas regulators and
the type of hose used to couple-up to cylinders. Here
are some of the main innovations:

• A new design of 'universal' regulator was developed
  that would operate using either butane or propane.
• A new standardised working pressure of 30mbar
  was introduced. Gas appliances now being installed

ⓘ Technical Tip

Neither propane screw couplings nor Calor clip-on couplings
have sealing washers. However, if you use a screw-on
butane regulator to suit Calor's 4.5kg butane cylinder, it
has a washer which *must* be changed regularly. A packet
of three washers costs pennies rather than pounds. Some
motorcaravanners think they can reuse the washer fitted
in the screw-on cap that's supplied with a refilled 4.5kg
cylinder. *Don't!* It's not made of the correct compound and
will soon be the source of a leak.

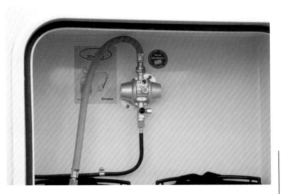

Since 2003 motorcaravans have usually been built with a wall-mounted 30mbar regulator. Customers choose their hose.

are set to work at this pressure and are labelled accordingly.

• The new 30mbar regulators are almost always fixed on the wall or ceiling of gas cylinder lockers, thereby forming part of a motorcaravan's factory-installed supply system. This practice means that regulators now receive manufacturers' soundness checks, together with the rest of the installation, before leaving the factory.

• The only component which a new owner has to purchase is a factory-made *high pressure* coupling hose with crimp-fit connectors. These connectors are important, and the types of hose clips hitherto used on low pressure hoses must not be fitted.

• High pressure hoses with different couplings are now manufactured. Whereas the connector for coupling to a wall-mounted regulator is standard, the connector on the other end has to suit the owner's choice of gas cylinder.

• Although there are coupling hoses to suit most types of cylinder connections used throughout Europe, a few systems require the owner to purchase an adaptor.

• Notwithstanding the benefits offered by wall-mounted regulators, a few German manufacturers (eg Dethleffs) still supply cylinder-mounted regulators instead. Although the latest types are 30mbar regulators handling both butane and propane, they still have to suit the owner's preferred type of cylinder.

Problems with the new system

The change to wall-mounted, butane/propane 30mbar regulators together with a high pressure coupling hose offers improved convenience when travelling in Europe. However, since the introduction of the new system there have been several incidents where

To minimise the chance of contaminated condensation running into a system, a 30mbar regulator should be high up.

Although regulators are now mostly wall-mounted, in this 2006 Dethleffs a 30mbar cylinder-mounting type is supplied.

Problems of gas blockages and evidence of an 'oily liquid' getting into systems was first reported around 2004.

motorcaravanners have experienced gas blockages and the consequent failure of their appliances.

There have also been reports of an 'oily liquid' appearing in the gas supply pipes as shown in the accompanying photograph. Intense investigation and laboratory analysis of the curious liquid has revealed that it contains a plasticising agent. It subsequently transpired that this was the product used in the manufacture of flexible rubberised hoses. It was duly concluded that this liquid was the cause of diaphragm failures in faulty regulators and the subsequent blockages.

A document published in January 2007 by The National Caravan Council (NCC) and available on the Council's website explained that in some circumstances, condensation seems to form in high pressure coupling hoses. With the passage of LPG, the condensate subsequently absorbs the plasticising agent used in the manufacture of flexible hoses. Furthermore, when a fixed regulator is mounted *lower* than the supply cylinder outlet, the resulting 'oily substance' is then able to trickle down the hose and enter a regulator's mechanism. This affects its performance and blockages might follow later.

In response to NCC recommendations, dealers are now remounting regulators at higher points in gas lockers so that any condensation can then run back into the cylinder rather than into the regulator. In addition, Gaslow has introduced a semi-flexible stainless steel pipe fitted with reinforcing ribs and covered with a steel braid. This is completely free of plasticising compounds and acts as a logical alternative to traditional rubber-composition coupling hose.

Time will tell whether these recommended measures will end the blockage problems and The National Caravan Council concedes that the phenomenon was totally unexpected. The published document also affirms that there is no inherent fault in either LPG or the individual components. It is interesting to note, too, that blockages don't seem to occur in systems that employ cylinder-mounted regulators.

Changeover systems

It's a poor design feature if a motorcaravan's gas locker only has space to accommodate one gas cylinder. Motorcaravanners need a subsidiary back-up supply, and when two cylinders are installed some owners have a manual or automatic changeover device fitted as well. This permits hasty switching when a supply cylinder runs out and eliminates the immediate need for disconnection. Several products are manufactured and there are changeovers to suit many combinations, including:

• Systems conforming to earlier British Standards with cylinder-mounted regulators
• Post-2003 supply systems with a 30mbar wall-mounted regulator
• Post-2003 supply systems with a wall-mounted regulator matched with a pair of Gaslow's refillable cylinders
• Post-2003 supply systems with a wall-mounted regulator and supplied by one Gaslow refillable cylinder paired with one normal propane cylinder.

As stated earlier, LPG is certainly a convenient product to use but it helps to have a knowledge of the gas supply components that enable you to get the best from your system.

Gaslow's semi-rigid stainless steel pipe, with or without a red handwheel, is often fitted instead of a rubberised hose.

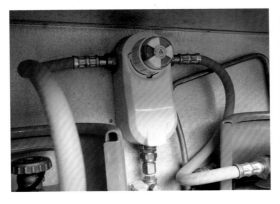

A variety of cylinder changeover devices is available, both for pre- and post-2003 gas supply systems.

CHAPTER FIFTEEN

COOKING AND HEATING

Although the majority of motorcaravans are fitted with gas-operated cooking and heating appliances, 230V hot plates and 12V fans are often fitted as well. In addition, there's increasing interest in appliances that run on petrol or diesel fuel drawn from the base vehicle's tank.

253

The stylish kitchen in this Auto-Trail Cheyenne is equipped with a large domestic stove.

Most British motorcaravanners like a hob fitted with a grill but few imported models offer this facility.

The increasing popularity of motorcaravanning throughout Europe has resulted in a lively export and import market. British-built models are purchased abroad just as some owners in this country drive motorcaravans manufactured in Belgium, France, Germany, Italy, Slovenia and Spain. However, this burgeoning interchange of products has drawn attention to national differences and the contrasting requirements of owners.

In Britain, for example, the majority of motorcaravanners want good cooking facilities, kitchen worktop space and a grill for their toast. Equally they expect to have electronic ignition to light the burners on their hob and consider that matches and hand-held devices are hardly appropriate in costly habitation vehicles. These expectations pose a problem for UK residents planning to purchase an imported model.

For example, German motorcaravans are often characterised by impressive washrooms bespangled with lights, in complete contrast to kitchens that are small and poorly equipped. That's what owners in that country usually want because they frequently take meals in restaurants and bars. Even though barbecues are popular, cooking indoors is low on the holiday agenda. In fact many Continental motorcaravans only have hobs offering two or three burners. Moreover, if their kitchens include an oven

Below right: The kitchen in this Dethleffs Esprit is pleasingly spacious but it doesn't include a four-burner hob with a grill.

Below: This tiny oven fitted in a Knaus Sport coachbuilt doesn't meet the expectations of many British owners.

it's usually small, worktop space is limited and grills are seldom installed.

You'll find exceptions, of course, and some UK importers add extra appliances retrospectively to meet the expectations of British clients. Conversely, British manufacturers whose models are built for export have different interior specifications designed to suit the contrasting wishes of foreign buyers.

One element which is universal, however, is the design of the supply system that serves gas-operated appliances. In this respect, check the accompanying panel describing supply control valves.

Having described the dissimilar expectations of owners, let's take a cook's tour of some kitchens.

Closing the sink and hob glass lids is the only way to obtain worktop space in this imported motorhome.

Technical Tip

Supply control valves

Since motorcaravans are usually equipped with several gas-operated appliances, a supply system is constructed to suit the provision. Typically a main trunk pipe from the cylinder and regulator subdivides into branches, thus providing individual supplies to individual appliances. To isolate separate items you'll normally find a bank of gas valves that control their operation. Isolation valves should be labelled and their designation is usually repeated in the owners' manual.

If you purchase a pre-owned motorcaravan and find the labels are missing, you can often follow the route of each branch pipe with the help of a torch and a mirror. When the respective functions have been noted, you can confirm your findings by igniting each appliance individually and then trying its shut-off valve. Having completed this check it's sensible to then add your own labels.

Many hobs fitted in imported models have to be lit using either a match or a hand-held igniter.
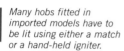

HOBS AND GRILLS

In all recently-built European motorcaravans it's obligatory for the burners on hobs to be fitted with a flame-failure device (FFD). On these burners, a small probe derives heat from the flame and creates a small electric current, which holds open an electro-magnetic gas valve. As the panel on page 185 describing FFDs explains, if a draught extinguishes the flame the probe cools, a coil spring in the gas valve shuts off the supply, and gas can't escape from the burner. It's a useful safety system. However, after lighting a burner its probe takes a moment to get warm – that's why you have to depress a control knob for a few seconds when a burner is first lit. Although they're a standard feature nowadays older hobs lack FFDs, but there's no requirement to update them retrospectively.

A close inspection of the burners may also reveal a second probe, which is a spark igniter. You'll seldom find these fitted on Cramer hobs, which were originally manufactured in Germany. If your motorhome has one of these you'll either have to purchase matches or a purpose-made igniter. Dometic, the latest owner of the company, has made assurances that Cramer hobs can be ordered with built-in spark igniters; in reality, few Continental manufacturers request this option.

On a different note, some British hobs are now being manufactured with a 230V hotplate amidst the gas burners. Moreover, drawing from practices adopted on narrowboats a ceramic hob that runs on diesel fuel has been introduced by Webasto for motorcaravan installation. It remains to be seen how popular these products become.

The diesel-driven ceramic top hob from Webasto is often fitted in canal boats.

As regards grills, these are normally only fitted to British motorcaravans, although some importers add them to foreign motorhomes as soon as they arrive at their UK showrooms. Most Continental manufacturers don't fit a hob with an integrated grill and it seems that motorcaravanners from other European countries see no use for them. One can only presume that they've yet to discover the pleasure of toast.

Finally, please read the accompanying panel on heating and hobs.

(i) Safety Tip

Heating and hobs

Never use a hob to act as a space-heating appliance. Admittedly, when a kettle is boiled or a saucepan is in use the living space gets warmer, but in some kitchens heat rising from a burner that isn't covered by a pan is sufficient to damage a locker or shelf fitted above it.

As a second safety warning, note that if the gas/air mix on a hob is slightly out of adjustment there's a possibility that small quantities of carbon monoxide are present in the products of combustion. For instance, if you find that the underside of cooking implements gets badly covered with soot this is a warning that the flame is incorrect. Get the hob checked by a qualified gas engineer at once.

That's why leaving an incorrectly adjusted hob running as a heater for a prolonged period can be extremely dangerous. A short article in a South Wales newspaper reported how two people did this in a campervan to keep warm at night; both were found dead in the morning.

Many British coachbuilts such as this Avondale Seascape are fitted with a large cooker complete with hob, grill and oven.

Above: Some owners are content with compact cooking appliances in their motorhome.

Below: Microwave ovens are being fitted more frequently but normally they'll need to run on a 230V hook-up.

OVENS

Whether you need an oven in a motorcaravan is a personal matter – some people who have a full-size domestic cooker at home don't often use it. That said, many British manufacturers install large cookers in coachbuilt motorhomes which undoubtedly claim a significant part of a vehicle's payload. Smaller products are normally confined to small coachbuilt models and van conversions; some don't offer an oven at all.

Microwave ovens have also gained in popularity and these have both supporters and detractors. Some owners contend that a microwave oven fitted at head height is dangerously situated when you're reaching for a hot mug of coffee. Others point out that you need a generous 230V supply to run a microwave, adding that the current draw is particularly high during the start-up period in a cooking cycle.

As far as the provision of ovens is concerned, some owners use their oven a lot, others don't want one at all. This makes things difficult for a manufacturer endeavouring to supply kitchen appliances that everyone likes.

(i) Technical Tip

Electrical consumption of microwave ovens

The cooking power of a microwave oven is often expressed in watts – a medium-sized product might be rated at 600W: compact models are 450W. This relates to their *output*.

However, motorcaravanners owning a microwave oven need to establish its *input* requirements, especially if they want to purchase a portable generator. To calculate this, a rough rule of thumb is to double the output and then subtract 10 per cent. In other words the absolute minimum wattage required from a generator to run a 600W microwave oven is 1,080W (1,200 watts – 120 = 1,080 watts).

SPACE HEATERS

The term 'gas fire' has long been superseded for good reason. Moreover, the word 'heater' is imprecise because motorcaravans are often fitted with two – one is a water heater, the other heats the living space.

This cutaway display unit shows how the burners in modern heaters are mounted in a room-sealed enclosure.

Gas fires

Thirty or so years ago caravans and motorhomes were often fitted with a 'gas fire'. These appliances had an exposed burner, and this was potentially dangerous. For example, a gas burner needs oxygen, and that was simply taken from the living area. Equally, there was no flue to discharge the products of combustion to the outside world. They were merely released into the living space.

Such fires were often lit with a match and risks of carbon monoxide emissions – described above in respect of hobs – were potentially a source of danger. This prompted the introduction of 'room-sealed' heaters.

Room-sealed space heaters

A 'room-sealed' heater has these features:

- The gas burner is mounted inside a sealed enclosure
- A duct or specially constructed inlet draws oxygen into the enclosure from *outside* the living space
- The products of combustion are returned directly outside via a flue system

Technical Tip

Exposed flame gas fires

If you buy an older motorcaravan fitted with a gas fire that has exposed flames and no permanently installed flue, get it removed and scrapped at once. It might even cause a fatality, and if it hasn't been checked by a qualified gas engineer do *not* use it.

It's much safer to discharge combustion fumes externally via either a wall- or roof-mounted flue.

This heat exchanger in a Truma heater includes an inspection port to show when the burner's alight.

- When the sealed enclosure gets hot, it warms up the air around it
- The enclosure, called a 'heat exchanger', is designed to release its heat efficiently into the living space
- There is either a warning light or a sealed inspection port to show that the main burner is alight
- A room-sealed heater can normally be left in operation all night – however, confirm that this is the case either by checking the Owner's Manual or seeking advice from a dealer.

Understandably, you can't light a burner using a match when it's mounted inside a sealed chamber. Instead, an efficient and reliable ignition system is utilised, and provided you have your heater serviced regularly neither Piezo nor electronic ignition systems are likely to fail.

Types of heater

Van conversions are often equipped with either compact gas heaters manufactured by Propex or the E Series products from Truma. These don't take-up wall space and can even be mounted in a small locker. Although the output of the Trumatic E 4000 fan-driven version achieves a useful 3.7kW, this type of product isn't normally used for heating the spacious interiors of larger coachbuilt models.

For that reason, many coachbuilt motorcaravans are fitted with wall-mounted room-sealed gas heaters

The E-Series blown air heaters from Truma incorporate a balanced flue/air intake and fit into very small spaces.

and the output of some models is augmented by a subsidiary mains-powered electrical element. The Trumatic S range is a popular example and models in the range offer thermal output levels from 1.85 to 5.5kW.

Apart from the fact that they take up wall space, these heaters are efficient performers. However, a separate water heater is also required, and these are described later in this chapter.

A third category of gas heaters, often known as 'Combination' or 'Combi' products, integrate both space and water heating tasks within one appliance. The Truma C range is one of the best-known examples, whereas Atwood's combination heater was withdrawn from production several years ago.

Depending on the model, Truma Combination heaters achieve thermal outputs between 2.0 and 6.0kW. They include a mains facility for alternative water heating, but it should be noted that some models don't include a 230V facility for space heating. In other words if your gas supply runs out unexpectedly this can leave you cold in winter.

Domestic fan heaters

Recognising that gas supplies can run out at inopportune moments, some owners take a small 230V portable domestic fan heater on winter trips as a back-up. These should be operated via a vehicle's RCD and MCB-protected mains system, described in Chapter Twelve. Whether the use of a 230V portable product in a confined space is a wise strategy is a matter of debate.

There are other considerations too. Many mains hook-up supplies at campsites don't provide sufficient current to run a domestic heater in the way you would at home. The amperage available at sites varies enormously and a 230V fan heater may overload a site supply if used on more than its lowest setting (see Chapter Twelve). That said, many owners exercise the appropriate caution and use one of these heaters if their gas system fails.

Truma wall-mounted appliances such as this one fitted in a Swift Sundance are efficient space heaters.

Not all models in the Truma C Range of combination heaters include a 230V space-heating facility.

Many winter users pack a domestic fan heater as a back-up item, but its consumption may be too great for some sites.

Most space heaters are fitted with a network of pipes so that warm air can be distributed throughout the living space.

To achieve an equitable distribution of ducted air throughout the living area, some heaters have an adjusting control.

Electrical assistance

The effectiveness of gas heaters is often enhanced by distributing their warm air through a system of ducts with the help of a 12V fan. This also enables you to heat a separate shower room and to control temperatures in other zones.

In spite of this you sometimes find that one end of a motorcaravan is cooler than the other. If that's the case, some heaters have a balance control fitted on the main duct at the point where it splits into two separate routeways. Some Carver and Truma wall-mounted heaters have this control adjacent to the fan itself. This may be hard to reach and some owners are unaware that it exists. A good owner's manual should provide you with details.

As regards the inclusion of fixed 230V space-heating elements in gas appliances, the operation of these is influenced by the same constraints applicable to domestic fan heaters. Moreover in some (but not all) gas heaters the electrical element can be operated simultaneously when the gas burner's alight. In the case of recent Trumatic S3002(P) wall heaters fitted with an additional

Several gas heaters can be fitted with a supplementary 230V element such as this Truma Ultraheat unit.

 **Useful Tip**

Spare parts

Two names traditionally associated with space and water heaters are 'Carver' and 'Truma'. In the mid-1980s the German company Truma supplied many components to Carver, which was based in Warwickshire. When this co-operative venture terminated the companies carried on independently. However, in the late 1990s Carver ceased production.

The supply of spare parts for many of Carver's products was then taken over by Truma, although this service might not continue much longer. However, a close replica of Carver's Crystal Water heater is now being manufactured and sold as the Henry GE. Some parts of this new appliance might be suitable for use in older Carver heaters.

The situation is less satisfactory with regard to Atwood combination heaters, which were fitted by several UK manufacturers including Murvi. Although the parent US company had established an Atwood base in Europe, this unexpectedly closed. Purchasers of pre-owned motorhomes fitted with these heaters find it hard to obtain spare parts.

Ultraheat electric element, different combinations of operation offer you:

500W from the electric element	Subject to site amperage
1kW from the electric element	
2kW from the electric element	
3kW (controllable) from the gas system	
Up to 5kW from the combined systems	

For winter sports enthusiasts this versatility is notably beneficial.

Wet heating systems
A few motorcaravans are fitted with a central heating system that uses radiators. The efficient 3000 Compact Alde system, for example, is highly regarded and is often installed in top specification models.

WATER HEATERS
Many small 'van conversions don't have the space to fit a water heater. This isn't a serious shortcoming and few campervan owners complain about boiling a kettle to produce hot water for washing-up. However, owners of coachbuilt models usually have higher expectations.

A large number of motorhomes are currently fitted with a Truma Ultrastore water heater.

A few older motorcaravans still have 'instantaneous water heaters' such as the appliances from Paloma and Rinnai. These operate with exposed burners and often have internal flue diffusers so they're no longer installed in new models. Instead, storage water heaters are preferred and the Truma Ultrastore is widely fitted.

That said, a lot of owners have fond memories of the Carver Crystal storage water heater, which was sold with and without a 230V heating option. Some motorcaravanners also believe that its installation is more compact than Truma's Ultrastore and the launch of the Henry GE certainly pleased many owners of older motorhomes. The fact that the Henry GE adopts the dimensions of its Carver predecessor means that a replacement appliance can be installed in the original compartment. The cut-out in the side of a vehicle doesn't need alteration either.

Another available storage heater with a well-established background is the Maxol Malaga. This has also been sold bearing a Belling Badge.

Regardless of different product detailing, one thing is common to all storage water heaters and that's the importance of draining them down before the arrival of frosty weather. Frost damage was described in Chapter Ten and water heaters may be irreparably affected if these precautionary measures are ignored.

A Henry GE water heater can be easily fitted in the place formerly occupied by a Carver Crystal product.

(i) Technical Tip

Payload considerations

Water is heavy and some motorcaravanners drain down a water heater before taking to the road. This might seem over-cautious but it's not a misplaced strategy if your vehicle is running close to its Gross Vehicle Weight. A Carver Cascade holds 9 litres (2 gallons), thereby taking up 9kg (19.8lb) of payload. A Truma Ultrastore has either a 10- or 14-litre capacity, which will add 10kg (22lb) or 14kg (30.9lb) to your load.

SAFETY

System safety checks

When you buy a new motorcaravan, its gas appliances will comply with the European regulations applicable to LPG appliances in leisure vehicles. In addition to a CE marking on the label, documents provided with your purchase will confirm their compliance with European Norms/British Standards and the fact that a qualified gas engineer has inspected and approved their installation.

Things are seldom as straightforward when you purchase a second-hand motorcaravan. Ideally, a pre-owned 'van will be supplied with a recently signed and dated certificate to confirm the integrity of the supply system and its appliances. If that's missing, a good service centre can arrange for a safety inspection to be carried out and will issue signed/dated documents to verify that the gas system is in safe working order.

This checking procedure should always be carried out before putting a pre-owned motorcaravan into commission. It only needs an appliance's gas and air mixture to be incorrect and there's a risk that carbon monoxide might be emitted. For peace of mind many owners also fit one of the carbon monoxide alarms sold at dealers and DIY stores.

Also bear in mind that a motorcaravan's gas appliances aren't used regularly throughout the year. During periods of inactivity it's not unusual for insects, moths and spiders to get into the air intakes or flues. In some instances this can upset the delicate air/gas balance; it can also upset the ignition process. For example, a pilot flame on a space heater might ignite but you subsequently find that the main burner then fails to fire-up. This is usually caused by obstructions – even a spider's web spun around the cowl on a roof-mounted flue can upset a heater's ignition process.

There's no doubt that routine and regular servicing of all gas appliances is essential and owners should

Modern gas heating appliances are complex products and DIY repairs should not be attempted.

265

Operating pressures

Appliances are built to operate at specific gas pressures and the recent change in standards and the labelling of products was discussed in Chapter Fourteen. This earlier chapter describes the purpose of gas regulators and the fact that today's products, which are designed to run at 30mbar, must not be fitted into older motorcaravans built with different systems.

Both the igniter and flame-failure device on a gas burner need cleaning and resetting periodically by a trained fitter.

check their manufacturers' advice for information about the nature and frequency of these operations.

Bear in mind, however, that within a four-hour standard habitation service appliances are only checked to see that they're working correctly. This basic service doesn't involve the disassembly of heating appliances and the cleaning of their internal components. That's usually an additional service, as it is with refrigerators.

Note, too, that the designs of modern heaters are complex and servicing work should never be tackled by an unqualified person. Furthermore, if you don't have the work carried out by a competent, trained gas specialist, important elements like gas ignition may cease to operate properly.

DIESEL AND PETROL HEATING

Pleasure boats and the cabs of long-distance lorries have been fitted with diesel-fuelled heating systems for many years, but it wasn't until 1998 that Murvi Motorcaravans worked closely with Eberspächer, a diesel heating specialist, to create a similar system for installation in Murvi van conversions. This later drew interest from manufacturers of larger models and in 2000 the author's self-built motorcaravan was the first UK coachbuilt to be equipped with an Eberspächer combined air and water heating system.

These products normally use diesel fuel drawn from the base vehicle's tank, although the company also makes similar units that run on petrol. Today, an increasing number of motorcaravans are equipped with diesel rather than gas heating systems, and these are supplied by Eberspächer and Webasto.

Broadly speaking there are three levels of provision:

1. Warm-air space heaters
Examples of these compact, enclosed appliances include Webasto's Air Top 2000, 3500 and

5000 fan heaters. The fan-driven Air Top 2000S is sufficiently compact to fit under a cab seat and is used by several van converters, including Middlesex Motorcaravans. Similar products include Eberspächer's Airtronic D2 (2.2kW) and D4 (4kW), which are often fitted under lounge seats in motorcaravans from Auto-Sleepers and Romahome. Recently Eberspächer also launched a system that pairs-up an Airlectric 230V unit achieving a 1kW output with an Airtronic heater.

A Webasto fan-driven diesel heater is compact enough to be fitted under the seat in most commercial cabs.

2. Combined water and space heater units

These are manufactured in several forms. The Eberspächer Combitronic Compact is enclosed in a casing that's often mounted under the floor. Choosing this location frees-up space in the living quarters and its components include a hot-water cylinder. The Combitronic has been installed in Autocruise CH coachbuilt motorhomes.

3. Combitronic Modular linked with base vehicle's cooling system

In this arrangement, the individual heating assemblies remain as separate modules for installation where the designer thinks best. In some circumstances there can even be a link with the base vehicle and that affords additional benefits.

The Eberspächer Airlectric 230V unit, which achieves a 1kW output, can be coupled to an Airtronic diesel heater.

In this Webasto installation, water heated by diesel fuel is taken to small radiators with fans mounted in the living area.

A coupled design involves extending the vehicle's water-cooling system so that hot-water pipes from the engine run through the living area too. Just as vehicle cabs have dash-mounted heaters distributing heat from the engine, an extended arrangement adds further small radiators with fans to distribute warm air in the living area.

In addition, piped hot water drawn from the engine runs through a coil in a copper cylinder to heat water for the shower, sink and wash basin. Effectively this is a miniature version of the copper cylinders fitted in many people's homes, and, like the ones in houses, the small Eberspächer cylinder also has a 1kW immersion heater that runs using a 230V hook-up as well.

While the vehicle is being driven, the engine creates hot water which circulates through both the copper cylinder and the fan-assisted space heaters. However, when the vehicle is parked and the engine switched off, Eberspächer's compact Hydronic boiler – usually mounted out of sight

Below: Sheathed in insulation foam, Eberspächer's copper cylinder with an immersion heater stores very hot water.

Right: Hydronic diesel heaters from Eberspächer can be fitted in the engine compartment. They have an impressive output.

Panels with Eberspächer space- and water-heating systems offer an impressive array of control options.

near the sump – can then be activated to take over the heating duties. An Eberspächer Hydronic heating system can be operated safely while you're driving, and that's a great help when the weather is cold.

Operation is controlled by a multi-function panel that can be activated manually as well as programmed to operate for up to three different periods in 24 hours; the timing facility can also embrace a seven-day operating regime. Remote control units are optional extras; so is a telephone activation feature.

Of course, some modular systems are fitted to run wholly independently of the base vehicle but if an Eberspächer installation is linked to a vehicle's cooling system the owner can then use a Hydronic unit to pre-heat the engine in winter. It can also work in conjunction with a dashboard heater so that a snow-covered screen can be cleared when the system is manually switched or activated by remote control. These facilities are extremely useful.

Conclusion
Diesel heaters are remarkably economical and mean that you only need LPG to run your fridge, hob, grill and oven. You therefore only need to carry smaller cylinders, which offers a weight-saving benefit, though this is usually offset by the larger Ah battery needed to run most diesel heater units and their air distribution fans.

One criticism is that some people find the noise of a diesel-fired system irritating, though others are more tolerant of it.

Gas appliances are undoubtedly the most common products used for heating motorcaravans, but diesel and electrical systems are now attractive alternatives.

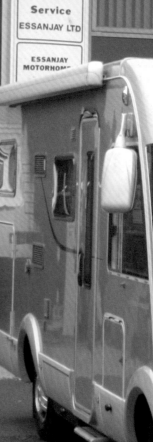

CHAPTER SIXTEEN

SERVICING AND
MOT TESTING

All motorists understand the importance of keeping a car serviced, safe, and MoT tested. However, in the case of a motorcaravan, there's another precautionary measure that owners have to take, and that's to have its conversion elements checked. The procedure is normally referred to as a 'habitation service', much of which relates to health and safety matters.

271

Some commercial vehicle workshops don't have sufficient access to accommodate large motorcaravans.

To conduct vehicle and habitation service operations, a ramp or inspection pit is an important facility.

The base on which a motorcaravan is built shares many features with other private passenger vehicles. For instance, it will be sold with an owner's manual, a service booklet and a list of approved service centres. But there's a snag. One might be misled into thinking that an international address list of commercial dealers would be just what owners of motorcaravans need. Unfortunately that's not the case. Many commercial service centres are often unable to accommodate motorcaravans because they're simply too large for their workshops.

A similar problem often occurs when a Ministry of Transport (MoT) test is needed. Approved test stations sometimes can't help because a vehicle is too tall for their workshop; unsuitable ramps, the position of a rolling road for brake testing and insufficient manoeuvring space also conspire to make things difficult. Not surprisingly, issues like this aren't always made clear when you take ownership of a motorcaravan.

Height nearly turned out to be a problem at this MoT station, which is otherwise able to test Class IV vehicles.

In response to this, the magazine, *Motorcaravan Motorhome Monthly* periodically publishes a list entitled 'Base Vehicle Servicing and MoT

Technical Tip

Base vehicle servicing and MoT

Further guidance about centres able to help motorcaravanners:
- In some areas, health authority ambulance servicing depots have started to carry out service operations and MoT tests on private vehicles. Check your local telephone directory.
- British Telecom (BT) motor transport workshops are sometimes able to service private vehicles.
- A local Road Transport Enforcement Department of the Vehicle Inspectorate is usually able to advise where heavy goods vehicles can be serviced and will give locations of MoT stations equipped to carry out Class IV MoT testing. Check your local telephone directory for Vehicle Inspectorate numbers. Additional information on the MoT test and the Vehicle & Operator Services Agency (VOSA) is given on pages 106-107.

The rollers for MoT brake testing aren't always positioned to accommodate the wheels on large motorcaravans.

– Motorhome-friendly garages'. At the time of writing this is a five-page compilation of readers' submissions listing 278 centres in 71 counties and major British cities. Each entry is accompanied by brief comments in which contributors describe their experiences.

Reprints of the latest *Motorcaravan Motorhome Monthly* listing can be obtained by telephoning 01778 391187. It's an invaluable guide for owners of large motorcaravans in general and coachbuilt models in particular. The accompanying 'Technical tip' panel adds further advice to anyone searching for suitable servicing facilities.

VEHICLE SERVICING OPERATIONS

It would be impossible here to list all the servicing operations applicable to base vehicles used for motorcaravans. Detailed schedules are often available from franchised dealers and succinct guidance is normally included in the service packs included with new vehicles.

Elements such as oil and filter changes form part of the routine operations, as do precautionary measures such as changing a cam belt. In many vehicles this is carried out on the basis of mileage covered as well as years in use. However, unlike commercial users, motorcaravan owners don't normally notch up high annual mileages, so it's usually age rather than mileage that decides when a vehicle's cam belt needs replacing. On some vehicles this should be done every five years and it's a requirement important to note. If a cam belt breaks, considerable

Above right: Changing filters and lubricants is among the many tasks involved in a base vehicle service.

Above: Tiny cracks were just starting to appear on this Fiat Ducato cam belt after five years in use.

engine damage can occur and repair costs are often extraordinarily high.

Servicing work on a base vehicle's engine, transmission and running gear are all-important but some issues relate to the conversion itself. So essentially there are two areas of attention:

1 Work on the base vehicle
2 Work on the conversion, referred to as 'habitation servicing'.

Motorcaravans built on AL-KO Kober chassis

Although a large number of coachbuilt models are built on Fiat's base vehicles, it was stated in Chapter Three that on many Ducatos and Peugeot Boxers the original chassis is sometimes removed before building a motorhome. An AL-KO Kober motorhome chassis is then fitted in its place, which means that the motorcaravan's rear axle runs on AL-KO's torsion bar suspension rather than its original springs.

Where there's been an alteration like this it's understandable that a Fiat servicing centre is unlikely to carry out checks and greasing operations on a product made by a different manufacturer. So who carries out these important operations?

To assist motorcaravanners, AL-KO Kober has a national network of service centres to assist owners of vehicles fitted with their chassis. Alternatively this part of a vehicle's servicing work can be carried out if you have a habitation service performed by a dealer who's a member of the Approved Workshop scheme, the first area of attention listed on an Approved Workshop service schedule sheet being 'Underbody' issues.

Whether work on an AL-KO chassis and suspension is included in a habitation service conducted by a dealer that isn't a member of the Approved Workshop scheme is something a customer would need to check. For instance, a habitation service specialist might reasonably claim that servicing

AL-KO Kober has a network of approved service centres that's useful to note if your motorhome is built on an AL-KO chassis.

suspension elements is hardly a 'living area' issue and should logically be included when base vehicle servicing is carried out. Either way, it's an area of attention that mustn't be overlooked – which is why it's included in Approved Service centre 'habitation service' schedules. So, too, are checks of body-to-chassis mountings.

Challenges linked with base vehicle service operations

Tasks like changing air filters in an engine compartment require good access and this is provided by base vehicle manufacturers when designing engine compartments and their bonnets. In the case of A-Class motorcaravans, however, bonnet lids form part of a glass reinforced plastic front panel designed by the converter rather than the vehicle manufacturer. Regrettably, there are some A-Class models where apertures intended to provide access to the engine bay are impracticably small. Some service specialists claim that one recent A-Class model yields insufficient space to replace an air filter when the bonnet is lifted.

A similar hindrance was noted on a recent coachbuilt model constructed on an AL-KO chassis. In this case the installation of underfloor water tanks completely obscured the axle tube's greasing points

Access to the engine on this 1999 Fiat Ducato is sensibly designed and filters are quite easy to change.

Access to the engine is good on this Hymer A-Class, but on some A-Class vehicles changing an air filter is a nightmare.

Carrying out an air pressure test on a gas supply system is an important safety element in a habitation service.

Flexible connecting hose can start to deteriorate over a period of years, and this is closely checked.

Low-level gas escape vents are checked to see that they're not obstructed; pipes are inspected as well.

which lubricate the torsion bar suspension units. Routine lubrication is not only essential for torsion bar operation; it is also a warranty requirement.

So converting a vehicle into a motorcaravan sometimes introduces servicing issues that don't become evident until later. That's why some potential purchasers seek advice from service centre staff to ascertain if servicing work is straightforward on a model they're planning to buy. Magazine technical tests also highlight such issues.

HABITATION SERVICE WORK

As pointed out earlier, a habitation service isn't merely restricted to safety checks within the living area. So let's look closely at the scope of the work.

In a full habitation service around 50 jobs need to be carried out, and this can take from three to four hours. In the schedules used by members of the Approved Workshop scheme these normally fall into the following categories:

1 **Underbody** – chassis, running gear, tanks, spare wheel, corner steadies.
2 **Ventilation** – openings, roof lights, fixed and opening ventilators, freedom of airflow, heating fan check.
3 **12V electrics** – road light operation, reflectors, fridge operation, interior lighting, leisure battery, wiring, fuses, pump, heater fans.
4 **Mains electrics** – inlet socket, connecting cable, earth bonding, RCD operation, permanent connections, visual and function check.
5 **Gas system and appliances** – leak test, regulator operation test, operation of appliances, pipe runs, flexible hose check/replacement, cylinder security, gas drop-out holes.
6 **Water system** – water pump, pressure/micro switch operation, grit filter cleaning, tap operation,

water filter, waste system, toilet seals, flush action, drain-down valves.

7 Fire safety – security alarms, smoke alarms, extinguisher type/expiry date, fire blanket location/ fixing.

8 Bodywork – sealant, door locks, hinges, body attachments, racks, aerials, locker boxes, floor panel condition, cab-seat swivel, furniture condition, window seals, blinds, rising roof (where fitted), damp test.

Optional work

Absorption refrigerator service
In a standard service, checks are carried out to verify that an absorption refrigerator is working properly on its three sources of power (described in Chapter Eleven). However, a full service of an absorption fridge as laid down by its manufacturers includes replacing the gas jet, realigning the igniter and cleaning the gas burner and flue. To accomplish these tasks, a service specialist will usually have to remove a fridge from a motorhome and transfer it to a workbench. The full operation incurs an additional fee, and fridge removal/reinstallation is sometimes a significant factor when determining the charge.

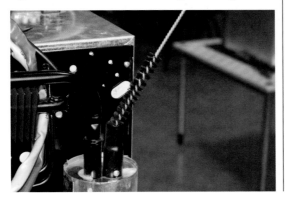

Where fitted, rising roof mechanisms are checked along with the security of accessories fitted to a motorhome body.

A fridge service is normally an 'optional extra'. To clean a burner tube usually involves removing the appliance.

Technical Tip

Independent specialists who can verify and issue certificates relating to the integrity of mains electricity and gas supply systems in leisure vehicles must have specific qualifications.

Mains electricity

To establish that a mains installation in a motorcaravan meets the latest technical requirements, an inspection can be carried out by either an approved contractor of the National Inspection Council for Electrical Installation Contracting (NICEIC), or a member of either the Electrical Contractors Association (ECA) or the Electrical Contractors Association of Scotland.

If there's no inspection certificate accompanying a pre-owned motorcaravan advertised for sale, it is in the purchaser's interests to arrange for the 'van to be inspected *before* the mains system is put into service. To find your nearest NICEIC specialist telephone 0171 582 7746, or to find an ECA member telephone 0171 229 1266.

Gas

The inspection of a gas supply system and the verification of its integrity should be carried out by a CORGI qualified specialist who has successfully completed a course which embraces training in LPG installations in leisure vehicles. CORGI stands for Council for Registered Gas Installers. Registration is a requirement for those who install and maintain LPG installations as laid down in the Gas Safety (Installation & Use) Regulations 1998.

Disassembly, cleaning and readjustment of gas heating appliances

When servicing is specified by the manufacturers of heating appliances, the work can also be included in a servicing operation for an additional fee.

Supply of Independent Certificates relating to the gas and electricity installations

At an Approved Workshop a standard service is carried out by experienced staff and certificates of the training courses they've attended must be placed on display in the service reception. However, if you wish to be supplied with separate gas and electricity approval certificates, workshops can arrange for appropriate independent contractors (described in the accompanying panel) to undertake the inspections. This will incur a further fee unless a service centre is large enough to employ staff who hold these industry-specific qualifications.

A professional calibrated damp meter is costly and several measures have to be taken to get meaningful readings.

Damp checks

An operation of particular importance included in a habitation service is a damp check. Like many other tasks, this has to be carried out annually in order to comply with the conditions laid down in a motorcaravan's conversion warranty. Even in older models, having routine damp tests carried out is strongly recommended; and while they're included in a habitation service, they can often be conducted by dealers as a separate operation, too.

Some owners wish to carry out checks themselves and several types of DIY damp-check meter are on sale. Unfortunately some of the cheaper products aren't always reliable, but few owners will want to spend a three-figure sum on a professional tester with its all-important percentage meter.

Even professionally calibrated models, which express moisture content as a percentage, aren't a lot of use in inexperienced hands. You need to know the conditions in which a meter will operate accurately and its results have to be interpreted correctly. For instance, in appropriate ambient temperatures readings between 0–15 per cent are considered acceptable. That's because there's natural moisture in some materials used in motorcaravan construction. However, readings between 16–20 per cent signify that further investigation is required, while readings over 20 per cent indicate zones where remedial work is urgently needed.

Readings are typically taken in 40 to 50 areas, and the findings should be recorded on line drawings and given to customers on completion of a test. Water ingress is always a matter of concern and the purpose of a damp check is to identify early signs of the incidence of moisture in the fabric of a motorcaravan. If damp is detected it's essential to take immediate action before it spreads. In fact anyone purchasing a pre-owned motorcaravan should enquire if a recent damp test report is included in the package. If it isn't, buyers should insist that one is obtained before they proceed with the purchase.

Service schedule

Working to a strict job list is important and when arranging to have your 'van serviced you should always ask to see the centre's service schedule *before* confirming the booking. Similarly, when the work is completed you should be given a copy of the completed schedule, signed, stamped and dated. This document should include comments arising from the technicians' scrutiny. For instance, early signs of condensation forming within a double-glazed window panel should be brought to an owner's attention.

These are standard procedures when a motorcaravan's habitation service is undertaken at an Approved Workshop. Unfortunately there have been incidences of non-accredited service 'specialists' completing the work but not providing customers with written documentation to confirm the operations they've carried out. That is wholly unsatisfactory.

Floor delamination

Where a bonded floor panel is fitted, a service check investigates if there's any sign of its plywood layers losing their bond with the insulation foam in the core. Composite 'sandwich' floors fitted in coachbuilt models are light, strong, and noted for good thermal insulation. However, their strength is badly compromised if the bonding adhesive fails and layers break away from each other. This is called 'delamination'. The condition can usually be cured if quick action is taken when a fault is detected. For this reason floor checking is included in habitation service work.

If a light bulb is found faulty during a habitation service, it's usually replaced as a matter of course.

Minor repairs and authorisations

When a service is carried out, it's not unusual for a technician to find faulty items. For example, an interior light might need a new bulb or a replacement fluorescent tube. Many centres will replace such small items as long as there's time to do the job within the allotted period for a service. And whilst the cost of small components will obviously be added to the invoice, most owners prefer such small jobs to be carried out there and then.

Making more expensive replacements is a different matter and this prompts an issue to raise when arranging a service. Get the dealer's assurance that a technician won't embark on costly repairs without gaining your permission first. Of course, 'costly' is a bit vague so you might agree a cost limit, as well as asking the service receptionist what procedures are followed when a serious problem is encountered.

Choosing a reliable service specialist

In the first few years of a motorcaravan's life, conversion elements will be covered by a warranty. However, converters of vans and manufacturers will clearly specify that habitation service work has to be carried out in accordance with conditions set down in the owner's manual. When the need for a service approaches, you'll also need to make sure that your chosen service centre receives the full approval of your motorcaravan's manufacturer. If there's any doubt, call the customer helpline and request that they approve, in writing, your nominated specialist.

Approved Workshop scheme

In the past there have been examples of poor standards of workmanship when conducting habitation servicing. To resolve this, an initiative was launched by The Camping and Caravanning

Dealers who are members of the Approved Workshop scheme are required to display a tariff of service charges in their reception.

Club, The Caravan Club, and The National Caravan Council.

Lengthy discussions followed and a nation-wide chain of Approved Caravan Workshops was established in 1999. The idea proved successful, and in 2003 centres specialising in motorcaravan servicing were also brought into the scheme. At that point the name was changed to Approved Workshop.

Before being accepted into the scheme, service centres have to undergo a lengthy and elaborate inspection conducted by an independent agency. The appointed agency, Jones Vening Ltd, also administers the scheme on a day-to-day basis and publishes a list of approved centres on its internet website, www.jones-vening.co.uk. In addition, the three member-organisations given above provide information on their own websites. However, approvals aren't set in stone and re-examination inspections are conducted annually to ensure that standards are maintained.

The accompanying panel contains further information about the scheme. It undoubtedly provides owners with assurances of a high standard of workmanship, procedural consistency, a detailed invoice and a clear customer complaints procedure. Centres are also obliged to display a full tariff of charges in the service reception, and that's something owners often want to see before making a booking.

Conclusion

Having your motorcaravan's base vehicle and habitation elements serviced regularly is important. However, be aware of the seasonal nature of motorcaravanning and book your vehicle for servicing operations well in advance of busy spells. Service centres become extremely busy from early spring onwards.

Useful Tip

Approved Workshops

The number of Approved Workshops is ever-increasing, although it should be noted that some specialise in touring caravans rather than motorhomes.

In one information leaflet, the Approved Workshop scheme is described as 'rigorous, uncompromising and designed to offer you, the customer, an assurance of first class service and value for money.' This a praiseworthy intention and the scheme offers many benefits to motorcaravan owners.

Note: There is no implicit suggestion that workshops that are not members of the Approved Workshop scheme are unable to provide owners with a professional and high standard of service. Some most definitely do offer good service and workmanship; but there are others that don't.

CHAPTER SEVENTEEN

WINTER LAY-UP

Most modern motorcaravans are heated, well-insulated and able to provide comfortable accommodation during the cold months of the year. However, circumstances sometimes dictate that you don't have the time to use your vehicle in winter. Before it's put into storage, however, you need to carry out several de-commissioning tasks.

283

If you're unable to use your motorhome in winter, some pre-storage work must be done.

If a vehicle is parked for long spells, fatigue cracks can develop on the tyres' sidewalls.

Since all but a few campervans are sold with heaters, many owners use their motorcaravans all year round. From a technical point of view this is ideal: mechanical equipment develops faults if it isn't used on a regular basis.

Occasional driving

Even if you don't take up full residence, an occasional drive in your motorcaravan is strongly recommended. If left unused for long spells items can seize up, including components such as the brake mechanisms. Moreover, if a vehicle isn't moved the side-walls of tyres soon start to deteriorate. That's because particular sections of the tyres bear all the loads, and localised fatigue cracks will appear.

Relieving the weight completely is possible if a motorcaravan is fitted with four motorised LevelTronic jacks. These also act as an effective security system. However, a LevelTronic installation isn't cheap and periodically moving a motorcaravan half a metre or so to rotate the wheels is a way of reducing localised side-wall damage. Taking short drives is even better.

Naturally you wouldn't want to take a vehicle out for a routine drive when salt is liberally sprinkled on snow-covered roads. And even though winter sports enthusiasts often use snow chains on motorhomes, these are tiresome to fit. However, it's always in an owner's long-term interests to keep a vehicle in regular use.

Winter breaks

If you do decide to drive your vehicle *and* use the living space, don't forget that a growing number of UK campsites are open for most of the year. Some site owners also organise annual Christmas and New Year celebrations and these functions are so popular that they have to be booked well in advance.

Many retired motorcaravanners also use their vehicles as a 'second home', and as soon as the weather gets cold they book a ferry and head for the sun. Countries such as Portugal and southern Spain are especially popular with owners from Britain.

Storage

Notwithstanding the advisability of keeping a vehicle in service, a large number of owners are obliged to park their motorhomes for extended periods. Some are able to keep their vehicle

Snow chains are often used by winter motorcaravanners but they're not easy to fit.

Vehicle security is enhanced when a storage specialist offers indoor parking facilities.

alongside the house; others have to use a secure storage compound.

Of course, some storage facilities are more secure than others. For instance, the off-season compounds created in remote corners of campsites are seldom as secure as purpose-made facilities. Furthermore, before selecting a storage venue always check the conditions of your insurance policy.

Unfortunately there *have* been incidents where motorcaravans have been stolen from insecure compounds, and in 1999 this prompted the inauguration of a trade organisation concerned with vehicle storage. A national register of inspected and secure sites was then compiled and storage companies wishing to gain membership have to pass a rigorous inspection of the premises. Further information about this initiative is provided in the accompanying panel.

In a wider context, you can find caravan and motorhome storage specialists listed in *Yellow Pages*. Additionally, if you're a member of one of the national caravanning clubs these have address lists available.

Caravan Storage Site Owners' Association

Recognising the need to combat motorcaravan theft, a professional trade association was instituted in 1999 to represent caravan and motorhome storage owners. Known as CaSSOA (Caravan Storage Site Owners' Association), this professional body demands a high level of security at its members' storage centres.

The initiative is closely linked with insurance companies, many of which offer discounts on premiums if a motorcaravan is stored at one of the approved venues. The growing national chain of CaSSOA centres currently exceeds 600 members.

When a storage site owner applies for CaSSOA membership, an inspector checks the facility and successful applicants are issued with a gold, silver or bronze designation to reflect the level of security. Inspection criteria take note of features such as site location, protection from the elements, security, safety and control of access.

Your nearest CaSSOA-approved centre can be accessed through the organisation's website, www.cassoa.co.uk, or by telephoning 01159 349 826. Bear in mind that some storage sites only accommodate touring caravans; others impose limits on the size of vehicle. These are matters you need to check. Also remember that there are many other secure storage sites located around Britain that are not members of the CaSSOA scheme.

LAYING-UP A MOTORCARAVAN

If you have to leave your motorcaravan unused for a long period, there are several tasks you need to carry out. The following section provides some basic guidance; more detailed information on water, gas, and refrigeration systems is given in earlier chapters.

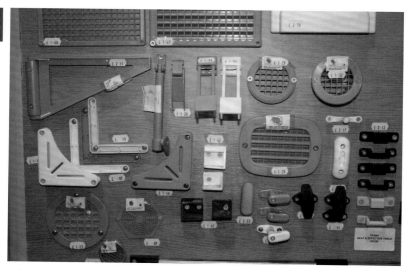

At the end of a season, there are often components in need of repair. It's a good discipline to get these replaced before parking-up your vehicle.

All taps have to be opened and the lever on this type of mixer tap must be centralised. The reason for this is explained in Chapter Ten.

Fresh water tanks are drained down in different ways. In this Swift Sundance's inboard container, a plug on a chain is merely withdrawn.

In this 2005 Dethleff's Esprit the water system is drained down by lifting a yellow lever that's conspicuously installed under a bench seat.

There's a red manual control to drain a Truma Combination heater, but it also works automatically and releases water when temperatures are low.

The water held captive in a taste filter cartridge can freeze, expand and split the casing. So remove the filter and buy a new one for later.

Even when it's drained, a waste tank's odour can creep up the pipes and enter the living area. So fit plugs in the sink, basin, and shower tray.

When all waste water and toilet flush water has been drained, it's a good time to add cleansing chemicals. A variety of types are sold for different purposes.

There are different ways to drain flushing water from bench and swivel-bowl toilets. This picture shows one of Thetford's 1990s bench-type models.

Just in case someone overlooked their toilet emptying duties at the end of the last trip, always remove the cassette for inspection.

Spray the rubber seal and cassette closure blade with Thetford's maintenance spray. Alternatively use olive oil, but no other types of lubricant.

When the cassette's replaced, always leave the release blade wide open. If closed, dampness on the blade causes it to stick firmly to the seal.

Interiors get damp easily and inexpensive dehumidifiers are often on sale. Leaving electric heaters running unattended is unwise.

When you've finished with an awning at the end of a season, check it's totally dry before packing it away. Mildew stains are hard to shift.

Dilemma! Leaving blinds down prevents the sun from fading interior fabrics, but blind manufacturers state that it weakens the recoil springs.

During a long lay-up, many owners transfer upholstery to a warm room in a house. This also makes a vehicle less likely to be stolen.

Once a refrigerator has been emptied the door should be left slightly ajar. Guidance on cleaning the interior is given in Chapter Eleven.

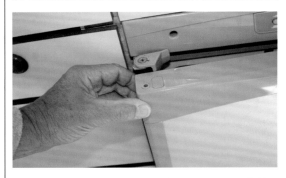

Motorcaravanners often remove a leisure battery during a lay-up period. When transferred to a bench its charge condition is easily monitored.

Check the cells in a lead-acid leisure battery, and if the liquid electrolyte doesn't quite cover the plates top them up with deionised water.

Engine batteries need to be kept in good condition and the trickle chargers used for Classic cars are also useful for motorhomes in storage.

A modern gas supply system is fitted with control valves on branches that serve different appliances. These should all be turned off.

If it's to be a long period of storage, it's strongly recommended that you remove gas cylinders. Important storage advice is given in Chapter Fourteen.

If you tow a trailer, spray an industrial lubricant like Tri-Flow on the plug and socket. Don't use WD40 here because it can react with this type of plastic.

Take precautions with regard to security, bearing in mind that some storage centres disallow devices that prevent a vehicle from being moved.

A few manufacturers make breathable covers to order. Both Specialised Accessories and Pro-Tec supply these products to motorhome owners.

Tip

Motorcaravan covers

If your motorcaravan is unused for extended spells, it might seem prudent to cover the roof with a large polythene sheet or plastic 'tarpaulin'. However, these materials sometimes attract damp, and condensation subsequently develops on the underside. In strong wind the flapping plastic can also damage paintwork and the surface of acrylic plastic windows.

Purpose-made motorcaravan covers manufactured using a breathable fabric are much better, even if a small amount of rain might penetrate some of the stitched seams. These products are also useful for keeping a vehicle free of green algae and bird droppings. However, you have to ensure that a motorcaravan is clean before fitting a cover because a film of dust acts as an abrasive when wind blows the fabric about. Some covers are costly, too, and can be quite a struggle to fit or remove – especially on large motorhomes with roof-mounted equipment.

Final notes

The list of tasks given above isn't claimed to cover every procedure appropriate for all kinds of motorcaravan. Other jobs might also be identified in your owner's manual, so check this with care because some of your appliances might be different from those discussed in this book.

If you've diligently carried out these close-of-season tasks, recommissioning your motorhome shouldn't take long. Before leaving home once again you'll want to set up your water system and try it out. Equally, you'll want to check fridge operation, the gas cooker, and so on, especially if you haven't managed to get your motorhome serviced. Add to this a tyre pressure check – not forgetting the spare – and you'll soon be ready to leave. Enjoy your return to the open road and the pleasures that lie just ahead.

CONTACT ADDRESSES

This address list was correct at the time of going to press. It includes specialist suppliers and manufacturers whose products and services have been mentioned in the text. Several of these firms have web sites which are easily found by using search engines.

As regards motorcaravan manufacturers and importers, the list in *Motorcaravan, Motorhome Monthly* magazine includes more than ninety addresses. Similar information is also published periodically in *Motor Caravan* Magazine, *Practical Motorhome* and *Which Motorcaravan*. Readers are strongly recommended to consult magazines for up-to date information on dealers, importers and manufacturers.

A.B. Butt Ltd,
Frog Island,
Leicester, LE3 5AZ
Tel: 0116 251 3344
(Solar systems and inverters)

ABP Accessories,
27 Nether End, Great Dalby,
Leicestershire, LE14 2EY
Tel: 08700 115111
(American RV accessories)

Adria Concessionaires,
Hall Street,
Long Melford,
Suffolk, CO10 9JP
Tel: 0870 774 0007
(Importer of High Top and
Coachbuilt models from
Slovenia)

A-Glaze paint sealant system
– See Creative Resins

Alde International (UK) Ltd,
14 Regent Park,
Booth Drive,
Park Farm South,
Wellingborough,
Northamptonshire, NN8 6GR
Tel: 01933 677765
(Central heating systems, gas
leak detector)

AL-KO Kober Ltd,
South Warwickshire Business
Park,
Kineton Road, Southam,
Warwickshire, CV47 0AL
Tel: 01926 818500
(AL-KO chassis and accessories)

Arc Systems,
13 Far Street,
Bradmore,
Nottingham,
NG11 6PF
Tel: 0115 921 3175
(Repair of all types of Carver
heater)

Autoglym,
Works Road,
Letchworth,
Hertfordshire,
SG6 1LU
Tel: 01462 677766
(Motorcaravan interior and
exterior cleaners)

Auto-Sleepers,
Orchard Works,
Willersey,
Nr. Broadway,
Worcestershire,
WR12 7QF
Tel: 01386 853338
(Wide range of van
conversions and coachbuilt
models)

Auto-Trail,
Trigano House,
Genesis Way,
Europarc,
Grimsby,
NE Lincolnshire,
DN37 9TU
Tel: 01472 571000
(Coachbuilt motorcaravans
and imported CI,
Rollerteam and Trigano
models)

Autovan Services Ltd,
32 Canford Bottom,
Wimborne,
Dorset,
BH21 2HD
Tel: 01202 848414
(Habitation inspection service
for buyers)

BeenyBox.co.uk,
Station Garage,
Trevu Road,
Camborne,
Cornwall,
TR14 7AE
Tel: 01209 711093
(Underfloor sliding storage
locker system)

Beetles UK Ltd, - See
Danbury Motorcaravans

Belling Appliances,
Talbot Road,
Swinton,
Rotherham,
South Yorkshire,
S64 8AJ
Tel: 01709 579900
Tel: 0870 458 4378
(Brochure hotline)
(Cookers, hobs and water
heaters)

Bilbo's Design,
Eastbourne Road, (A22)
South Godstone,
Surrey,
RH9 8JQ
Tel: 01342 892499
(Van conversions)

Bradleys,
Old Station Yard,
Marlesford,
Suffolk,
IP13 0AG
Tel: 01728 747900
(Mail Order supplier of ABS
repair kits and paint products
for plastic)

Brian James Trailers, Ltd,
Sopwith Way,
Drayton Fields Industrial
Estate,
Daventry,
Northamptonshire,
NN11 5PB
Tel: 01327 308833
(Car and other trailers)

British Car Auctions Ltd,
Sales & Marketing
Department,
Expedier House,
Portsmouth Road,
Hindhead,
Surrey,
GU26 6TJ
Tel: 01428 607440
(Motorcaravan auctions)

Brownhills,
Six UK branches
Tel: 0800 374941
(Wide range of British-built
and imported models)

**Bulldog Security Products
Ltd,**
Units 2, 3, & 4,
Stretton Road,
Much Wenlock,
Shropshire, TF13 6DH
Tel: 01952-728171/3
(Bulldog security devices and
posts)

C.A.K. - See Caravan
Accessories

Calor Gas Ltd,
Athena Drive,
Tachbrook Park,
Warwick, CV34 6RL
Tel: 0800 626626
(Supplier of butane, propane
and LPG products)

E.E. Calver Ltd,
Woodlands Park,
Bedford Road,
Clapham,
Bedford, MK41 6EJ
Tel: 01234 359584
(Indoor motorcaravan storage)

**The Camping & Caravanning
Club,**
Greenfields House,
Westwood Way,
Coventry, CV4 8JH
Tel: 024 7647 5448
(Club with large number of
motorcaravan members)

Campingaz
Coleman UK Inc.,
Gordano Gate,
Portishead,
Bristol, BS20 7GG
Tel: 01275 845024
(Supplier of Campingaz
butane and LPG appliances)

The Caravan Club
East Grinstead House,
East Grinstead,
West Sussex, RH19 1UA
Tel: 01342 326944
(Club with large number of
motorcaravan members)

**Caravan Accessories (C.A.K.
Tanks) Ltd,**
10 Princes Drive Industrial
Estate,
Kenilworth,
Warwickshire, CV8 2FD
Tel: 0870 757 2324
(Components, electrical
products, appliances, water
accessories)

The Caravan Centre,
Unit 3A,
Gilchrist Thomas Industrial
Estate,
Blaenavon, NP4 9RL
Tel: 01495 792700
(Specialist dealers supplying
caravan/motorhome parts)

Caravanparts.net,
Unit 5,
Grovehill Industrial Estate,
Beck View Road,
Beverley,
East Yorkshire, HU17 0JW
Tel: 01482 874878
(Supplier of the Henry-GE
water heater)

**The Caravan Seat Cover
Centre Ltd,**
Cater Business Park,
Bishopsworth,
Bristol, BS13 7TW
Tel: 0117 941 0222
(Seat covers, new foam, new
upholstery, made-to-measure
curtains)

Carcoon Storage Systems Int,
Orchard Mill,
2 Orchard Street, Salford,
Manchester, M6 6FL
Tel: 0161 737 9690
(Power & charge system: Mail
Order direct)

Carver products - See Miriad
Products and Truma (UK)

Cave and Crag,
Market Place, Settle,
North Yorkshire, BD24 9ED
Tel: 01729 823877
(Supplier of Kyham Tents and
annexe awnings)

Ceuta Healthcare,
41 Richmond Hill,
Bournemouth,
Dorset, BH2 6H7
Tel: 0800 0975606
(Milton sterilising products
and water treatment
additives)

**The Council for Registered
Gas Installers (CORGI),**
1 Elmwood, Chineham Park,
Crockford Lane, Basingstoke,
Hampshire, RG24 8WG
Tel: 0870 401 2200

CEC Plug-in Systems -
Contact your motorcaravan
dealer

Creative Resins Distribution,
7, The Glenmore Centre,
Castle Road,
Eurolink, Sittingbourne,
Kent, ME10 3GL
Tel: 01795 599880
(Mail Order supplier of
A-Glaze Total Surface
Protection)

CRiS
Dolphin House,
New Street,
Salisbury,
Wiltshire, SP1 2PH
Tel: 01722 413434
(Motorcaravan Registration &
identification Scheme)

Crossleys,
Unit 33A, Comet Road,
Moss Side Industrial Estate,
Leyland,
Lancashire, PR26 7QN
Tel: 01772 623423
(Major body repair and
rebuilding work)

Danbury Motorcaravans/ Beetles (UK),
Unit 1,
Bristol Mineral Works,
Limekiln Road, Rangeworthy,
South Gloucestershire,
BS37 7QB
Tel: 0870 1202356
(VW Type 2 Campervans with modern conversions, Type 2 VW Brazilian imports, supply of retrofit interiors)

Design Developments,
24 Carbis Close,
Port Solent,
Portsmouth,
Hampshire, PO6 4TW
Tel: 023 9237 9777
(Barry Stimson design consultant and motorcaravan manufacturer)

DLS Plastics,
Occupation Lane,
Gonerby Moor,
Grantham,
Lincolnshire, NG32 2BP
Tel: 01476 564549
(Plastic components, plumbing items for motorcaravans)

Dometic Ltd,
99 Oakley Road,
Luton,
Bedfordshire, LU4 9GE
Tel: 01582 494111
(Refrigerators, air conditioners, Seitz windows, toilets.)

Driftgate 2000 Ltd,
27 Little End Road,
Eaton Socon,
St Neots,
Cambridgeshire, PE19 8JH
Tel: 01480 470400
(Manufacturers of XCell mains inverters; X-Calibre stage chargers)

Drinkwater Engineering - see TVAC
(Air suspension systems, chassis work and motorhome weight upgrades)

Driver and Vehicle Licensing Agency (DVLA),
Swansea, SA99 1BA
Tel: 0870 2400010
(Guidance on vehicle registration; notification of changes to a vehicle)

Driverite Air Assistance Systems
(Air assistance units available through dealers - NOT full air suspension)

Eberspächer (UK) Ltd,
10 Headlands Business Park,
Salisbury Road,
Ringwood,
Hampshire,
BH24 3PB
Tel: 01425 480151
(Petrol and diesel-fuelled space & water heaters)

Elecsol Europe Ltd,
47 First Avenue,
Deeside Industrial Park,
Deeside,
Flintshire, CH5 2LG
Tel: 0800 163298
(Elecsol carbon fibre leisure batteries)

Electrical Contractors Association (ECA),
3 Buenavista Gardens,
Glenholt,
Plymouth
Tel: 01752 700981
(Mains supply system checking)

Electrolux Leisure Appliances
- See Dometic

Elsan Ltd,
Elsan House,
Bellbrook Park,
Uckfield,
East Sussex, TN22 1QF
Tel: 01825 748200
(Manufacturers of toilets and chemicals)

Essanjay Motohomes,
Unit 2,
Sovereign Business Park,
48 Willis Way,
Poole,
Dorset,
BH15 3TB
Tel: 01202 683608
(Motorhome servicing, components)

Exhaust Ejector Co Ltd,
Wade House Road,
Shelf,
Nr. Halifax,
West Yorkshire, HX3 7PE
Tel: 01274 679524
(Replacement acrylic windows made to order)

Exide Leisure Batteries Ltd,
Customer Services,
6-7 Parkway Estate,
Longbridge Road,
Trafford Park,
Manchester, M17 1SN
Tel: 0161 786 3333
(Exide base vehicle and leisure batteries)

Explorer Group,
Explorer House,
Delves Lane,
Consett,
Co Durham, DH8 7PE
Tel: 01207 699000
(Manufacturer of Compass and Elddis motorcaravans)

EZRise Trailer Solutions,
Unit 1, Croft Court,
Butts Close,
Redmarsh Industrial Estate,
Thornton Cleveleys, FY5 4JX
Tel: 01253 865862
(Air lift & lower trailers for motorcycles, mobility scooters etc)

Farécla Products Ltd,
Broadmeads,
Ware,
Hertfordshire, SG12 9HS
Tel: 01920 465041
(Caravan Pride G3 acrylic window scratch remover, GRP surface renovator)

Fenwicks Superior Products,
Fir Tree Farm,
Nantwich,
Cheshire, CW5 8JR
Tel: 01270 524111
(Cleaning products, window scratch remover)

The Farnborough VW Centre,
10 Farnborough Road,
Farnborough,
Hampshire, GU14 6AY
Tel: 01252 521152
(High quality VW campervan restorations)

Fiamma accessories - Contact your motorcaravan dealer

Froli Kunststoffwerk Fromme GmbH,
Liemker Strasse 27,
D-33758 Schloss Holte-Stukenbrock,
Germany.
Tel: 49 (0) 52 07 - 95 00 0
(Froli bed support systems)

Fun Tech Microcar from Secma, France – See QPOD

Gardner of Wakefield Ltd,
76 Wakefield Road,
Flushdyke, Ossett,
West Yorkshire, W5 9JX
Tel: 01924 265367
(Protective covers for accessories)

Gaslow International,
The Manor House,
Normanton-on-Soar,
Leicestershire, LE12 5HB
Tel: 01509 843331
(Gas leak gauges, refillable cylinders, LPG components)

GB-Sol,
Unit 2,
Glan-y-Llyn Industrial Estate,
Cardiff Road, Taffs Well,
Cardiff, CF15 7JD
Tel: 029 2082 0910
(Semi-flexible lightweight solar panels)

General Ecology Europe Ltd,
St. Andrews House,
26 Brighton Road,
Crawley, RH10 6AA
Tel: 01293 400644
(Nature Pure Ultrafine water purifier)

GE Protimeter PLC,
Meter House, Marlow,
Buckinghamshire, SLW 1LW
Tel: 01628 472722
(Professional moisture meters)

Grade UK Ltd,
3 Central Court, Finch Close,
Lenton Lane Industrial Estate,
Nottingham, NG7 2NN
Tel: 0115 986 7151
(Status TV aerials, flat screen/ DVD players and accessories)

Grangers International Ltd,
Grange Close,
Clover Nook Industrial Estate,
Alfreton,
Derbyshire, DE55 4QT
Tel: 01773 521521
(Awning proofing and cleaning products)

HBC International A/S,
Fabriksparken 4,
DK9230 Svenstrup, Denmark
Tel: +45 70227070
(Professional system for repairing aluminium body panels)

Hornchurch Motor Caravan Centre,
5–7 Broadway Parade,
Elm Avenue,
Hornchurch,
Essex, RM12 4RS
Tel: 01708 444791/443782
(Custom-made roof racks, cycle/motorcycle racks, ladders)

IH Motor Campers,
Great North Road,
Knottingley,
West Yorkshire, WF11 0BS
Tel: 01977 677118
(Van conversions and low profile coachbuilt models)

International Tool Co,,
Unit 82,
Tenter Road,
Moulton Business Park,
Northampton, NN3 6AX
Tel: 01604 646433
(Mail Order: Tyre pressure gauges for motorhome use)

Isabella International Camping Ltd,
Isabella House,
Drakes Farm, Drakes Drive,
Long Crendon,
Buckinghamshire, HP18 9BA
Tel: 01844 202099
(Isabella and Ventura awnings, alteration, repair and reproofing)

JC Leisure,
Strand Garage,
A259,
Winchelsea,
East Sussex, TN36 4JT
Tel: 01797 227337
(Van conversions)

Jenste,
The Stables,
Pashley Farm, Ninfield Road,
Bexhill-on-Sea,
East Sussex, TN39 5JS
Tel: 01424 893880
(RYD Live/neutral polarity changeover unit)

Jonic,
Unit 5,
Woodgate Park,
White Lund Industrial Estate,
Morecombe,
Lancashire, LA3 3PS
Tel: 01524 67074
(Memory foam, fitted sheets, mattress protectors, duvets)

Just Kampers,
Unit 1,
Stapeley Manor,
Long Lane,
Odiham,
Hampshire,
RG29 1JE
Tel: 01256 862288
(VW Camper and Transporter parts 1968–2004; accessories)

Khyam freestanding tents and awnings – see Cave and Crag

Lab-Craft Ltd,
22B King Street,
Saffron Walden,
Essex,
CB10 1ES
Tel: 01799 513434
(Electrical appliances, lighting units)

Lattoflex Bed Systems,
Thomas GmbH + Co.
Sitz- und Liegemöbel KG
Walkmühlenstrasse 93
27432 Bremervörde,
Germany
Tel: 0049 4761 979138
(CaraWinx mattress support systems)

Leveltronic,
Ares Engineering,
Via Brenta 7,
36010 Carrè,
Italy
Tel: +39 0445 720021
(Electric lifting and levelling automatic jacks; UK installers)

Lowdham Leisure World,
(Midlands),
Lowdham Road,
Gunthorpe,
Nottinghamshire, NG14 7ES
Tel: 0845 6349411
(Selling models from Explorer Group, Swift Group and imported ranges)

Magnum Mobiles and Caravan Surplus,
Unit 9A,
Cosalt Industrial Estate,
Convamore Road,
Grimsby, DN32 9JL
Tel: 01472 353520
(Caravan/Motorcaravan surplus stock; bespoke building services)

Marquis Motorhomes,
Head Office,
Orchard Works,
Willersey,
Nr. Broadway,
Worcestershire,
WR12 7QF
Tel: 08000 26 77 77
(Hire and buy scheme, chain
of dealers)

Maxview,
Common Lane,
Setchey,
King's Lynn,
Norfolk,
PE33 0AT
Tel: 01553 813300
(TV aerials, satellite TV
products, free guidebooks)

Mer Products,
Whitehead House,
120 Beddington Lane,
Croydon,
Surrey, CR0 4TD
Tel: 020 8401 0002
(Cleaning products)

Middlesex Motorcaravans,
22 Station Parade.
Whitchurch Lane,
Edgware,
Middlesex, HA8 6RW
Tel: 020 8952 4045
(Complete and part-build van
conversions; Westfalia pre-
owned imports)

Milton Sterilising Products
– See Ceuta Healthcare

Miriad Products Ltd,
Park Lane,
Dove Valley Park,
South Derbyshire,
DE65 5BG
Tel: 01283 586060
(Spares for heating, water
appliances and other
accessories)

Morco Products Ltd,
59 Beverley Road,
Hull, HU3 1XW
Tel: 01482 325456
(Water heaters, accessories)

**The Motor Caravanners'
Club,**
22 Evelyn Close,
Twickenham,
Middlesex, TW2 7BN
Tel: 020 8893 3883
(Club for motorcaravanners)

**Motorhome Information
Service,**
Maxwelton House,
Boltro Road,
Haywards Heath,
West Sussex, RH16 1BH
Tel: 01444 458889
(Information about
motorcaravans and general
guidance)

**Munster Simms Engineering
Ltd,**
Old Belfast Road,
Bangor, Co. Down,
Northern Ireland, BT19 1LT
Tel: 02891 270531
(Whale pumps, taps and
plumbing accessories)

Murvi,
4 East Way,
Lee Mill Industrial Estate,
Ivybridge,
Devon, PL21 9GE
Tel: 01752 892200
(Van conversion specialist)

**The National Caravan
Council,**
Catherine House,
Victoria Road,
Aldershot,
Hampshire, GU11 1SS
Tel: 01252 318251
(Trade association for
caravans and motorhomes)

**National Inspection Council
for Electrical Installation
Contracting,**
(NICEIC)
Vintage House,
36-37 Albert Embankment,
London, SE1 7UJ
Tel: 020 7564 2323
(Certification of motorcaravan
wiring for mains electricity)

The Natural Mat Company,
99 Talbot Road,
London, W11 2AT
Tel: 0207 9850474
(Slatted sprung beech bed
systems, anti-condensation
underlay)

**Noise Killer Acoustics (UK)
Ltd,**
103 Denbydale Way,
Royton,
Oldham, OL2 5UH
Tel: 0161 643 8070
(Noise reduction systems for
motorcaravans)

**O'Leary Spares and
Accessories,**
314 Plaxton Bridge Road,
Woodmansey,
Nr Beverley,
East Yorkshire, HU17 0RS
Tel: 01482 868632
(Caravan/motorcaravan
accessories)

Omnistor,
Unit 11,
Birch Copse,
Technology Road, Poole,
Dorset, BH17 7FH
Tel: 0844 800 9949
(Outdoor blinds, cycle racks
and storage boxes)

Paintseal Direct,
34 Cross Street,
Long Eaton,
Nottinghamshire, NG10 1HD
Tel: 07783 300 377
(Paint protection systems
containing DuPont™ Teflon®)

Parma Industries,
123 High Street,
Wickham Market,
Suffolk, IP13 0RD
Tel: 01728 745700
(Wheel trims, dashboard
plastic veneer, general
accessories)

Plug-In-Systems - Contact
your motorcaravan dealer

Propex Heat Source Ltd.,
Unit 5,
Second Avenue Business Park,
Millbrook,
Southampton, SO15 0LP
Tel: 023 8052 8555
(Propex compact blown air
gas heaters; Malaga Mk II
water heater)

Pro-Tec Covers,
202-206 Leeds Road,
Bradford,
West Yorkshire, BD3 9PS
Tel: 01274 780088
(Breathable covers for
motorcaravans)

Pro-Tow
Unit 1,
565 Blandford Road,
Hamworthy, Poole,
Dorset, BH16 5BW
Tel: 01202 632488
(Car-a-Tow towing frames;
Solar Solutions solar panels)

PWS,
Unit 5,
Chalwyn Industrial Estate,
Old Wareham Road,
Parkstone, Dorset, BH12 4PE
Tel: 01202 746851
(Racks, protector bars,
custom-made tow bars)

Pyramid Products Ltd,
Unit 1,
Victoria Street,
Mansfield,
Nottinghamshire, NG18 5RR
Tel: 01623 421277
(Awnings, Gazebos, wheel
clamps and accessories)

QPOD (Fun Tech) Microcars,
Motorpoint,
Fenny Bridges,
Honiton, EX14 3BG
Tel: 0870 241 4804
(QPOD Microcar from Secma,
France, formerly called the
Fun Tech)

Reich UK,
91 Hednesford Road,
Cannock,
Staffordshire,
WS12 3HL
Tel: 01543 459243
(Importer of accessories
including the Fuse Control)

Remis UK, - Through
accessory dealers
(Internal blinds, flyscreens,
and roof windows)

RoadPro Ltd,
Stephenson Close,
Drayton Fields,
Daventry,
Northamptonshire,
NN11 5RF
Tel: 01327 312233
(Accessories, chargers,
reversing aids, TVs)

RYD Polarity reversal switch
– See Jenste

**Sargent Electrical Services,
Ltd,**
Unit 39,
Tokenspire Business Park,
Woodmansey,
Beverley, HU17 0TB
Tel: 01452 678987
(12V controls and panels)

Seitz Windows, - See
Dometic

**The Selfbuild
Motorcaravanners Club,**
www.sbmcc.co.uk
(Web-based; Large
membership of builders and
potential builders)

Sew 'n' So's,
42 Claudette Avenue,
Spalding,
Lincolnshire,
PE11 1HU
Tel: 01775 767633
(Bespoke awnings, bags and
covers)

SF Detection Ltd,
Hatch Pond House,
4 Stinsford Road,
Poole,
Dorset,
BH17 0RZ
Tel: 01202 645577
(Carbon monoxide detectors,
LP Gas alarms)

SHURflo Ltd,
Unit 5,
Sterling Park,
Gatwick Road,
Crawley,
RH10 9QT
Tel: 01293 424000
(Water pumps)

Silver Screens,
P.O. Box 9,
Cleckheaton,
West Yorkshire,
BD19 5YR
Tel: 01274-872151
(Insulated window covers)

**The Society of Motor
Manufacturers and Traders,**
Forbes House,
Halkin Street,
London,
SW1X 7DS
Tel: 0171 235 7000
(Specialist Sub-
Committee concerned with
motorcaravans)

Solar Solutions – See Pro-Tow

Sold Secure Trust,
5c Great Central Way,
Woodford Halse,
Daventry,
Northamptonshire, NN11
3PZ
Tel: 01327 264687
(Test house conducting attack
tests on security devices)

Specialised Accessories,
Concours House,
Main Street,
Burley-in-Wharfdale,
Ilkley,
West Yorkshire, LS29 7JP
Tel: 01943 864828
(Motorcaravan breathable
covers)

Spinflo, Ltd, - See Thetford
(UK) Spinflo

Glen Dimplex Cooking,
Stoney Lane, Prescot,
Merseyside, L35 2XW
Tel: 0151 426 6551
(Stoves UK Grills, Hobs,
Ovens)

Swift Group Ltd,
Dunswell Road, Cottingham,
East Yorkshire, HU16 4JX
Tel: 01482 847332
(Manufacturer of Ace,
Bessacarr, & Swift
motorcaravans)

Symonspeed Ltd,
Cleveland Garage,
1 Cleveland Road, Torquay,
Devon, TQ2 5BD
Tel: 01803 214620
(Air assistance units and SOG
toilet system)

TB Turbo Ltd,
Turbo House,
Port Royal Avenue
Off Willow Lane,
Lancaster, LA1 5QP
Tel: 01524 67157
(Autoclutch, Turbo conversion,
intercoolers, LP Gas tanks,
engine chips)

Technicol Ltd,
The Studio,
112 Hardwick Lane,
Bury St Edmunds,
Suffolk, IP33 2LE
Tel: 02392 588588
(Ventair 15 mattress anti-
condensation underlay)

TEK Seating Ltd,
Unit 32,
Pate Road,
Leicester Road Industrial
Estate,
Melton Mowbray,
Leicestershire, LE13 0RG
Tel: 01664 480689
(Cab seating, seat swivels,
seat bases and upholstery)

The 12Volt Shop,
9 Lostwood Road,
St Austell,
Cornwall, PL25 4JN
Tel: 01726 69102
(Twelve volt electrical
components)

Thetford (UK) Spinflo,
4-10 Welland Close,
Parkwood Industrial Estate,
Rutland Road,
Sheffield, S3 9QY
Tel: 01142 738157
(Norcold refrigerators, toilets
and treatments, Spinflo
cooking appliances)

Towsure Products,
151-183 Holme Lane,
Hillsborough,
Sheffield,
South Yorkshire, S6 4JR
Tel: 0870 60 900 70 (Sales
Hotline)
(Retailing and Mail Order
Accessories)

TOWtal,
332 King Street,
Fenton,
Stoke-on-Trent, ST4 3DA
Tel: 01782 333422
('A' Frames, electric brake
actuators, trailers, scooter
racks, tow bars)

Truma UK,
Park Lane,
Dove Valley Park,
Foston,
Staffordshire, DE65 5BG
Tel: 01283 586050
(Space and water heating
systems, gas components,
Carver spares)

**TVAC (Incorporating
Drinkwater Engineering),**
Enterprise Business Park,
Centurion Way,
Leyland,
Lancashire, PR26 6TZ
Tel: 01772 457116
(Air suspension systems,
chassis repair and weight
upgrades/downgrades)

Tyron Safety Band (UK) Ltd,
Manor House Stables,
Normanton on Soar,
Leicestershire, LE12 5HB
Tel: 0870 744 6911
(Distributor of Tyron Safety
Band)

Van Bitz,
Cornish Farm,
Shoreditch,
Taunton,
Somerset,
TA3 7BS
Tel: 01823-321992
(Strikeback Thatcham-
Approved security, gas alarm,
Battery Master)

**The Vehicle & Operator
Service Agency,**
91/92 The Strand,
Swansea,
SA1 2DH
Tel: 0870 60 60 440
www.vosa.gov.uk/
(To apply for an SVA test and
for general enquiries)

Ventura Awnings – See
Isabella International

V & G Caravans,
107 Benwick Road,
Whittlesey,
Peterborough,
Cambridgeshire,
PE7 2HD
Tel: 01733 350580
(Replacement replica panels
in GRP)

Waeco UK Ltd,
Unit G1,
Roman Hill Business Park,
Broadmayne,
Dorset,
DT2 8LY
Tel: 01305 854000
(Compressor refrigerators,
reversing aids, navigational
aids)

Watling Engineers Ltd,
88 Park Street Village,
nr. St. Albans,
Hertfordshire, AL2 2LR
Tel: 01727 873661
(Specially designed towing
brackets)

Webasto Products UK Ltd,
Webasto House,
White Rose Way,
Doncaster Carr,
South Yorkshire,
DN4 5JH
Tel: 01302 322232
(Diesel-fuelled heaters, water
evaporative air conditioners)

Whale water accessories
– see Munster Simms

Wheelhome,
Tip's Cross,
Blackmore Road,
Hook End,
Brentwood,
Essex,
CM15 0DX
Tel: 01277 822208
(Specialist building compact
motorcaravans from MPVs)

Wayfarer Estates,
The Street,
St Nicholas at Wade,
Birchington,
Kent,
CT7 0NP
Tel: 01843 845888
Importer of Wingamm
coachbuilt models from Italy.

Witter Towbars,
Drome Road,
Deeside Industrial Park,
Deeside,
Chester,
CH5 2NY
Tel: 01244 284500
(Towbars and cycle carriers)

W4 Ltd,
Unit B,
Ford Lane Industrial Estate,
Arundel,
West Sussex,
BN18 0DF
Tel: 01243 553355
(Mains 230v kits, socket
testers, ribbon sealants)

Young Conversions,
Unit 47,
Barton Road,
Water Eaton,
Bletchley,
Milton Keynes,
Buckinghamshire, MK2 3BD
Tel: 01908 639 936
(Full or part conversions,
conversions for disabled
users)

ZIG Electronics, Ltd,
Saxon Business Park,
Hanbury Road,
Stoke Prior,
Bromsgrove,
Worcestershire, B60 4AD
Tel: 01527 556715
(12V controls, chargers, water
level sensors and gauges)

21st December, 2007
© John Wickersham

INDEX

301